This book is dedicated to

Seyed Zia-ul-Hassan Jaffery

A man of discipline in every sense of the word

Printed in memory of the marhumeen of the Khimji family

The Fourteen Infallibles

A compilation of speeches and lectures by

Dr. Sayed Ammar Nakshawani

sayed ammar press

The Fourteen Infallibles

A compilation of speeches and lectures by
Dr. Sayed Ammar Nakshawani

1717 Pennsylvania Ave NW #1025
Washington, DC 20006.
Phone: 202-559-9123
Email: info@umaamerica.net
Brought to you by The UMAA Publishing House.

Printed in the United States of America

Contents

About the Author

Dr. Sayed Ammar Nakshawani is regarded as one of the most powerful speakers in the Muslim world. He was born in 1981 and graduated from the University College London, as well as the London School of Economics. He was then awarded with an MA in Islamic Studies from Shahid Beheshti University in Iran. Dr. Nakshawani completed his PhD thesis at the University of Exeter He has lectured at the university in Classical Islamic History and then pursued further studies at the Islamic Seminary in Damascus, Syria. Currently he is a visiting scholar at the Centre of Islamic Studies, University of Cambridge.

Acknowledgments

I wish to thank all the individuals who helped, supported and contributed to this work, particularly the transcriber who wishes to remain unknown, and my hard-working editor, Kawther Rahmani, for her dedication and diligence and to Tehseen Merali of Sun Behind The Cloud Publications for her help in publishing the work.

My special thanks to Professor Hamid Mavani, Professor Sajjad Rizvi, and Dr. Liakat Takim for their valuable comments; to Yahya Seymour, Nisar Visram, Nebil Husayn and Ahmed Virani for their insight and useful comments; to the Hamam family, Murtaza Kanani and Haider Ali Hashmi for their generosity; to the community in Dar es Salaam, Tanzania for the recordings of my lectures; to the Abidi Foundation for their unrivalled support in publishing this work; and lastly to my beloved parents who instilled love of The Fourteen in my heart.

Your rewards are with the Almighty.

Foreword

The Muslim community was confronted with a major crisis of authority and leadership right after the Prophet's death in 632: Who would succeed him? The Shi'is who comprise about 20% of the global Muslim population believe that the Prophet had explicitly appointed his cousin and son-in-law, Imam 'Ali b. Abi Talib as his temporal and religious successor. The central and pivotal evidence advanced by the Shi'is in favor of Imam 'Ali's succession is the tradition of Ghadir Khumm. This tradition is named after the place where the Prophet delivered his "Farewell Sermon" in the last year of his life in March 632 on his way back to Madinah after completing the hajj. Upon reaching a crossroad from where the pilgrims would disperse, he introduced Imam 'Ali as the mawla of the community.

The Shi'is interpret this word as explicit evidence of the Prophet's designation of Imam 'Ali as his successor in both the political and religious spheres, and even more so, as the Prophet was commanded to designate him based on a qur'anic directive: "Messenger, deliver that which has been sent down to you from your Lord; for if you do not, then you would not have delivered His message. God will protect you from people" (5:67). The Sunnis do not dispute this incident's veracity; however, they assert that it is no more than an admonition to the Muslims to provide his cousin and son-in-law due respect and honor, especially since some discontent and displeasure had been directed toward the latter on account of how he had distributed the booty after returning from an expedition in Yemen.

Since mawla has multiple meanings, one should search for other hints, signs or contextual indications (qara'in muttasilah) within the text of the Prophet's sermon. The most important qarinah is the question that

Prophet Muhammad posed to the pilgrims, immediately prior to designating Imam 'Ali as his successor: "Am I not entitled to a greater right over you than you have upon yourselves?" Others have cited external pointers (qara'in munfasilah) such as the fact that the Prophet delivered this sermon after halting in the middle of the desert in scorching heat and, afterward, told those present to convey his message to those who were absent (fa-l-yuballigh al-shahid al-gha'ib). Other qara'in include people congratulating Imam 'Ali after the Prophet concluded his sermon and poems composed on the spot by Hassan b. Thabit to celebrate this event. 'Allamah Amini provides ten qara'in (internal and external) related to this event.

The essence of the Imamate can be gleaned from the letters sent by Imam Husayn to the people of Kufa and Basra. In response to the Kufans' persistent appeals after Yazid's assumption of the caliphate in 680, that he lead and guide them toward the truth (al-haqq wa al-huda) and throw off the yoke of Syrian domination, he writes: "…who is an imam (ma al-imam) except one who acts according to the Book (al-hakim bi al-Kitab), one who upholds justice (al-qa'im bi al-qist), one who professes the truth (al-da'in bi din al-haqq) and one who dedicates himself to [the essence of] God (al-habis nafsa-hu 'ala dhat Allah)?" In his reply to the Basrans, Imam Husayn forcefully attributes his exclusive entitlement to the rank of Imam, to his having inherited the Prophet's charisma and to his distaste for rupturing the community over the issue of leadership:

> We are his family (ahl), those who possess his authority (awliya'), those who have been made his trustees (awsiya') and his inheritors (wuratha'); we are the ones who have more right to his position among the people (ahaqq al-nas) than anyone else. Yet, our people selfishly laid claim to this exclusive right of ours and we consented [to what they did] since we hated disunion and desired the well-being [of the community]. However, we know that we have a greater claim to that right, which was our entitlement (mustahaqq 'alay-na), than those who have seized it.

The work in your hands covers the exemplary lives of the Prophet, the Lady Fatima, and the Imams. In addition (and tangentially), it deals with the theological doctrine of the Imamate that remains so pivotal and crucial in Shi'i Islam that, one can argue, it has colored the entirety of Shi'ism. These collected transcribed lectures were delivered in Dar-es-salaam, Tanzania, in Ramadan 2011 by Sayed Ammar Nakshawani (Ph.D. Exeter, 2011) a much sought-after and eminent speaker and lecturer. He is a scholar with a solid grounding in both the traditional and academic studies of religion in general and of Islam in particular. This enables him to act as an ambassador, interpreter, and/or translator of the corpus of literature on the Fourteen Infallible Guides (ma'sumin) from the primary Arabic sources and/or academic language to a delivery that is clear, crisp and understandable by the general public. More significant, in my view, is his zealous aspiration to transform these paragons of virtue and exemplary models from mythical figures, miracle workers, or victims of oppression and injustice into role models for us today so that we can attempt to follow in their footsteps and embrace a worldview that is morally, ethically, and spiritually sound. In fact, this was the objective that he had set for himself at the beginning of the lecture series. He has fulfilled it admirably.

I anticipate that these kinds of works will be received with enthusiasm by Muslims in general, especially those living in the West who are searching for relevant and pragmatic guidance. As this work is intended for the general public as opposed to scholars, and since he is speaking from a vantage point of an insider of the faith tradition with its attendant presuppositions, assumptions, and premises, Dr. Nakshawani has provided no footnotes or annotations.

May Allah (swt) reward him for his noble efforts in transforming the lives of the ma'sumin from abstraction into practical guidance. May He reward the reader, and may He endow all of us with felicity as well as the capability and capacity (tawfiq) to abide by His Will and Pleasure. Amen.

Wassalamu 'alaykum,

Dr. Hamid Mavani
Assistant Professor
School of Religion
Claremont Graduate University

May 8, 2012 / Jumad al-thani 17, 1433

Introduction

In Imami theological circles the members of the Household of the Holy Prophet (pbuh) are referred to as The Fourteen Infallibles. Namely, the Prophet (pbuh) himself, his daughter Fatima (as), his son-in-law Ali (as), then his grandsons Hassan (as) and Hussein (as) and the nine descendants from Hussein (as): Ali b. Hussein (as), Muhammad b. Ali (as), Ja'far b. Muhammad (as), Musa b. Ja'far (as), Ali b. Musa (as), Muhammad b. Ali (as), Ali b. Muhammad (as), Hassan b. Ali (as) and the twelfth Imam known as al-Mahdi (ajfs).

The principle aim of the examination of their biographies is three-fold. The first reason is to apply their lessons in our life, because when we dissect the lives of these personalities we must ask ourselves, "What of their lives over one thousand years ago affects our lives today in 2012? Which of their standpoints, which of their ethics, and which of their principles can relate to my standpoints, my ethics and my principles today? Which situations did they face in their life may I be facing in my life?" When we come to dissect the lives of every one of these leaders, it should not just be a theoretical discussion about when they were born, or how many children they had, or whom they were married to. While that type of knowledge is important, what is equally important, and what should really be important, is a practical discussion that examines the way their lives can affect our lives. Which circumstances did they fall into which we may fall into as well? We find that the first of the important points in dissecting the biographies of these fourteen infallibles is that we want their lives to relate to ours.

A frequent complaint about early history is that "When people discuss the biographies of the fourteen infallibles, they do not relate history to our life today. We hear all these great stories but we do not see a relationship to what we face today." The irony is that every one of those fourteen infallibles, at one point or another in their life, faced a situation that we will face in our life. Either they faced circumstances with their family or with their friends or with their enemies or with people of the same faith or with people of different faiths that will relate to us. Thus we need to dissect how they reacted to those circumstances.

All things considered, when we take them as role models in our life, it is not because they were from the line of the Prophet (pbuh); there were many people from the line of the Prophet (pbuh). Rather these members from the line of the Prophet (pbuh) were the ones whom he instructed us to hold on to in many of his hadith, alongside the Quran. Therefore, the first point as to why we are going to dissect their biographies is that we need to take as many lessons from the anecdotes of their lives as possible because there is no point in only taking life-lessons from Ali b. Abi Talib (as) or from Hussein (as). One must ask, which lessons can I take from Musa b. Ja'far (as)? Which lessons can I take from Muhammad al-Jawad (as)? Which lessons can I take from Hassan al-Askari (as)? There is a tendency in our communities to focus on a couple of Imams from the infallibles and neglect the others. This series of lectures will firstly seek to dissect the biography of every Imam and then ask ourselves which lessons from their lives are applicable to our own.

The second point in examining the biographies of the fourteen infallibles is that there are four key questions every human being will ask in their life which these fourteen personages have answered in their lives. What are these four key questions which a Hindu will ask…a Sikh will ask…a Jew will ask…a Buddhist will ask…a Christian will ask…or an atheist will ask? In short, every human being will ask these four key questions.

The first of them is a metaphysical question; the second is a cosmological question; the third is a psychological question and the fourth is an ethical question. There is not a single human being who does not go through a moment in their life without asking these four questions, and there is not a single moment in the lives of those fourteen holy personages where they have not answered each of them. What are these four questions?

The metaphysical question...Is there an unseen force who is the cause of the effect that we are today? Is there a God or is it Mother Nature? This is a metaphysical question. It goes beyond the physical world and towards the unseen.

The cosmological question...How did this universe begin? Many people ask this question. The psychological question...What is my role in this world? The ethical question...How do I behave with other human beings, and is there a difference when the person is from my religion or from another?

These four questions are the four most important questions in the psyche of any human being. Thus the second reason we are analyzing the biographies of the fourteen infallibles is to discover what their answers were to these questions. For example, what did Ali (as) say about the metaphysical? What did Ja'far as-Sadiq (as) say about the ethical? What did Ali b. Musa (as) say about the psychological? What did Hassan b. Ali (as) say about the cosmological? We want to see how their holistic approach to the world can provide answers for mankind in the 21st century, be they Muslim or not.

The third reason we are going to dissect the lives of the fourteen infallibles in this series is because we as Muslims have committed injustice to these fourteen holy personalities. How have we done this? We have cocooned them for ourselves rather than share them with other religions. How many of us have explained Ali b. Musa al-Ridha (as)'s golden medical dissertation to the Sikh community? How many of us have discussed the maxims of Ali b. Abi Talib (as) with a Buddhist? How many of us have dissected the bravery of Hussein (as) outside of Karbala and then discussed it with a member of the Jewish community?You should realize that these fourteen infallibles were not meant solely for Muslims, rather they are the property of every human being. We make them the property of Islam alone, and thus we have committed an injustice. How many of us can sincerely say that we have discussed our Imams with our non-Muslim brethren? Some will say, "Okay. I discussed Imam Hussein one day with one of my non-Muslim friends." Ask him, "How about Ja'far al-Sadiq (as)? Did you discuss him? Or did you discuss Muhammad al-Jawad (as)'s knowledge with your non-Muslim friends?"

When these fourteen infallibles were chosen as a guidance for people, they were chosen as a guidance for mankind, not just for Islam. Islam came as a religion to allow for the evolution of the growth of mankind. What was the role of the fourteen? Their role was to allow for the growth and evolution of the human being, an evolution that helped the growth of every human being, not just the Muslim. Notice Gandhi. Does anyone ever say "Gandhi, the Hindu?" Or do they say, "Gandhi, the humanitarian?" When they look at Martin Luther King, do they say, "Martin Luther King, the Christian?" Or do they say, "Martin Luther King, the humanitarian?" What we need to do at the end of this series is take the fourteen out of the cocoon of Islam and allow the whole world to learn from their lives, from their principles, and from their ethics. Generosity, is it an Islamic principle or a human principle? Patience, is it an Islamic principle or human principle? Forbearance, is it an Islamic principle or a human principle? All of the traits from these Imams are human principles. Any human being can relate to a patient human being. You do not need to belong to Islam to say, "Patience is a virtue." Thus the third reason to dissect their biographies is to allow them to be seen as universal role models.

The methodology used in reconstructing this era in Islamic history will be developed by answering a few key questions:

- Can we reconstruct Islamic history or is history "his story?"
- How important is "intertextuality" for us to have a rounded picture of the lives of the fourteen infallibles?
- What are the sources that we are going to use to discuss the lives of the fourteen infallibles and why is it important that we use our sources as well as the sources from other schools of thought in Islam?
- Concerning these fourteen or these twelve masumeen…was it a made up notion after the twelfth Imam went into *ghayba* (occultation), or does evidence appear in discussions concerning them before the twelfth Imam?
- Why is it important for Biblical religions like Judaism and Christianity to discuss the lives of the infallibles because of the chapter of Genesis in the Bible?

The first question that arises amid the discussions of the biographies of the infallibles is whether or not we can really reconstruct Islamic history reliably. What does this mean? There are certain people who oppose this reconstruction of Islamic history. What are their objections?

Sceptics argue that we Muslims have two problems with reconstructing early history, referring to the first three hundred years that we will be discussing here, from the time of the Prophet (pbuh) up to the twelfth Imam (ajfs). They say there are two reasons we cannot reconstruct our history. The first reason, which is very interesting, is that they say that all the books that are being used as references (and which I am going to use as well) for the dissection of the lives of the infallibles were books which were written after the year 300 AH. So they turn around and state, how could you rely on books that are so late to discuss people who were so early? What do they mean?They argue that early Islamic history was oral; it wasn't written. In the time of the Prophet (pbuh), everybody used to orally narrate the history of the Prophet (pbuh). The hadith narrate, "I heard the Prophet say…I saw the Prophet do…" It was all oral. They argue, "it was late in Islam that you wrote down your history." So the first objection that they have in reconstructing Islamic history is that your written material on early history is very late. How can you be so sure that your written material discusses something three hundred years before? How can you be sure that it is reliable?

Their second objection is that history is nothing but "his story." Their complaint pertains to the objectivity of those sources you would like to use. How do you know the author isn't writing history in a way that only promotes his theology or his political opinion? This is a very interesting point. When I am an author of a book of history, am I going to write objectively, or am I going to write in a way where I am going to look after my own people? That is why they are of the opinion that history is "his story." He looks back, or he looks at whom he likes, or he makes him look great, he makes him say great words, he makes him sound like he was brave; and he looks at who he dislikes and he makes him look bad and weak and negative and so on. We cannot begin with the biography of the infallibles unless these two objections are answered because they are very valid objections.

Let's take the first objection. They say, for example, your book, The History of al-Tabari, was written over three hundred years after

Muhammad died. Or they say, for example, your book, like the book of al-Baladhuri, Ansab al-Ashraf, was written more than two hundred years after Muhammad died. Or they say, al-Kamil fi'l-Ta'rikh by b. Athir was written a few hundred years after Muhammad died. Or they say, your books (referring to Shi'a books), like al–Kafi, were written three hundred years after Muhammad died. Or for that matter book such as Man La Yahduruhu al-Faqih were written much later. Thus we ask ourselves, why were these works compiled so late? If I am going to use books that were written three hundred years after Jamal, Siffin and Karbala, how do I know these books are actually telling the truth? There is a big gap of time, isn't there? For example, Karbala took place in the 61st year after Hijra, while al-Tabari was writing about it 250 years after Karbala. How do I know that he was reconstructing it exactly the way it should be? They claim all our material was oral, people would hear each other but no one began writing until much later. So now how do we reply to both these objections?

This is a very important matter that needs to be understood. The reply to both these objections has to be understood very well, because the moment you can reply to both, you can reconstruct Islamic history. The first reply to the group who say your books are late, we reply:

1- *Does a "solid core" of history exist from these books even though they are late?* There is a concept called the "solid core." What does the "solid core" mean? Fred Donner and Montgomery Watt said, "Even though you may have many books which are late, a solid core exists which allows you to paint a picture of early history."

Is the event of Saqifa narrated in all the books? Yes, there is a solid core about Saqifa. Similarly, there is a solid core for the Battle of Jamal as well. Do all of them talk about Siffin? Yes. Do they talk about the Battle of Nahrawan? Yes. Do they say Karbala happened? Yes. I'm not going to talk about what motivated the author. I'm focusing on whether I have a solid core to work with. Because when I want to dissect Imam number one until Imam number twelve, I need to make sure that the solid core that I have, whether it is from my school or another school in Islam, I need to make sure the solid core exists. Jamal happened... Siffin, Nahrawan, Karbala, Mukhtar, Abdullah b. Zubair, the Abbasids, the Umayyads, Harun, Ma'mun - the solid core for these historical facts clearly exists.

2. *Even if a book is written later, what stops me from finding a chain that goes back all the way to the Prophet (pbuh)?* If I write a book three hundred years after the Prophet (pbuh) died, I meet someone who is older than me. Then, for example, I will ask him, "Did you ever hear anything about the Prophet (pbuh)?" He'll say, "Yes, I heard him say". We reply by saying, "our authors show us the chain of narrators and the chain goes all the way back to early works." 'Abd al-Razzaq as-San'ani has a book called al-Musannaf. It is one of the earliest books of fiqh. What does as-San'ani do in this book? He takes a hadith on fiqh and gives you the chain. Do you know why? Because he knew there would be a day in 2012 when someone would say, "Your book of fiqh is late. How do you know Muhammad actually gave that theory of fiqh?"

So what did as-San'ani do? He says, "Okay, let me tell you how I got this hadith. I got it from b. Juraij, who got it from Ata, who got it from Umar b. Khattab, who got it from the Prophet (pbuh)." So he has given me a chain. Or in another hadith he says, "This is from b. Ishaq, who got it from Zuhri, who got it from b. Zubair, who got it from Zubair who got it from the Prophet."

Just because a book is written late does not mean you do not have a chain that goes all the way back to the Prophet (pbuh).

3- *Even if my early history was oral, and just because there was a lot of oral transmission, does that mean there was no one writing at home?* So when you tell me that, "The early Islamic history was oral," I reply by saying, "Okay, most people were narrating orally; does that mean no one was writing anything at home?" There is an article by the famous academic Etan Kohlberg, a professor of Islamic studies at the University of Tel Aviv, who says that the fifth Imam was referring to a book called Kitab Ali. So what he is saying is that when Imam al-Baqir (as) was discussing a hadith, he was referring to a book called 'Kitab Ali.' This means that Ali b. Abi Talib, even though most of his words were transmitted orally, was also writing a work at home. There was already a work that was being produced. And that is why even Abdullah b. Zubair, who lived for about sixty years after the Prophet (pbuh), always said in his works, "Which 'Sahifa' (transcript) did you get that particular narration from?"

We can go a step further than this too. When they tell me all your books of history are late, I reply to them, "What is early to you? Give me a date that is early and I will give you a source." To them, the term "early" is vague. They are playing with us psychologically by telling us, "Your books are late," so I tell them, ""What is early? Give me a date. If I give you a book from that date, will you admit that I can reconstruct Islamic history clearly?" Therefore, we have replied back to the first group.

The second group is even more interesting. The second group says, "History is 'his story.' How do you know you can trust that writer? Of course he is going to write books which praise Ali and condemn Mu'awiya because he is from your (Shi'i) school. So when he writes history he is writing 'his story.' He is not going to write history the way it should be written." Then they give two brilliant examples to support this.

There are two scholars who are famous historians and theologians; one is called Abu Bakr al-Baqillani and the other is called Ahmad b. Yahya al-Baladhuri. The sceptics say that, "You attack Mu'awiya because you say that the books of history claim that Mu'awiya was not a good person, but the people you get your hadith from, like Bukhari, who says that he was a bad person, was working for the Abbasid government. Do you think an Abbasid is going to write history by writing nice things about the Umayyads? Naturally, his political affiliation may affect the way he writes history. Similarly, al-Baqillani was an Asharite in his theology. Therefore, when he writes history, is he not going to write history with an Asharite vision? Ahmad b. Yahya al-Baladhuri was the chief judge of Mutawakkil; if he was the chief judge and he was an Abbasid, of course he is going to hate the Bani Ummayah because the Banu Abbas seized power from the Bani Ummayah."

Thus the second school of sceptics says, "You Muslims cannot reconstruct your history because your authors write history with the lens of their theology or their politics. They do not write it objectively."

How do we reply back to them? We reply back by saying:

1- If al-Baqillani, for example, or al-Baladhuri (both of whom were Abbasids), is writing history with the lens of the school that he follows, that means he cannot praise any Umayyad, because if he is an employee of the Abbasids, he would never be allowed to praise anyone from Bani Ummayah. Yet al-Baladhuri has many narrations where he praises people who were caliphs of the Bani Ummayah. If al-Baladhuri was biased in his history and he wasn't objective, then he wouldn't praise the Bani Ummayah. But if you read the work of al-Baladhuri, you will find very clearly that he praises, for example, Umar b. Abdul Aziz. He was the one who stopped the la'na (cursing) of Imam Ali (as) in the Friday prayer. He is also the one who gave the land of Fadak back to the sons of Lady Fatima (as). Umar b. Abdul Aziz was an Umayyad caliph. If Muslim historians are writing "their story," then al-Baladhuri should not praise Umar b. Abdul Aziz as he was with the Bani Ummayah and al-Baladhuri was with the Bani Abbas.

We have many great historians in Islamic history who are objective. One must not ignore the efforts of Fuat Sezgin, Harald Motzki, Hossein Modarressi, Gregor Schoeler and Behnam Sadeghi in recovering literature from the first century (in addition to the second). Sezgin and Modarressi have paved the way for retrieving lost works by utilizing the works of medieval "scholar-bibliophile-booksellers" and scouring the intellectual tradition for fragments and recensions of early works, and noting extant manuscripts. Motzki, Schoeler and Sadeghi have utilized innovative techniques with hadīth collections that preceded the influential third century to identify reports that historically emanated from Companions about their recollections of the Prophet. When they need to praise their associates, they will praise them; but when they need to praise the opposition, they will praise them as well.

2- What makes you think that there was a crystallized ideology in many of these people's minds at the time? They say, "Some of these scholars, they already were crystallized in their opinion and that's why they are not objective in their history." Who told you they were crystallized in their opinion? Many of them were still trying to understand how Islam developed. There wasn't such a thing as a prototype, for example, a follower of the Ahl us-Sunnah (Sunni school of thought). There was someone who in his theology was following Ashari and in his fiqh (Islamic jurisprudence) was following Abu Hanifa. Can you call him someone who is crystallized? No. In his theology he follows one scholar and in his fiqh he follows someone else.

In other words, what are we arguing? We argue that when someone replies by commenting that history is "his story," we reply, yes, there may be moments where a person's opinions affect the way they write the history but many of our historians are objective.

Now that leads me to discuss the next methodology that is essential when reconstructing Islamic history: If we are only going to use historical sources to discuss the biography of the fourteen infallibles, we are going to find ourselves in a debate that is weak. They will keep coming back to us and they will keep saying, "...but it is a book of history and you cannot rely on history, and history is only writing 'his story.'"

So do you know what theory we are going to use in these biographies? We are going to use the theory of "intertextuality." Why should I discuss the biography of the Imams only from historical sources? Why do not I use different genres of Islamic literature? Julia Kristeva was the person who initiated the theory of intertextuality. She said, "When you want to discuss a particular figure in history or a particular nation, do not discuss them from one genre of literature. Use different genres of literature and discuss them because then you will allow yourself to see different codes of knowledge coming out from different areas of literature." What does this mean?

I mean, why should I only focus on history? Why don't we also use books of jurisprudence, which are known as books of fiqh? And why don't we use books of theology, which are known as books of kalam? And why don't we use books of belles-lettres, or Arabic literature, which are known as books of adab? When I want to dissect the life of Ja'far as-Sadiq (as), I do not need to just look at history. If I look at history books for Ja'far as-Sadiq (as), someone will come to me and say, "...but that historian is just being favorable to Ja'far as-Sadiq." So I say, "Okay, I won't just use books of history. I am going to look at all of the books of history on Ja'far as-Sadiq (as), and the books of fiqh on Ja'far as-Sadiq (as), and the books on theology of Ja'far as-Sadiq (as), and the books of adab and Arabic literature on Ja'far as-Sadiq (as)." Tell me, won't that give me a more holistic picture of Ja'far as-Sadiq (as)?

Numerous people, when they dissect the Imams, what do they do? They use only books of history and then someone will say, "Well, how is this book reliable?" So here, we shall use different genres of literature. Again, someone may turn around and say, "Why different genres of literature?" History will give me a narrative; fiqh will show me how much they contributed to this religion's legal system. If I take a book of early jurisprudence, I will show how Muhammad al-Baqir (as) is in a different league than anyone around him. If I only examine a book of history, I will only look at Muhammad al-Baqir (as) in terms of family, wife, children and wars. If I use a book of fiqh, I can show you Muhammad al-Baqir (as)'s legal knowledge of salat, sawm, zakat, hajj, khums and so on. But then I'm not going to stop there. Let me look at Muhammad al-Baqir (as) also from the viewpoint of theology; let's look at his sermons on predestination and free will. Let's look at his sermons on the importance of God's Mercy to mankind. Let's look at his sermons on theological issues about sin and the different types of sin.

Now look, I have Muhammad al-Baqir (as) from history; I have Muhammad al-Baqir (as) from fiqh; I have Muhammad al- Baqir (as) from theology, but I do not end there. I'm also going to look at Muhammad al-Baqir (as) from Arabic literature. Let us also look at the eloquence of Amir al-Mu'minin from Arabic literature - the khutba (sermon) of Imam Ali (as) where he does not use the letter "alif" even once. Or the khutba of Imam Ali (as) where he was asked, "Can you give a sermon without using a letter of the Arabic alphabet which has a dot?" He gave an entire sermon without using any of the letters with dots. If I use a book of history, Ali b. Abi Talib will be narrowed down to simply being a historical figure. Let me show Ali (as) from history, Ali (as) from fiqh, Ali (as) from theology, Ali (as) from Arabic literature. Then you will see why they are on a different level from those who surrounded them.

Now if someone asks, what are the sources you are going to use? The following are the sources I am going to use in discussing their biographies:

From history, I am going to use the works of al-Baladhuri, al-Tabari, b. Athir, Ya'qubi, and Mas'udi. These are going to be my historians.

For theology, I am going to use the works of Sheikh al-Mufid, Sharif al-Murtadha, al-Tawhidi, Qadhi Abdul Jabbar, and Qadhi al-Nu'man.

In fiqh, I'm going to use the works of al-Fiqh al-Akbar of Abu Hanifa, Kitab al-Umm of Imam al-Shafa'i, Malik's Muwwata, and the works of later jurisprudents like al-Jassas, and I will even be taking snippets from the works of al-Bukhari and Muslim and al-Nasa'i.

In Arabic literature, we are going to use al-Jahiz and Abu Hayyan al-Tawhidi.

So now we have four genres of literature to examine fourteen human beings. In addition to these sources I will also use the works of Abu al-Faraj al-Isfahani, such as Maqatil al-Talibiyyin, Kitab al-Aghani; the works of later historians and academic specialists like Aqqad, Tushtari, Lawasani, and Amin.

We will use all these works, and we won't just focus on historical works, but we will use the theory of intertextuality. Let's see how these texts, when they interact with each other, will provide you with the holistic figure that is the member of the household of the Prophet (pbuh).

However, then another question arises from the beginning, and the question is an interesting one: Give me the reference of one narration which mentions the Prophet (pbuh) talking about these twelve people, but before your Mahdi went into occultation.

Why? Because there is a theory that is being spread now that the idea of the infallibles is an idea that was concocted after the Mahdi. They do have a point here in this particular area because it is not easy to find a narration where the Prophet (pbuh) says, "These are the twelve Imams after me," by name. Someone might say, but it is in al-Kafi. Yes, but al-Kafi was written after the occultation. Someone may arqgue, it is in Man la Yahduruhu ul-Faqih, but that too was written after the occultation. Wasa'il ush-Shi'a, Bihar ul-Anwar , were all written after the occultation.

They say, "You want to discuss the idea of the twelve Imams after the Prophet (pbuh), but you do not even have an early narration about the Prophet (pbuh) mentioning them. All your narrations about them somehow come to us after they have all died. Why should we not suspect that someone came later and formed a theory where he picked out twelve and he said that 'the Prophet (pbuh) said follow these twelve?'"

You can contact many scholars and play the devil's advocate, and say, "Mawlana, can you show me a hadith where the Prophet (pbuh) says, 'These are the twelve after me, and these are their names,' and show me a hadith in a book which was not written after the occultation in a book which was written during their lives?" The moment you can answer this question then you can move on with the discussion, and I can tell you that it is not an easy question to answer; because there are many who come and tell you, "Where is this hadith about the Masumeen? I see the hadith is very late."

So yes, there is a chain that goes back to the Prophet (pbuh), and even though we do have chains that go back to him, we need a simpler argument, which is as follows:

We do have references that we can build to highlight why we need to discuss these fourteen or these twelve infallibles.

1- The first reference is in the book of al-Bukhari, who wrote the famous Sahih. He lived in 196 Hijra until the middle of the third century. In Sahih al-Bukhari, he mentions very clearly that "the Prophet says, 'After me there will be twelve caliphs; all of them are from the Qureish.'" Already we have the number twelve, isn't it? But did Bukhari write the Sahih after the twelfth Imam or before? Before. It was the beginning of the third century, thus before the time of the twelfth Imam (ajfs).

2- The sixth Imam had four hundred usul. His disciples would write his hadith; from these four hundred usul, only sixteen remain. There is an article on these usul by Etan Kohlberg, professor of Islamic studies at Tel Aviv University. He writes about these usul of Ja'far as-Sadiq, and which of them remain. Many of these hadiths were burnt or removed; only sixteen currently remain and they are in Iran. Thus, the manuscript of those sixteen usul have remained. Of these sixteen, there is one that is vital, and which is with us until today. The manuscript is called al-Asl Abu Saeed al-Asfari. He lived in the time of Imam as-Sadiq (as). Abu Saeed says that, "the Prophet (pbuh) says, 'There are twelve successors after me...'" and he named them from Imam until Imam.

3- The great companion of the Ahlulbayt (as), Fadl b. Shadhan, has a book called Kitab al-Ghayba. Fadl b. Shadhan was a companion, according to some, of the eighth, ninth, tenth and eleventh Imams. Fadl b. Shadhan has a hadith where the Prophet (pbuh) mentions the names of each of the twelve. Fadl b. Shadhan lived before the appearance of the twelfth Imam. If he had lived after, one could have supposed that the names were concocted.

4- Then there is a Zaydi leader. From our Zaydi brothers in Yemen, one of their great leaders was Qasim al-Rassi. He has a book called al-Rad ala ar-Rafidha, which means "A Reply to the Rejecters" (referring to the people of the Imamiyya school of thought). In this book he talks about our ninth Imam. He says, "And some of their Imams, according to them, know all that is guidance and faith as a young child…." Al-Rassi was living in the time of the ninth Imam. He does not say, "Muhammad al-Jawad...," but refers to him as "the Imam of the Rafidha…" proving that the idea of Imams was not an idea made after the twelfth Imam. It was a belief that had already existed at the time.

This is not an easy concept to grasp but understand that these documents are vital to show that there was already a discussion about the twelve infalllibles in the times of the Imams.

Is it only us, as Muslims, who need to dissect history? No. In the Bible the chapter of Genesis has a fundamental verse which highlights the fact that God has always promised the human being that his message would continue in a certain line. It is mentioned in Genesis, Chapter 17, Verse 18-20.

When Sarah could not give children to Abraham, she said, "Marry my maidservant Hagar." Hagar then gave birth to Isma'il. This story is discussed in the Bible in the chapter of Genesis. When she gives birth to Isma'il, it says in the Bible that "…she gave birth to the baby and a spring of water gushed." After that it says, "God says to Abraham, 'I will bless the generations of Isma'il, and make them blessed, and make them fruitful, and make them a large nation, and allow them to have twelve princes from his line.'"

In other words, when we are going to dissect the biography of the infallibles in this series, understand that this dissection is not just an Islamic or even an Imamiyya dissection, it is a dissection which is the responsibility of every one of you to spread to your non-Muslim brethren that God did promise that there will be twelve princes with a large nation from the line of Prophet Isma'il (as).

Lecture 1

The Holy Prophet Muhammad (pbuh)

The Holy Prophet of Islam occupies a prominent position within the religion of Islam and is revered as the greatest personality within the religion. He is a man whose life has to be examined in depth for there are many lessons to be learnt and indeed many examples to be derived. And he is indeed a man whose biography has been unfortunately very much undervalued and indeed very much underestimated. Therefore it is vital that we discuss his biography from the day that he was born until the day he died in order that we are able to, firstly, take as many practical lessons from his life and apply them in our own lives; and secondly, remove any misconceptions that surround his biography, for there was a period in Medieval Europe when he was seen as being the devil incarnate or as being the false Messiah, the Antichrist. Therefore, there is a need for us to examine his biography so that we present him in his true light - as a mercy for mankind and a moral exemplar for everyone.

The Significance of the Prophet (pbuh)'s Date of Birth

The Holy Prophet (pbuh) was born in the year 570, known as the "Year of the Elephant." The Arabs did not have a calendar dating system as such. They would look at what was the most important event in that particular year and then name the year after that event. For example, if there was a famous personality who died, they would name the year after that personality. Or if there was a war that took place, they would name the year after that war. The year within which the Prophet (pbuh) was born was called "Am ul-Feel," the Year of the Elephant. This was because of an incident that took place involving an army of elephants.

At that time in Arabia there were people who would visit the Ka'aba. In Yemen there was a church that was built by an Ethiopian man by the name of Abraha. [Bear in mind the words "Ethiopian," because Abraha's niece was Bilal al-Habashi's mother. When Abraha's niece was caught as a prisoner, she got married within one of the Arabian tribes and gave birth to a son by the name of Bilal. Hence, when Bilal is said to be of the people of Habash, it is because of his mother's uncle being Abraha, who was an Ethiopian, yet was the governor of Yemen.]

Abraha had always been envious of the fact that there were people who would visit the Ka'aba rather than his church in Yemen. He attempted to send emissaries and ambassadors to go towards the Ka'aba and tell the Arabs, "Leave your place of worship because your place has been polluted. Originally you were people of Abraham, but now you worship idols. It is better that all of you come to my church in Yemen and make my church the main center of the area." When he noticed that his emissaries were not successful, the narrations tell us that he decided it was better for him to take his army and march to the Ka'aba with an army of elephants. Hence, within the religion of Islam there is a chapter called "Surat al-Fil," which is chapter 105 of the Quran. The chapter begins, "Have you not seen how your Lord dealt with the People of the Elephant?" because, although Abraha arrived in Mecca with elephants, he had brought only a few elephants with him; as we know, elephants are of a size where there only needs to be a few for them to capture your attention. When he came towards Arabia with these elephants, there were people who were unquestionably scared. That is why the main person who thwarted his plans was Abdul Muttalib, the grandfather of the Prophet (pbuh).

Abdul Muttalib told the people to hide in the desert hills. So they went to hide there in the desert hills and then Abdul Muttalib was chosen by the people to meet Abraha. Notice from the beginning of the biography of the Prophet (pbuh) we see that the line of Abraham through Isma'il is still looking after the birthplace of Isma'il. Earlier on, we said that in Genesis, chapter 17, verse 18-20, says that "God promised Abraham that in the line of Isma'il there will be twelve princes who are part of a fruitful generation..."

Abdul Muttalib entered Abraha's tent. Abraha was sitting down. When Abdul Muttalib entered the tent, Abraha looked at him. He saw quite an imposing figure; he told him to sit down and then said to him, "What is it that you want?" Abdul Muttalib said, "I want my camels." Abraha said, "Sorry?" Abdul Muttalib said, "I want my camels. You took my camels. I want my camels returned back to me." Abraha looked at him and said, "Do you know when you entered my tent I had a lot of respect for you, but now I have lost all that respect." Abdul Muttalib said, "Why?" Abraha said, "When you entered my tent, I thought this is a man who will want to protect his 'black cube,' known as the Ka'aba, but instead all you want is the camels?" Abdul Muttalib said, "That house has a Lord of its own to protect it; and I am the protector of my lot of camels. I want my two hundred camels given back to me!" Abraha said, "Get out! Get out! There is no agreement between us."

Abdul Muttalib came back a second time to persuade him; again Abraha wouldn't agree. Abraha decided that he would take his elephant (most of the other narrations indicate another six or seven elephants) and march towards the Ka'aba. They marched towards the Ka'aba and the Quran put it quite beautifully when it said, "Have you not seen how your Lord dealt with the People of the Elephant? Did He not ruin their plan? And He sent against them flocks of birds, striking them with stones and petrified clay. And thus He reduced them to rotten chaff."

What did Allah do? He ensured that "you plan and I plan, but I am the greatest of planners." These elephants were ready to achieve victory. The narrations state very clearly that some birds pelted them with stones until the opposition army was defeated.

In other words, the Arabs had not began the Hijra calendar in the year in which the Prophet (pbuh) had been born. We know the Hijra calendar began after the Prophet (pbuh) migrated from Mecca to Medina. So from that time on they named their years 1 AH, 2 AH, 3 AH and 4 AH and so on, but before that they named their years according to the major incidents which happened in them.

There is a difference in the date of the Prophet's birth within the various schools in Islam. Our brothers in other schools celebrate his birth on the 12th of Rabi ul-Awwal whereas we celebrate his birth on the 17th of Rabi ul-Awwal. It is vital that this is not a cause of friction between us. Why? Ayatollah Montazeri used to stress on this week as being a week of unity between Muslims because all of us share a common denominator, and that is the life of our Prophet (pbuh). Therefore, it should be the case where our leaders and congregations go to the mosques of our brothers on the 12th of Rabi ul-Awwal and celebrate with them, and our brothers are welcomed into our mosques to celebrate with us on the 17th. Thus, there is a difference of opinion, and in the historical research you will find, barring Sheikh al-Kulayni, most of the others will say that he was born on the 17th of Rabi ul-Awwal.

The Initial Years of the Prophet (pbuh)'s life

The Prophet (pbuh)'s first few years of life were not easy. Imagine that your father passes away in first few years of your life; according to some narrations, it was only a few months into his life. Since his father Abdullah passed away, the Prophet (pbuh) therefore was born an orphan; hence the Quran says, "Did we not find you an orphan?" His mother Aminah did what most Arabs did with their babies at the time. If you were of the noble aristocracy of Mecca, what would you do with your baby? Eight days after the birth of their babies, the Meccan aristocrats would take them to the desert to be suckled and breast-fed by a wet nurse. Someone may ask, "Why couldn't his mother suckle him? Why did she have to take him to the desert?"

There were a number of reasons the Arabs, and especially the aristocrats, would take their babies to be raised in the desert. The reasons why the Arab aristocrats would send their infants to be raised in the desert are very important to understand because they have a major role to play on the upbringing and the psyche of the Prophet (pbuh).

The first reason is that it allows you to grow up in an environment where you are independent and a free thinker for the first few years of your life. In the desert there aren't buildings or forests surrounding you, nor are there lots of humans and shops, or markets and trade. It is open in the desert. You can sit there and look at the creation and reflect upon your creation and your meaning and role in life. The Arabs who would send their babies to have their first eight or ten years in the desert would want that baby to be living in a world where they would grow up as a child who is not told what to think, but is rather shown how to think.

The second reason was because Mecca's climate was not a healthy climate for children both in terms of what they saw and what they breathed. Imagine you are a child growing up in an environment where you see baby girls being buried alive? Is that a good start to your life? Or you see people performing tawaf (circumambulation) of the Ka'aba naked. The Arabs used to go around the Ka'aba naked because they said, "God created us free so there is no need for clothes; clothes are impure. Let's go and circumambulate His house like how He created us," completely naked. The Prophet (pbuh)'s mother wanted him to grow up in the desert so he would not see this.

The third reason was that Mecca's wind and climate was hot and unhealthy. There were pests and epidemics. So his mother made sure that he was sent there.

Most narrations say that there were two women who breast-fed the Prophet (pbuh), and Abdul Muttalib chose both of them. The first lady to have breast-fed the Prophet (pbuh) was Thuwayba, the servant of his uncle Abu Lahab. Before Muhammad (pbuh) announced his prophethood, Abu Lahab used to love the Prophet (pbuh) because he was his younger brother's son. So first Aminah asked Abdul Muttalib who should breastfeed their son and he said, "Thuwayba." Thuwayba also suckled Hamza because the Prophet (pbuh) and Hamza's ages were very similar. That is why when the Prophet (pbuh) was one day told to marry Hamza's daughter, he said, "We cannot because we suckled from the same wet nurse."

The other lady who Abdul Muttalib chose was Halima Sa'adiyya. Halima Sa'adiyya was a pious God-fearing lady. Halima Sa'adiyya herself would say, "I saw vast riches and goodness affect my life the moment I started to suckle the Prophet (pbuh)."

Some narrations in Islamic history try and tell us that when the Prophet (pbuh) was with Halima as a two-year-old, "he remembered" he was sitting down one day; two men came, opened his chest, gave him a "heart transplant" because there was the black dot of Satan (Satan) on his heart, so they put a new heart in and Muhammad was pure after that day.

We of course differ with this idea because even if someone has the dot of Satan, it is not on their physical heart. The dot on the heart is metaphorically referring to being on one's "nafs" (self or ego) therefore a change of the heart is not needed.

On the contrary, the Prophet (pbuh) was born with this purity. He did not need people to open him up, perform an operation, and then move on. The Quran says, "Have We not expanded for you your breast (which was able to take in knowledge)?" Therefore, some narrations say that Halima saw this happening to the Prophet (pbuh), but we differ with this completely.

Halima twice went back to Aminah, the mother of the Prophet (pbuh), and said to her, "Do you want to take him back to Mecca?" Aminah twice replied back to her saying, "O Halima, keep him there because I see diseases and epidemics which will affect him."

Some people ask the question, "If God loves Muhammad so much, why let him have such a difficult beginning as an orphan?" - meaning why did not God allow him to have a natural beginning like everyone else and have a father and a mother?

When the Imam was asked this question, he replied, "God wanted to ensure nobody protected and brought up Muhammad but Himself." He wanted to ensure that the Prophet (pbuh) would not show obedience to anybody, even from his early life, except Himself. Sometimes your parents may sway you one way or the other. Even though his parents were loyal believers in the message, God wanted to be the One who oversaw his development. Therefore you find that his father died when he was young, then his mother died, and then his grandfather Abdul Muttalib looked after him.

His grandfather died within a couple of years, so his uncle Abu Talib brought him up. His uncle Abu Talib acts as a backbone not only to him, but also to the message of the religion of Islam. Abu Talib preferred his nephew even above his sons. His wife Fatima bint Asad was exactly the same. When the Prophet (pbuh) buried Fatima bint Asad, he said, "This is my mother. This is the lady who preferred me above her sons. This is the lady who used to clothe me and wash me and look after me and she is the one who nourished me."

So notice these were the two who looked after him, and that is why there is a certain question that is asked: "What do we know about him before the age of forty?" In a few moments we will examine his life after the age of forty, but if you were to ask many Muslims, "Tell us about your Prophet before the age of forty," many would be unaware of his biography. Notice that before the age of forty, when Abu Talib was bringing him up, the Prophet (pbuh) would latch on to him everywhere he went to the extent that Abu Talib himself narrates, "One day I was about to leave for Syria on a commercial expedition. The young Muhammad was only twelve, and he latched on to me as I was leaving. When he latched on to me, it hurt me that my nephew was an orphan, so I said to myself, 'Let me take him with me.'"

The narration states that he took him towards Syria. On the way towards Syria they walked passed a monastery. The monk saw these people coming. They said to him, "We are coming here to reside for the night."

The monk looked at him and said to Abu Talib, "All of you can come and are welcome to eat what you want to eat, but Abu Talib, I want to ask you a question." Abu Talib said, "What is it?" He said, "You know that young man walking alongside you? Bring him along with you tomorrow as well." Abu Talib said, "Very well, I will bring him tomorrow." The next day when Abu Talib came, the monk looked at him and said, "Where is the young man?" Abu Talib said, "My nephew?" The monk said, "Yes." Abu Talib said, "He's just over there." The monk said, "Call him towards me."

And this is one of our proofs within Islamic theology that he was already inspired with the knowledge of God and the knowledge of his mission. It is not the case that he became a Prophet at the age of forty and was now told to announce his prophethood. He knew about his prophethood beforehand because that monk came to him when he was the age of twelve and said to him, "In the name of Allat and Uzza…"

As soon as the Prophet (pbuh) heard this, he said to him, "Do not mention those names in front of me. Those are the most detested names to me." They were the names of the idols of Qureish. Then the monk said, "I want to give you some sadaqa." The Prophet (pbuh) said, "We do not accept sadaqa."The monk then said to him, "Can I see the mark between your shoulders?"

He allowed him to see the mark between his shoulders and then he looked at Abu Talib and said, "Abu Talib, if you did not know already, then know that this young man is the Prophet whom Jesus spoke about, and whom Moses spoke about, and beware of the enemies that he is going to face." Abu Talib said, "How did you know?" He said, "When you were walking and Muhammad was next to you, I saw every tree bow down after Muhammad passed by."

The Prophet (pbuh)'s Love for Justice

Even after the age of twelve the Prophet (pbuh) had this innate love for justice and the removal of oppression. One of the greatest incidents that happened in his youth was at the age of twenty, and years later he would always refer back to this. At the age of twenty he joined a group called "Hilf ul-Fudul." What was this?

In Arabia many people would come to the markets. They came from outside the market area and would bring their goods as well, and the people of Arabia would buy them. One of these people came from the Banu Zabid tribe (or some say Banu Zubayd) to sell some of his goods to 'As b. Wa'il, the father of Amr b. 'As. When he sold these goods, he said to 'As, "Give me my money." 'As replied back to him, saying, "What money?" He said, "You've just taken my goods and I want my money back." 'As said, "There's no money for you and you are a stranger in our land. You are not going to get your money back and I am one of the aristocrats of Arabia so you might as well forget about it."

This person was so enraged that he went on one of the mountains of Arabia and said, "O people of Arabia! I have come as a stranger to your land and I have been involved in a business transaction. None of you have sought to help me when this man has taken my right. At least one of you speak up!"

A twenty year old man named Muhammad spoke up for him. He got up and said, "It is unjust for us to be like this with a person who is a guest in our location; and secondly, how can we be unjust when the goods have been sold in a business transaction? Let's form a league which looks after the rights of business employees and protects transactions within the Arabian state."

How old was he? Only twenty, and there was still no announcement of his prophethood; but from that young age the first sign that people noticed was that he was a man who spoke out against injustice.

In 2012, how many of us speak out against injustice, whether it be injustice against Muslims or non-Muslims? Our Prophet (pbuh) did not look at that man and say, "Well, that man is not a Muslim so I am not going to speak up for his right." Whenever we see any oppression anywhere in the world, we must speak out against that oppression because our Prophet (pbuh) taught us this even from the time of his youth. This is the first lesson that we can take from him.

Not only did he achieve this at the age of twenty, later on he achieved two attributes which the Arabs would honor him for. They gave him the title, "as-Sadiq" (the Truthful) and "al-Amin" (the Trustworthy). Notice that the Arabs did not know that he was a Prophet nor did they receive any book from him, but they were concerned with his ethics as a human being.

When a flood affected the Ka'aba and it was damaged, they needed to put the Hajr al-Aswad (the black stone) back into the Ka'aba after repairs were made. The Arabs fought with each other about who would put the Hajr al-Aswad back in its position. One tribe said, "We should put it back." Another said, "We should put it back." A third said, "We should put it back!" They said, "Okay, let's do this. The man who walks into this meeting next will be the one who chooses which tribe puts it back." As soon as he walked in, they did not say, "Muhammad has walked in." They said, "as-Sadiq…al-Amin has walked in!" The focus wasn't on the name; the focus was on the morals of the man.

Today in Islam there is too much focus on names and not morals. When he began his prophethood, or even before he began, he did not just come in front of the people and say, "People! I am a Prophet. Follow me!" You need to have those attributes where, for forty years, no one can find a black dot on you.

Yet do you know what we do as humans? If you give us a white piece of paper and there is a black dot in the middle and you ask us, "What is on that paper?," we will say, "A black dot." None of us will focus on the white, will we? We love to focus on the dots. Even if there is so much white about someone's character, all we can remember is the black dot; whereas the Prophet (pbuh) did not allow them to point at one black dot - he was Sadiq and Amin.

Therefore, when he came to announce his prophethood, he said, "Did you not call me as- Sadiq? Did you not call me al-Amin? When the Hajr ul-Aswad was to be placed in the Ka'aba, was I not the one who said, 'O you four tribes, do not fight each other. One of you hold one part of the cloth, another hold a second, a third hold the third, and the fourth hold the fourth part of the cloth; all four of you carry the Hajr ul-Aswad and I will pick it up from you and I will place it inside.'"

The Aim of his Prophethood

1- To spread awareness

When he announced his prophethood at the age of forty, the question arises, what was the aim of his prophethood? The aim was nothing more than allowing mankind to meditate and reflect on their existence, in order that, after meditation and reflection, mankind not only had respect for themselves but they had respect for other creations of God as well.

We made our Prophet (pbuh)'s religion complicated, whereas his mission from the beginning was a mission that was simple. Arabians were in Jahiliyya (Age of Ignorance). If any society is stagnant, it means that it is a society that does not reflect; and when the human does not reflect, then he is the cause of a virus in his society.

When the Prophet (pbuh) began his mission, did he begin his mission by saying, "All of you, must pray right now!"? Did he say, "All of you, it is Shahr Ramadan…Fast! Fast!" "All of you, keep a beard!" or "All of you, wear hijab!"? He began first by saying, "Mankind, reflect on your existence. Have an hour of reflection, it is greater than seventy years of worship." Today's Islam is too dogmatic. It is too focused on halal… haram…halal…haram…wajib…makrooh…halal…haram. Is this what the Prophet (pbuh) brought to mankind?

The first part of the Prophet (pbuh)'s mission was to emphasize that a true human being is one who is reflecting on his role in this world. The moment he reflects, everything else will fall into place. The Muslims of today focus on the jigsaw pieces and have forgotten the puzzle.

Miqdad, a close companion of the Prophet (pbuh), says, "In those early days in Islam I heard the Prophet through one hadith saying, 'An hour of reflection is greater than a year of worship'; Then I heard b. Abbas say that the Prophet said, 'An hour of reflection is greater than seven years of worship'; Then I heard another companion say that the Prophet said, 'An hour of reflection is greater than seventy years of worship.' So I decided that I was going to go to the Prophet and ask him, how is it that in one hadith you are telling the people an hour of reflection is greater than a year of worship; then in a second you are saying it is greater than seven years of worship; then in a third you are saying it is greater than seventy years of worship?"

When he asked the Prophet (pbuh), the Prophet (pbuh) said, "Miqdad, come with me. Let's ask the first person." They asked the first person, "How do you reflect?" He said, "I look at the creations of the heavens and the earth and I think to myself that these could not have come by an accident." The Prophet (pbuh) said, "His one hour of reflection is greater than a year of worship." Then they went to the second and said to him, "How do you reflect?" He said, "I think about the Day of Judgment and the questions I am going to be asked, about what I did in public, and what I did in private." The Prophet (pbuh) said, "His one hour of worship is greater than seven years of worship." Then they went to the third and asked, "How do you reflect?" He said, "I am going to be very frank with you, I think about the hellfire and I get scared." The Prophet (pbuh) said, "His one hour of reflection is greater than seventy years of worship." Why? Because the moment you think about the hellfire it will make you change your ways quite quickly.

Thus the Prophet (pbuh) began first by saying, "One hour of reflection in this religion is greater than seventy years of dry worship." You can fast and pray, and fast and pray, and fast and pray, but if you fast for thirty days in the year and for the other three hundred and thirty-five days you are not reflecting on your life, on your role, on your meaning, on your objectives, then you have not understood the true message of the religion of Islam. On the other hand, the moment you reflect on your creation that you were one day insignificant, you weren't worth mentioning, you came from something that when you look at it you are disgusted, then you may look at those around you and say, "If I am so low, then why am I so arrogant to those who are around me?"

That is why, when the Prophet (pbuh) first began his mission at the age of forty, he asked people to reflect on their existence.

2- To eradicate racism and respect all of mankind

Then he brought their attention to the disease of racism in their society. Why? Because he knew that when the human reflects upon things, he will never be a racist. Am I better than another just because I am a certain color? No. We are both sons of Adam created from dust. Thus in the first part of his prophethood he spoke out against any type of racism.

How did Bilal come to Islam? Bilal came to Islam when he saw Ammar b. Yasir captured one day. When Ammar was captured, the early aristocrats of the Qureish looked at Ammar and said, "O Ammar, are you the one who is trying to come forward and say that Muhammad's religion is the one we should follow?" Ammar said, "Yes." He said, "Explain to me Muhammad's religion." Ammar said, "The Prophet talks of one God and that God is Merciful to His creation. He has given them free will and has a Day of Judgment where He will judge us, but He will not judge us on our race. He will judge us according to our consciousness of His presence."

Bilal was standing there. Bilal was then still a slave. At that moment, one of the members of the Qureish said to Bilal, "Bilal torture Ammar." Bilal said "No." He said, "What? Bilal! You black slave, torture Ammar!" Bilal said, "No." He said, "How dare you, Bilal! We brought you up. Torture him!" Bilal said, "I have never heard of a message where a man with my skin complexion is protected, where a man of my skin color is honored."

Notice here that when Bilal came towards Islam, it was because there was the avenue of reflection by the Prophet (pbuh). He allowed the religion to be intellectually spread, not emotionally.

In Medina when the Prophet (pbuh) said, "I want someone to call for prayer," the people came forward and asked the Prophet (pbuh) whom he would assign to call for prayer. The Prophet (pbuh) said, "Bilal, go up and give the adhan." Therefore the Prophet (pbuh) destroyed racism from the beginning.

He preached the fact that not only should we respect people from different races, but we must also learn to respect people of different religions. In the early years of his prophethood, his companions were being tortured, so he said to Ja'far b. Abu Talib, "Ja'far, go to Abyssinia. Leave with the companions." Ja'far said, "Where shall we go?"

The Prophet (pbuh) said, "Ja'far, go to Abyssinia because you will meet a Christian priest." Notice the message. On the first level he wants to remove racism, then encourage respect towards other human beings, and then to other religions, because if their principles are the same as ours then they are closer to us than people of our religion who are hypocrites without our principles. Thus Ja'far went to Abyssinia and met the Christian priest. Amr b. 'As was alongside Ja'far. When Ja'far came, the Abyssinian priest asked, "Who are these people?"

Ja'far replied by saying, "We are people who believe in all the prophets and the final prophet of God, who spoke about Jesus, son of Mary." When the priest heard this, he said, "What does your book say about Jesus, son of Mary?" He said, "Our Book says that Jesus, son of Mary, was born from a virgin birth and a chapter is named after his mother Maryam."

The Prophet (pbuh) could have said, "But he is a Christian and he believes in the crucifixion of Christ and we do not believe in that." On the contrary, the Prophet (pbuh) said, "He is a believer in God and there are more similarities between us than there are differences." Look at the attitude the Muslims have today. They do not look at a human being as a fellow member of humanity rather they look at them as disbelievers.

Thus the early message of Islam was: no racism and respect people of other religions because those people have principles that we preach and understand. Thus, because of this, Ja'far was able to stay in Abyssinia and build the early Muslim community in Africa.

3- To empower women

In the early years of Mecca the Prophet (pbuh) preached not only respect of other human beings and other religions but also the respect of the other gender. The Prophet (pbuh) saw that femAl infants were being buried alive; these people had no morals. Even someone like Umar b. Khattab himself narrates, "In the days of Jahiliyya before Islam came, we used to bury our daughters alive. There are two things, one of which makes me cry and the other makes me laugh. The one that makes me laugh is that we used to worship a god made out of dates. During our worship, when nobody was looking, we would take a date and eat it. By the end of our worship that god was dead. That used to make me laugh. The area that used to make me cry was when I buried my daughter alive. My daughter held onto my beard as I was burying her. But I got the spade and I hit her and I buried her alive."

Thus, the Prophet (pbuh) made them first reflect on their existence, then he made them respect fellow nations and reject bigotry, then he commanded tolerance towards other religions, and then he led them to respect the role of woman in society. He knew that if women were given rights there would be great nations. He established that first, women were not to be buried alive; then women were to inherit and not be inherited; and dowries were to belong to women. In the days of Arabian Jahiliyya, the dowry went to the father of the girl, not the girl. Then he said, "Heaven lies underneath the feet of the mother."

One day a young Jewish man who became a Muslim came to the Prophet (pbuh) and said, "O Prophet, my mother is Jewish but I am a Muslim. How do I treat her now that I have become a Muslim?" The Prophet (pbuh) said, "You treat her better than you used to treat her before." He went home and started to do all the chores; his mother looked at him and said, "Ever since you became a Muslim, you behave like this. Why?" He said, "My Prophet tells me that heaven lies underneath your feet." She said, "If this is what the Prophet (pbuh) preaches, then I want to join the religion of this Prophet."

4- To Set the Standard for the Highest and Perfect Morals

As a result of his moral system, even his enemies would respect him, so much so that many of them would keep their trusts with him.

He lived in Mecca for thirteen years and then he migrated to Medina and lived there for ten years. On the night that he left Mecca, he left Ali b. Abi Talib behind to sleep in his bed. Was this the only role of Ali b. Abi Talib (as)? No. Ali b. Abi Talib (as) had a second role. "O Ali, after you have left my bed, the next day return the trusts of my enemies that they entrusted with me."

Imagine the enemies of Qureish saying to the Prophet (pbuh), "We do not believe in you, we hate you, you are crazy…do you mind looking after this gold necklace for us?" Because it was an ethical trait where even though the person is his enemy he as a Prophet (pbuh) of God has not come to make enemies. If he can show that he is trustworthy, then let his enemies deposit [their belongings] with him. Thus, after living in Mecca for thirteen years, he moved on to Medina.

5- To respect all religions and encourage literacy

At the age of 53, when he went to Medina, they fought him in battles. Many people say, "Muhammad spread his religion by the sword." The reality is that those battles were defensive battles and not offensive battles. Were they defensive battles which only protected Muslims? No. The Quran says in chapter 22, verse 39-40, "And had repelled not God some people by others, verily had the monasteries been pulled down and the churches and the synagogues and the mosques in which God's name is much mentioned."

I ask you, that if this Prophet (pbuh) came to spread his religion by the sword, why is the Quran talking about churches and synagogues? Islam was trying to say that when we are defending ourselves in Medina we are looking to defend every single area of worship that says "There is only one God." It is not just for the Muslims. The Quran says, in chapter 3, verse 64, "Say, 'O People of the Book! Come to a word common between us and you that we worship none but God and shall not associate anything with Him and some of us take not others for lords other than God."

After those early battles, you even notice his focus on the message of education. After the Battle of Badr, when he takes prisoners, his companions said to him, "Let's kill them." He said, "No. Let's treat them well and make a proposition to them." They said, "What?" He said, "We will ransom them if they teach ten of our people how to read and write."

From the beginning the message in Medina was focused on education: "Seek knowledge from the cradle to the grave…Read until the final moments of your life…The value of a believer is their knowledge, their wisdom." Thus the Prophet (pbuh) introduced the idea of reading and writing among the Muslims because he knew that these skills were the basis of a great society.

Then, after establishing himself as the head of the state in Medina, he created treaties called "The Constitution of Medina" and the "Pact of Najran." The Constitution gave the Jews the freedom to worship in their synagogues and the Pact gave Christians the right to worship in their churches, alongside the Muslims who would worship in their mosques. He emphasized that there was nothing wrong with having a society with multi-religious dimensions.

6- To Spread Mercy and Compassion through Forgiveness and Patience

And even after that, in Medina, when the Prophet (pbuh) was ordered by His Lord to go back to Mecca, which he had not visited ever since he was expelled…when he returned to Mecca, his companions said, "Let's go back and fight those Meccans!" He said, "No, we will conduct a peace treaty with them." They said, "What do you mean by a peace treaty? Surely it is our chance to destroy these people's lives, to finish them like they tortured us." The Prophet (pbuh) said, "No. Let us have a peace treaty and allow them to be opened up to the mercy of the religion of Islam."

When the Prophet (pbuh) entered Mecca victorious, he taught us another ethical lesson of forgiveness. Many Muslims find it hard to forgive today. People find it hard to forgive a person who wrongs them, or a person who they see committing a wrong. You tell them, "But the years have gone by. Maybe the person has changed or repented." But they refuse, whereas their Prophet (pbuh) was the most forgiving of men.

When Mecca was conquered, there were two people who approached the Prophet (pbuh) and he forgave them. The first of them was Wahshi, the man who mutilated the body of his uncle Hamza to the extent that Hind, the mother of Mu'awiya, cut so many pieces of Hamza's body that she made a necklace for herself. This Wahshi ripped Hamza's chest apart. When Mecca was conquered, Wahshi, Abu Sufyan, Hind and people like Habbar b. Aswad, thought to themselves, "We are never going to be forgiven by Muhammad; Muhammad is going to enter Mecca and is going to execute us for what we did."

Wahshi and Habbar said, "But we hear Muhammad is a man of Mercy and that his religion is merciful and forgiving. He came to perfect the akhlaq of man." So they said, "Let us go and approach him." Wahshi went to him and said, "O Prophet of God, forgive me. I was in the days of ignorance. I did not know about the message of Islam. I heard rumors about you but they were not true. Prophet (pbuh) of God, forgive me for what has happened." And the reply was, "O Wahshi, you are forgiven. Now leave this area."

Then Habbar b. Aswad came forward. One of the Prophet (pbuh)'s stepdaughters was pregnant. She was going towards Medina. Habbar wanted her to miscarry, so on her way to Medina, he came and scared her in such a way that she ended up miscarrying her child. When the Prophet (pbuh) heard this, he was saddened. So when Habbar came to the Prophet (pbuh) after the conquest of Mecca, he said, "O Prophet of God, I am the cause of the miscarriage of your grandchild. I scared her in a way that led her to miscarry, but I was ignorant and they deceived me about your behavior and your character. When I see you now, I see a man of morals. Please allow me to be forgiven." We must ask ourselves, as Muslims today, how forgiving are we of our brothers, sisters, aunts, uncles, grandparents and cousins?

The Prophet (pbuh) told him, "You are forgiven by Allah. Do not worry over what you have done." The Prophet (pbuh) knew that the basis of a great community is all of these ethics of tolerance, patience and forgiveness. We must take our morals from him. Some of us have to be patient in our marriages; some of us have to be patient with our children. He too had to be patient with his marriages and his children. He had married a lady by the name of Shamba. Narrations say that this lady was the daughter of Amr al-Ghaffariyya. When she saw the Prophet's son Ibrahim die, she said, "You know, if you were a Prophet of God, God would not have made your son die; I'm leaving you!" and she left. Do you know how much patience you need to have when you are married to someone and they speak like that to you? But the Prophet (pbuh) was patient.

He had another wife by the name of Malika. Once she heard someone say that, "Muhammad is the cause of your father's death." She took all her possessions and left. Sometimes in life we complain about what we have to face, but our Prophet (pbuh) had to face more than us. He used to say, "Patience is to faith like the head is to the body." There can be no body without a head and there can be no faith without patience. Even he had to see a lot of his children die. His son Ibrahim died, his son Qasim died, even his son Abdullah died. Some of us today ask, "Why did our children die? Why did my friend's child die?" When we say, "The Prophet (pbuh) is an example," it is because everything that we face, the Prophet (pbuh) faced in his life as well.

7- To Leave Behind a Legacy of Perfect Morals

That is why, before he died, he did what any great leader would do. He made it clear to his people that "even though I am dying, I will first ensure that I will leave behind guidance for you." He left behind guidance on the Day of Ghadir when he raised the hand of Ali and made it clear to the people that "I will never leave this world without ensuring that there is a guide for you who continues to protect the message in the way I gave you the message."

But his final act was a true act of charity. In Islam, causing a fellow human being to smile is an act of charity. When his daughter Fatima came towards him when he was dying, there is a narration that states that first she cried and then she smiled. In this one act, the Prophet (pbuh) was showing us that, from the beginning of his life until the end, ethics and morality was the message of his biography. When Fatima turned around and they asked her, "Fatima, you cried and then smiled?" She said, "I cried because he told me that he was about to pass away; but then I smiled because he told me that I would be the first from his family to join him."

Notice from the beginning until the end he was a man who brought a smile onto the lives of humanity, and left with a smile, and that is why until today it is not only Islam that respects him but others as well.

Guru Nanak, the founder of the Sikh religion, believed that "Muhammad was an agent of Brahman." Some Christian priests have been quoted as saying, "Although we do not believe in the Prophet, he was a moral exemplar to mankind." And there are no better words than the words of Gandhi when he said, "It is impossible that millions are attracted to this man because of his sword. No, it was not his sword. It was his pledges which he kept and his simplicity in his life and his devotion to his family and friends that made this man the man that he was." Gandhi then said, "I was saddened when the second volume of his biography ended because I wish I had learnt more about this man, a man whom there is none like, Muhammad."

May Allah's Peace, Mercy and Blessings be upon him and his purified family.

Lecture 2

Lady Fatima Zahra (as)

Lady Fatima (as) was born in the year 615 and died in the year 633 (11 after Hijra). She is revered as the greatest woman in the history of the religion; a lady from whose life many extraordinary lessons may be learnt and many examples may be derived; and a lady who is revered for her sacrifice, humility, bravery and for her devotion towards the message of the religion of Islam. There is no lady in the history of the religion of Islam who has been seen as a role model in the life of billions of people in the world today like "the Lady of Light"; to the extent that the Prophet (pbuh) himself would say, "There are four women who are seen as the women of paradise: Asiyya (the wife of Pharaoh), Maryam (the mother of Jesus), Khadija (the wife of the Prophet) and Fatima Zahra."

Unfortunately, however, her biography has not been given the attention that it deserves, and so here we seek to examine her biography in depth in order that we may be able to learn as many lessons as possible.

Lady Fatima (as)'s Parents

Lady Fatima (as)'s father was the Holy Prophet of Islam (pbuh); her mother was a renowned lady by the name of Khadija bint Khuwaylid (as). The Prophet (pbuh) and Lady Khadija (as) share ancestry in the fifth descendant of their lineage. Lady Khadija (as) was the daughter of Khuwaylid, son of Asad, son of Abdul Uzza, son of Qusay; and the

Prophet (pbuh) was Muhammad, son of Abdullah, son of Abdul Muttalib, son of Hashim, son of Abd Manaf, son of Qusay. Therefore, in the fifth generation, there is an ancestral link between the two of them.

Lady Khadija (as)'s family was one of the most revered families in Arabia; each member of her family held a lofty position. Lady Fatima (as)'s grandfather, Khuwaylid, alongside Abdul Muttalib, were the chief patrons of Qureishi society when it came to the protection of the Ka'aba. The two main people in charge of the Ka'aba were Abdul Muttalib and Khuwaylid. Khuwaylid's original name was "Khalid," but in Arabia if your name was Khalid, your nickname would become Khuwaylid; or for example, if your name was "Jabir," your nickname would be "Juwayber." Thus even when Abraha led his army, Khuwaylid and Abdul Muttalib were the two people who were in charge of the Ka'aba at the time. Therefore, Lady Fatima (as)'s great grandfather was the protector of the Ka'aba, alongside Abdul Muttalib.

Another famous personality from her mother's line was her uncle Usayd. He was Lady Fatima (as)'s mother's brother. Usayd too had a prominent position in Arabian society. They used to call him "the just man of the Arabs." In the days before the Prophet (pbuh) announced his prophethood, if someone came with a set of goods and wanted to sell them in Arabia, there was no guarantee of him getting his money. During those days the Arabs formed a group called "Hilf ul-Fudul," or the League of Justice. This group originated because one day a man from a tribe came towards Arabia and wanted to sell his goods, but he realized that these people had taken his goods and were not going to give him his money back. The narrations state that this man complained on the mountain saying, "O people of Mecca! I have come as a guest to you; you have taken my goods without honoring my income. This is unjust and oppressive!" There were two men who stood up for this man; one of them was the Prophet (pbuh) and the other was Usayd. Khadija's uncle Usayd then joined this group and called it "Hilf ul-Fudul." Sometimes it is also translated as "The Federation of the Confederates." Thus a number of tribal leaders came together and formed this league of justice, which took the responsibility of protecting the rights of anyone who came to Arabia to conduct a business transaction .

Lady Khadija (as) also had a cousin (some say he was her uncle) by the name of Waraqa b. Nawfal. According to narrations he was of the monotheists. There was a group of people who were still following the message of Abraham, and Waraqa was one of them. Narrations state that he was one of the first men who spoke out against burying female infants alive. As mentioned previously in regard to Arabian society, it was a common practice for the female to be buried alive. The Quran mentions the practice, saying, "When one of them is given the news of a female, his face darkens with anger and he is in a state of grief." The reason that they would bury the femAl alive was because, in their opinion, she was of no use to them economically; for example, she was not going to stand in the markets with them or manage the stalls. Another reason was that, if there was a war, she would be of no use as she would not be able to fight or help in that war; moreover, they thought she could bring embarrassment to the tribe if she decided to run off with a man of another tribe. Thus it was more convenient for them to bury the females. Waraqa would stand in front of the Arabs and say, "O people of Arabia! If it is money that you look for, then I do not mind paying you; but please stop burying these females alive! This is unjust and barbaric!"

In other words, Lady Fatima (as) had many members from her mother's side who played a prominent role in Arabian society and all of them were monotheists who believed in the oneness of God.

Lady Khadija (as) suffered a setback very early on in her life. The narrations state that Lady Khadija (as)'s parents passed away, leaving her to be the inheritor of the family business along with her sister Hala and her two brothers, Awam and Usayd. Many people attack the religion of Islam saying, "Women do not have a role in business and they cannot go out and earn their own income," whereas Lady Khadija, from the very beginning, looked after her family business following the death of her parents. However, Mecca was not very conducive for business. Mecca used to hold three fairs a year but the real business took place elsewhere. In those days the Arabian caravans would travel to two specific places for trade: in the summer months the caravans would go to Syria and in the winter they would go to Yemen.

In Syria there were a variety of products that they could buy and Yemen was particularly famous for its coffee. Lady Khadija (as) would send her caravans to these two places. Lady Khadija (as) had a servant by the name of Mayserah; one day she said to Mayserah, "I want you to employ someone who can look after my caravans." Mayserah said, "Who exactly are you looking for?" She said, "I'm looking for somebody who knows how to travel in the desert and who can be weary of the highway thieves at night and who has the ability to understand medicine." Mayserah said, "Very well. I will go on this journey, and if I see anyone with these attributes, I will tell you."

At the time Abu Talib used to take the Prophet with him to Syria. When Mayserah was on his journey he found out about the Prophet's reputation as someone with a fantastic memory; someone who could glide through the deserts and was not scared of the highway thieves. So when Mayserah returned he said to Lady Khadija (as), "Khadija, I have found a man and they call him, 'as-Sadiq (the truthful),' and 'al-Amin (the trustworthy).'" She said, "What's his name?" He said, "Muhammad in Abdullah." She said, "Very well then, why don't we employ him for our business?" Mayserah then went to Abu Talib and said, "O Abu Talib, will you allow your nephew to join our company?" Abu Talib said, "By all means. Khadija is the daughter of Khuwaylid; Khuwaylid was a friend of my father. It would be an honor for us to have our nephew join your company."

Lady Khadija (as) had told Mayserah from the beginning, "Tell Muhammad I will double his commission if he comes back successful." This shows her generosity as a businesswoman. The Arabs used to call her "Amirat Qureish," or the Princess of the Qureish. She was not called this because of her great business ventures but because of the generosity and large heartedness she used to show in dealing with her workers. Some Muslims today can be the stingiest with their employees; sometimes they go through every loophole to be able to go below minimum wage. Their thinking is "How can I squeeze as much as possible from my worker?" This is extremely un-Islamic. On the contrary, Lady Khadija (as) was willing to double his commission depending on how well the Prophet (pbuh) did. She then told Mayserah to give her a report about his behavior.

Mayserah went with the Prophet; they traded and came back with double the profits. Mayserah came to Lady Khadija (as) and said, "You know, I have seen something that I have never seen in my life." She said, "What is it?" He said, "It's not about the 100% profits that we made; it is just that I have never seen a human being like this man." Lady Khadija said, "What do you mean?" He said, "His memory is unbelievable; when he trades with people he deals with them with humility, but there is something that he does that I have never seen another human being living in this entire area do." Lady Khadija said, "What is it?" He said, "When he finishes a transaction, he leaves the market and goes to sit by himself and he begins to whisper something as if he is meditating between himself and a force on this earth which nobody can know. I see that Muhammad is not consumed by the business, rather the business is a servant of Muhammad."

Today many of us are consumed by our businesses while our daily prayers are completely ignored; we neglect our families and tend to become irritable. All the Islamic principles begin to leave us - whereas the Prophet used to leave and sit and speak to the Lord by himself as if he was in constant gratitude for what he had earned.

On hearing this, Lady Khadija (as) said, "Very well. Then tell Muhammad that now that he has done this for me in Syria, I will triple his commission if he does well in Yemen." The Prophet (pbuh) achieved tremendous success in Yemen as well.

One day Lady Khadija (as) was talking to her friend Nafisa and said, "I have never seen anyone like this man, the success he has brought me, the humility and trustworthiness he has." Nafisa said, "Khadija, for how long?" Lady Khadija said, "What do you mean?" Nafisa said, "For how long will you remain unmarried? How many proposals have you had from the Qureish that you keep rejecting?" So Nafisa suggested that she marry the Prophet (pbuh). She said, "If he has all these qualities, then what are you waiting for?" Lady Khadija said, "Okay, then you take the proposal."

Thus match-making between couples was going on from the time of the Prophet. Today in our communities we question this match-making. It was a commendable practice that brought Khadija and the Prophet (pbuh) together. So Nafisa went to the Prophet and said, "Muhammad, I have someone for you for marriage. Would you be interested?" The Prophet asked, "Who?" She said, "Khadija." The Prophet said, "Khadija…for me?" This statement is a clear indication of that lady's greatness. Imagine if the Prophet (pbuh) says this about someone, then how pure must that human being be? He said, "Would she accept someone like me?" Nafisa said, "I know she will."

When Abu Talib was told about this proposal he had a smile on his face like he had never had before. Abu Talib said, "Very well, I will take the proposal to Khadija's house and to honor this marriage I will present the cloak and the staff of Abdul Muttalib." the Prophet (pbuh) was made to wear a black turban and an agate (aqeeq) ring and they went with the proposal.

One would think that, because Lady Khadija was wealthy, she would ask for a high dowry, but someone who knows that contentment in life is better than a high dowry will not ask for a high dowry. The Prophet (pbuh) said, "The worst of women is the one who asks for a high dowry."

For the Prophet (pbuh) and Lady Khadija (as), the dowry was set at 400 gold coins, and thereafter the marriage was conducted. They broke all the stereotypes in their marriage. In Arabia a woman had to be equal to a man on three levels and greater than him in one; whereas a man had to be greater than a woman in other areas. A woman had to be equal to a man in wealth, age and descent and greater than him in terms of her looks. The man had to be greater than a woman in wealth and height. So here Lady Khadija (as) was wealthier than the Prophet (pbuh) and a couple of years older than him.

Abu Talib then prayed, "In the name of Allah, the Most Beneficent, the Most Merciful. We are the children of Abraham from the line of Ishaq and Isma'il. It is my honor to bring Muhammad b. Abdullah to Khadija bint Khuwaylid…" and he continued the sermon after which the marriage took place. [Some people are of the opinion that Abu Talib died a disbeliever, but this sermon is one of the many proofs of his belief in Allah.]

One would think that when they got married their early years would be easy because on one side you have Lady Khadija (as) and on the other side you have the Prophet (pbuh); Allah loved the two of them and so they should have had no problems whatsoever. But on the contrary, they had the most difficult early years. It was as if Allah was showing us that, if in your early years you cannot have children, then the creation I loved more than any other creation could not have children (who stayed alive in their early years) either. The Prophet (pbuh) had a son Qasim who died; he had another son, Abdullah, who died as well. One can very well imagine that when he used to walk in the streets of Mecca, especially after he had announced his prophethood and had been married for a while, people would mock him by saying, "Abtar!," meaning, "the one with no line." Al-'As b. Wa'il, who was the father of Amr b. 'As, an ardent enemy of Islam, used to mock the Prophet (pbuh) every time he would see him.

Lady Fatima (as)'s Birth and Childhood

Thus, sometimes in life we are tested with our wealth, health or our education or with our children; there is no one on this earth who will not be tested in one of these four areas of their lives. The Prophet (pbuh) therefore had to patiently ignore the people mocking him until Allah revealed the verse, "Verily, We have granted you Abundance!" This was when Allah blessed the couple with Lady Fatima (as).

It is narrated within the traditions that when Lady Fatima (as) was born, the Prophet (pbuh) would frequently smell her and say, "From Fatima emanates the aroma of Jannah."

When Lady Khadija (as) was about to give birth to Lady Fatima (as), none of the women of Mecca came to help her. They said to her, "You married Muhammad, the imposter, the magician, the sorcerer! Do not expect us to help you when you give birth!"

But Allah is the Best of Helpers! Normally as a lady you want your sisters and mother and family around you; but when nobody was around Lady Khadija, the hadith states that Allah sent four women from the heavens to help her give birth to Lady Fatima (as): Maryam, the mother of Jesus; Eve, the wife of Adam; Asiyya, the wife of Pharaoh; and Kulthum, the sister of Musa.

When Lady Khadija (as) gave birth to Lady Fatima (as), it was the year 615, which was the most turbulent time for the Prophet (pbuh) in his prophethood. When the young Fatima was about two or three years old, the Qureish had placed economic sanctions on the Prophet. The Banu Hashim were confined to Shi'b Abi Talib (the Valley of Abu Talib) for three years where Lady Khadija spent all her money to provide food for the Muslims who were staying there. When the Prophet would sleep, Lady Khadija would stay awake to protect him. She would eat from the plants there so that the Prophet could eat whatever was healthy for him. Thus Lady Fatima (as) was witnessing the hardships her family had to endure at the hands of the Qureish.

After the sanctions, and upon returning from Shi'b Abi Talib, Lady Khadija developed a fever, from which she eventually passed away. Thus Lady Fatima (as), after only a few years of her life, became an orphan. All she had in her life now was her father. Now she witnessed her father being mocked, ridiculed and abused on several occasions. For instance, once the Prophet was in prostration near the Ka'aba. Lady Fatima (as) who was five or six years old at the time was sitting there. All of a sudden Abu Jahal came with the feces of a camel and poured it on the Prophet. Lady Fatima (as) went up to her father and said, "O father, do not worry; I will clean it up for you." She brought a cloth and helped her father wipe off everything. This was just one of the several occasions in which she would assist her father. That is why, whenever she would walk into a room, the Prophet would stand up for her in respect and say, "Fatima Umm Abiha! Fatima is the mother of her father!"

The wife of Abu Lahab used to collect firewood, burn it and then throw it on the Prophet while he would be walking on the streets. She would even place thorns outside his house so that he might step on them and hurt himself. Lady Fatima (as) would remove those thorns from her father's feet and clear the pathway for her father outside the house. No lady equaled that loyalty to the Prophet after her.

When the Qureish eventually wanted to kill the Prophet, he said to her, "O Fatima, I'm about to leave Mecca to go to Medina. There is a young man who will sleep in my bed tonight. That man who sleeps in my bed tonight will bring you to Medina tomorrow." She said, "Who, O my father?" He said, "Ali b. Abi Talib." She said, "Very well. Has he accepted to sacrifice his life for you?" He said, "He told me, 'O Prophet! It is the greatest honor for me to sacrifice my life for you tonight.' So tomorrow you, Fatima bint Asad (mother of Imam Ali), and Fatima, the daughter of your uncle Hamza, will all go with Ali b. Abi Talib after he has returned the trusts to the people. You will meet me in Quba. I will be waiting there for you."

Lady Fatima (as) narrates, "The son of Abu Talib took us to Medina; on our way to Medina the people were chasing us, and all of a sudden all of them were facing Ali b. Abi Talib, who was standing in front of us." They said to Ali, "Ali! Give us the women now! Her father has escaped but we will never allow them to escape!" [A look appeared upon his face that only reappeared when Lady Fatima (as) died. It was the same look he gave to the person who said to him, "We will exhume every single body in Medina until we reach Fatima's body and exhume it as well." The person later said, "When Ali b. Abi Talib looks at you like that, you do not bother fighting him."]

Thus, when the Qureish said that, Ali b. Abi Talib looked at them. They attacked him. Ali b. Abi Talib defended all of us and we finally reached Quba." Meanwhile, the companions at Quba said to the Prophet, "O Prophet, why are you waiting? Medina awaits you!" He said, "I will not enter Medina without Ali." By the time Imam Ali b. Abi Talib reached Quba, he was tired and injured, but they left for Medina soon after.

Lady Fatima (as)'s Marriage to Imam Ali b. Abi Talib (as)

Lady Fatima (as) was continually witnessing her father's relationship with Imam Ali b. Abi Talib (as). She saw the Prophet (pbuh) embracing Imam Ali b. Abi Talib (as) as his brother during the event of the first brotherhood in Medina. When the Prophet (pbuh) paired every Muhajir with an Ansar, the people asked the Prophet (pbuh), "O Prophet, who is your brother?" Prophet (pbuh) said, "Ali is to me like aron was to Moses; Ali is my brother."

It was only natural after seeing her father's sentiments regarding Imam Ali b. Abi Talib (as) that she eventually chose to marry him. After the Battle of Badr, many people proposed to her. For instance, Abu Bakr, Umar, and Abdur Rahman b. 'Awf, all came forward and proposed but the Prophet refused them all. Abdur Rahman b. 'Awf told Imam Ali, "Ali, what are you waiting for? This lady is waiting for you; there is nobody else."

Imam Ali b. Abi Talib (as) with all his humility wondered if he had the financial means to propose to her. Eventually the proposal was brought to the Prophet and the Prophet said, "I will ask Fatima."

Lady Fatima (as) would refuse everyone by verbally saying, "No," to her father, but with Imam Ali b. Abi Talib (as) she remained silent, which was a sign of approval. At that moment, the Prophet said to Imam Ali b. Abi Talib (as), "What do you have to offer as maher (dowry)?" Imam Ali b. Abi Talib (as) said, "O Prophet, I have a shield, a horse and a sword, and nothing else."

The Prophet said, "O Ali, as for your horse, keep it so you can use it to irrigate the land as a job for you to earn your income; as for your sword, keep it because that sword will defend the religion of Islam; and as for your shield, sell it."

Imam Ali b. Abi Talib (as) sold his shield and received 480 dinars for it. He used this sAl to provide the maher of Lady Fatima (as). However, Imam Ali b. Abi Talib (as) did not get married immediately. 'Aqil, Imam Ali b. Abi Talib (as)'s brother, saw him one day and said to him, "Ali, it is been a month now since your proposal has been accepted. What has happened?"

Imam Ali b. Abi Talib (as) said, "I am shy to go to the Prophet and ask him about the wedding. I know he has accepted me but I do not want to question him about the date of the wedding. I do not want to place a burden on the Prophet." 'Aqil said, "Okay, leave it to me." 'Aqil went to Umm Ayman and told her about the situation, who then spoke to Umm Salama who then spoke to the Prophet. When Umm Salama told the Prophet, he said, "Let the son of Abu Talib come and approach me; why is he shy towards me? I will arrange for the wedding plans."

The Prophet (pbuh) came to Imam Ali b. Abi Talib (as) and said, "Ali, do you want to get married?" Imam Ali b. Abi Talib (as) said, "Yes, O Prophet." "So why have not you told me? I have accepted you." "O Prophet, I did not want to put a burden on you." "It is not a burden, O Ali. Talk to me." "O Prophet, where do you want to celebrate it?" "You say." "Can we use the house of Harith b. Nu'man?" "You know, we have exhausted Harith b. Nu'man, but let us ask him."

They approached Harith and asked if they could use his house and he said, "O Prophet, my house does not belong to me. It belongs to you and Allah! Everything I earn from this world is a trust from Allah and you are his Prophet. Use my house for the marriage." So his house was used and everybody came for a very simple ceremony.

Lady Fatima (as) did not have a very beautiful dress to wear as she was living on the means of her father. Narrations state that the night before her wedding her father got her a lovely dress. She was looking at the dress and admiring it, when someone knocked at the door. A person said, "O family of the Prophet! I am someone who is poor and has nothing and I have come to the house of mercy. I beg of you to give me something."

Lady Fatima (as) heard this and thought to herself, "I will give the other dress that I have," but then she remembered the verse of the Quran that said, "Lan tanalul birra, hatta tunfiqu mimma tuhibbun. You will never achieve righteousness until you are willing to give away that which you love the most!" She loved her new dress and so she went to the person at the door and said, "Here is my dress. It is new. Go and sell it and inshallah it will bring you a good income."

How many of us live in this world but allow the world to live in us? If there is even a single spot on the wedding dress, people have been seen to explode in a tantrum!

When Lady Fatima (as) was asked why she gave her dress away, she said, "Because the Quran says, 'You can never achieve righteousness unless you are willing to give away that which you love the most'; I loved this dress but I wanted Allah to see me as someone righteous."

Thus, on her wedding day, she was wearing her old, patched-up dress. Just then the Prophet came to her and said, "Fatima, hurry get ready." She said, "Why?" He said, "Jibra'il has just come to me with a dress which Allah has honored from Jannah."

When you give for the sake of Allah, you think Allah will not give back to you? Thus the blessed couple got married.

In his house Imam Ali b. Abi Talib (as) had a jug, a jar and a mattress along with a couple of gifts given by people. This couple was arguably the greatest couple in Islamic history, and this is how they began their marital life. This is where Lady Fatima (as) was applying the lessons she had learnt from her mother Khadija on how to live a simple life.

Her honeymoon was carrying water for the soldiers at the Battle of Uhud. In the Battle of Uhud, she came with thirteen other women carrying water, and she said, "Where are the soldiers of my father?" They would say to her, "You are Fatima!" She would say, "I am like all the rest of you." She treated all the wounds of Imam Ali b. Abi Talib (as) on that day. She was only married to him for less than a year and she was patching up the wounds on his body.

After this, Allah blessed them with the most beautiful children: Imam al-Hassan (as), Imam al-Hussein (as), Sayyeda Zaynab and Umm Kulthum. Umm Kulthum was one and a half years old when her mother died.

When you look for the sacrifices or examples of altruism given in this world, go no further than the house of Fatima Zahra (as). She was the most devoted wife and a source of peace for her husband. She never ever used her tongue to put her husband down. There are a number of stories in Islamic History which reveal to us how she never wanted to trouble Imam Ali b. Abi Talib (as) with anything.

One day Imam Ali b. Abi Talib (as) came home and said to his wife, "You look ill." She said to him, "I am. Is it possible to get me one pomegranate?" "Why did you not tell me?" "I did not want to trouble you. Father says, 'Whichever lady makes a demand from her husband that is beyond his means, Allah will remove her from divine Grace.' My father also told me, 'Never trouble Ali b. Abi Talib.'" "Fatima, this is no trouble at all. Only one pomegranate and you call it trouble? I am going to get it for you."

He bought a pomegranate and was on his way back to his house when he saw an old lady sitting on the ground. She looked at him and said, "O son of Abu Talib, I am ill; do you mind giving me something to eat?"

He looked at the pomegranate and was thinking about Lady Fatima (as). So he cut the pomegranate in half and gave one half to her. He went back to Lady Fatima (as) and said, "O Fatima! Here is half a pomegranate."

She said, "Jazakallah khairu jaza (May Allah reward you with the best of rewards)!" He said, "Aren't you going to ask me why it is only half?" She said, "Tell me." He said, "On the way back I saw this old lady who was ill. I cut half and gave it to her." She said, "May Allah reward you the best of rewards that you helped a servant of Allah and you helped me as well."

Suddenly there was a knock on the door. It was n who said to them, "O family of the Prophet, I have come to you with a message from the Prophet." Imam Ali b. Abi Talib (as) said, "What is it?" He said, "Here are nine pomegranates for the act of Ali b. Abi Talib." Imam Ali b. Abi Talib (as) looked at n and said, "I do not believe this is from the Prophet." Salman said to him, "Why?" Imam Ali b. Abi Talib (as) said, "Because the Prophet says that when you do a good deed Allah rewards you with ten!" Salman said, "Truly, you are Ali b. Abi Talib!" He then took out the tenth pomegranate.

On another occasion Imam Ali b. Abi Talib (as) said to Lady Fatima (as), "Fatima, why are you looking pale?" She said, "I am alright." "No, tell me." "There is no food in the house." "Why didn't you tell me?" "I do not want to trouble you, O son of Abu Talib." "Let me go and bring something home."

So Imam Ali b. Abi Talib (as) went to borrow one dinar so he could buy some food for the house. On his way he met Miqdad and greeted him. Miqdad hurriedly said, "W'alaykumus Salam," and walked away. Imam Ali b. Abi Talib (as) found it strange as Miqdad never walked away so fast from him. Imam stopped him and said, "Miqdad, wait. Where are you going?" "Do not worry about it, O son of Abu Talib." "Miqdad, come back. What is it?" "Wallah, I have no money at home and my children's eyes have sunk in their sockets; I have given away all my money to the poor and I have nothing left." "Miqdad, here. Take this dinar."

That dinar was meant to buy food for the Imam's house, but this family is the family of sacrifice. Imam went to the mosque to offer Salat ul-Maghrib. The Prophet was leading the prayer. After the Prophet finished the prayer he turned around and said, "Where is Ali b. Abi Talib?" They said, "He's here." The Prophet said, "Ali, I want a favor from you." Imam said, "What is it, O Prophet of Allah?" The Prophet said, "Ali, I want to come to your house for dinner tonight."

It was as if Imam may have thought to himself, I went out to get food for home. I have given away my dinar, and now my father-in-law, who just happens to be the greatest man in this religion, wants to come home and eat with me.

Imam went back home with the Prophet (pbuh) and Lady Fatima (as) opened the door for him. She looked at her husband and he gave her that look to tell her he had someone with him for dinner. It was as if he was saying, are you ready to hear what I am going to tell you? Imam said, "Fatima, someone has come for dinner." She said, "Who?" Imam said, "Your father." She gave him the look wherein she was asking, "What do we do about the food?" Imam said, "I do not know."

The narrations state that this lady's connection with Allah was so pure that she went to the kitchen and called out, "Ya Allah! When Jesus, son of Mary, called you and said, 'O Allah, send us food from Jannah,' you sent him food from Jannah; I am the daughter of your Prophet. I am Fatima and I ask you for some food for my father."

At that moment Jibra'il came down with food for Fatima (as) and she was able to feed her father.

In other words, when the verse was revealed, "Wa yut'imuna al-ta'am 'ala hubbihi miskinan wa yatiman wa asira…(and they give away food in their love to an orphan, captive and a prisoner)," that wasn't the first time they gave anything away. Every day of their lives they were giving. This family of Fatima and Ali were giving throughout their lives solely for the pleasure of Allah.

Lady Fatima (as)'s Involvement in Politics

In the crucial year before he died, the Prophet had to face the Christians of Najran in the event of Mubahila, for which the Quran said, "Say to the Christians we will bring our women, you bring your women; we will bring our sons, you bring your sons; we will bring our selves, you bring your selves…."

Here we ask the question, "In Islam, is a woman allowed to be involved in politics?" In the 21st century we see that a woman cannot have any role in politics, but in the Islam of Muhammad, a woman was an ambassador in politics. The Prophet (pbuh) did not say, "A woman cannot be involved in politics because she is not mahram for the other man" or "a woman cannot be in politics because politics is only for men" or "a woman cannot be in politics because she has to wear hijab." Why did he take Fatima to meet the Christians? He could have easily kept her at home.

This tells us that a woman has as much a role in building the community as a man. Unless women become involved in participating in the future of a community, communities in the Muslim world will never be built. When the Prophet went to meet the Christians, Lady Fatima (as) was with him along side Hassan, Hussein, Ali and himself. The Christians looked at all of them and said, "We swear by God that we will not enter the Mubahila with these five because the amount of light that shines from their faces, if it told the mountain to move, the mountain would move from its position.

Thus Lady Fatima (as) was involved in politics from that day forward. When the Prophet was dying, he said to his daughter, "O Fatima, come near me." He whispered something to her. She first cried and then she smiled. She cried because he was about to die and she smiled because he said to her, "You will be the first to join me."

After the Prophet died, she did not leave Islamic politics. She highlighted to us that Mubahila was not a one-off political situation for her. After the death of the Prophet (pbuh), the Muslims usurped Fadak, a piece of land the Prophet had gifted to her in honor of her mother Khadija, who had given away so much for Islam. They usurped it by bringing forth an argument saying, "Prophets do not leave behind inheritance."

Lady Fatima (as) gave two memorable khutbas (sermons) at the time, which proved that the Quran was very much a part and parcel of her life. She said, "You tell me I cannot inherit? Solomon inherited from David, did he not? Yahya inherited from Zachariah, did he not?" She recited verse after verse from the Quran to prove her claim. She did not just sit at home as a victim when they usurped her right; on the contrary, she came out and fought for her right, exemplifying that I am the daughter of the Prophet, and when I see political injustice I do not remain silent. I have as much a role to play in the political system as every man does in Arabia. When she spoke she shattered and silenced them. So much so that the man who was in charge of the empire said, "Very well, Fatima. I will return Fadak to you." But then his friend intervened and said, "If you give Fadak back to her, then on the same basis [of her testimony], you will also have to admit that, due to the event of Ghadir, the caliphate too belongs to her husband!" And so her claim was rejected.

Lady Fatima (as) was the talking Quran. As followers of Lady Fatima (as) we too must absorb the Quran into our lives. Lady Fida served Lady Fatima (as) for many years. In the last twenty years of her life Lady Fida only spoke in words of the Quran, meaning she never gave an answer except by using the words of the Quran because she used to say, "The Quran encompasses all matters in life; I can answer you with the words of the Quran." The following is an example of her conversation:

One of the companions narrates that, "Once I saw a lady who was stranded in the desert. I came up to her and said, 'Excuse me, are you lost?' She looked at me and she said, 'Qul salam fa sawfa ya'lamun - Say Salam 'Alaykum for they shall soon know.' (43:89) 'Oh I'm sorry, I'm sorry. Salam 'Alaykum. Are you in need of guidance?' 'Wa man yahdi Allah fama lahu mim mudil - Whoever Allah guides can never be misguided.' (39:37) 'Are you a human or are you a genie?' 'Ya Bani Adam, khudhu zinatakum 'inda kulli masjidin wa kulu washrabu wala tusrifu - O children of Adam! Adorn yourself at every time with prostration, and eat and drink, and do not be extravagant.'(7:31) 'Okay, where have you come from?' 'Ula'ika yunaduna min makan ba'id - They are like those who are called to from a place far off.' (41:44) 'Where are you going?' 'Wa lillah 'ala al-nas hijjul bayt man istata' ilayhi sabila – It is incumbent upon mankind the pilgrimage to the house for those who can afford to journey there.' (3:97) So how many days has your kafila been lost for? 'Wa laqad khalaqna al-samawat wa'l-ard wama baynahuma fi sittat ayyam - And indeed created we the heavens and the earth and what is between them in six days.' (50:38) 'Very well. You must be hungry.' 'Wama ja'alnahum jasadan la ya'kuluna al-ta'am wama kanu khalidin - We did not create them as bodies who do not eat food.' (21:8) 'Very well, very well; by the way, there is a camel over there. Run after it! It is going towards hajj!' 'La yukallif Allah nafsan illa wus'aha - Allah does not put a burden on a soul unless he can handle it (meaning, I cant run that much).' (2:286) 'Okay, very well. Then I will sit on the camel and you sit behind me.' 'Law kana fihima aliha illa Allah la fasadata - If there were gods other than Allah there would be disorder (meaning, I cannot sit behind you because you are not mahram to me).' (21:22) 'Very well. You ride the camel and I will walk.' 'Subhana alladhi sakhara lana hadha wama kunna lahu muqrinin - Hallowed is He who subjected this unto us and we were not able to attain this.' (43:13)

As she was riding the camel, all of a sudden from faraway the man saw four people. He said to her, "Who are those four?" She said, "Al-Mal wal banun zinatul hayatad dunya - Wealth and children are an adornment of the life of this world."(18:46) He said, "Okay, what are their names?" She recited the verses about Prophet Dawud, Prophet Muhammad, Prophet Musa and Prophet Sulayman (peace be upon them all) thus indicating to him the names of her sons. So the man said, "Okay, now I know their names." Her sons approached her and said, "Mother, are you alright? Are you being looked after?" She said, "Ya abati ista'jirhu inna khaira manista'jarta al-qawi al-amin - O my father, employ them; verily the best of those whom you can employ is the strong and trusted one (meaning, give him his due for he was truthful and trustworthy)." (28:26)

The man looked at her and said, "Lady Fida, thank you for giving me my due," to which she replied, "Wallahu yarzuqu man yasha' - Allah gives sustenance to whomsoever he Wills!" People often asked her, "How can you speak like this?" She would say, "If all your life you have lived at the university of Fatima Zahra, isn't it but natural that you will be speaking the Quran?"

Lady Fida found it most difficult to see Lady Fatima (as) lying on her bed with a broken rib. The daughter of the Prophet got injured when she was crushed between the wall of her house and the door. Because of that she miscarried the child that she was carrying.

The following are some of the references concerning the fact that certain prominent personalities brutally attacked the house of Lady Fatima (peace be upon her)

- al-Shahrastani, reported from Ibrahim ibn sayyar al-Mu'tazili al-Natham: "Umar kicked Fatima's stomach on the day of allegiance until she miscarried and he yelled: 'Burn her house and whoever is in it' and in it were Ali, Fatima, al-Hassan and al-Hussain" (al-Milal wa al-Nihal, by al-Shahrastani v1, p 57)

- al-Safadi, also reported from al-Natham: "Umar kicked Fatima's stomach on the day of allegiance until she miscarried Muhsin" (al-Wafi bil Wafiyat, by al-Safadi, v6, p 17)

- al-Baladhuri, reported from Sulaiman al-Taymi, from Abdullah bin Aon – "Abu Bakr asked Ali to support him, but Ali refused, then Umar went toward Ali's house with a burning torch. At the door he met Fatima who said to him: "Do you intend to burn the door of my house?" Umar said: "Yes"! (Ansab al-Ashraaf, by al-Baladhuri Ahmed bin Yahya bin Jaber al-Baghdadi, v1, p 586)

- Ibn Abd Rabbuh reported in regards to the ones who did not pay allegiance to Abu Bakr : "They are Ali, al-Abbas, Zubair and Sa'd Ibn Ubadah. As for Ali, Abbas and Zubair, they stayed in the house of Fatima until Abu Bakr sent Umar to get them out of Fatima's house and told him: 'if they refuse, fight them'. He took a torch to burn the house and Fatima met him and told him: 'O' son of Khattab are you here to burn our house?' He said: 'yes, or you enter what the Ummah has entered in' [i.e swear allegiance to Abu Bakr]". (al-Iqd al-Fareed, by Ibn Abd Rabbuh al-Andalusi, v5, p 13)

- Ibn Qutayba al-Danyuri, reported: "Umar asked for wood, and told those people inside the house (i.e. the house of Fatima peace be upon her): 'I swear by Allah who has my soul in his hand, that if you do not come out, I will burn the house.' Someone told Umar: 'O Aba Hafs (i.e. father of Hafsa) Fatima is inside the house!'. Umar said: 'So what! It doesn't matter to me who is in the house." (al-Imama wa al-Siyasa, by Ibn Qutayba, p 12)

• al-Juwayni al-Shafi'i, relying on the Isnad of Ibn Abbas, that the Prophet (peace be upon him and his pure family) said: "As for my daughter Fatima (peace be upon her), when I saw her, I remembered what she will have to endure after me. It is as if humiliation entered inside her house, violating her privacy, confiscating her rights, depriving her of her inheritance, breaking her side, causing her to miscarry as she will call: `O Muhammed!' but there will be none to respond to her. She will seek help, but she will not be helped. She will remain after me grieved, depressed, weeping" (Fara'id al-Simtayn, by al-Juwayni al-Shafi'I, v2, p 34)

• al-Siyuti was among the ones who reported that Abu Bakr regretted what he had done to Lady Fatima (peace be upon her) as he said: "I wish I had not searched for Fatima's house, and had not sent men to harass her." (Musnad Fatima by al-Siyuti p 34, Al-Mu'jam al-Kabeer by al-Tabarani v1 p 62, History of al-Tabari v3 p 430, al-Iqd al-Fareed, by Ibn Abd Rabbuh v2 p 254,)

In a polemical treatise written in response to the argumentation of a Shi'i scholar Ibn Mutahhir al-Hilli (d. 726/1326) entitled Minhaj al-Sunnah al-Nabawiyyah, Ibn Taymiyyah does not deny the event but rather offers a unique justification for Abu Bakr's ordering of the attack/raid on the house of Fatima, he uses the term Kabasa which denotes "forcefully entering" in describing Abu Bakr's party's action, but then justifies the action by offering the interpretation that Abu Bakr was merely thoroughly checking that nothing from the treasury of the Muslim State was in the house of Fatima so that if it were, it could be distributed to more deserving individuals.

This does raise the question as to whether or not Ibn Taymiyyah in his diligence and attempt to not reject authentic historical narratives at the expense of the polemical spin of others, recognised that the origins of the narrative which had been utilised by Shi'a polemics was originally a well-documented event which had its precedent in primarily the earliest Sunni collections of recorded history.

Just before Lady Fatima died, she said to Imam Ali, "O son of Abu Talib, tell me…did I ever trouble you in your life?"

Asma narrates that, "I saw Ali b. Abi Talib wash the body of Lady Fatima. I saw him go to the corner of the ghusl room and cry. I said to him, 'O son of Abu Talib, why do you cry? You lifted the gate of

Khayber!' He said to me, 'O Asma, I was washing the body of Fatima and my hands came across one of her broken ribs.'"

When Imam Ali b. Abi Talib (as) carried the body of Lady Fatima (as), Imam Hussein (as) ran to the chest of his mother and began to cry, saying, "Mother, it is me Hussein!" There is a narration, which states that Jibra'il came at that moment and said, "O Ali, remove Hussein from the chest of his mother because the angels are lamenting and cannot bare to see Hussein on the chest of his mother!"

Lecture 3

Imam Ali b. Abi Talib (as)

Imam Ali b. Abi Talib (as) was born on the 13th Rajab in the year 600 and died on the 21st of Ramadan in the 40th year after Hijra (660 CE). He occupies a prominent position within the religion of Islam and is revered as one of the greatest leaders in Islamic history; he is a man from whose life many extraordinary lessons may be learnt and many examples may be derived, and a man who was seen as the embodiment of knowledge, generosity, valor, bravery and dedication towards the religion of Islam.

His Parents and Childhood

The Imam's parents, Abu Talib and Fatima bint Asad, were both followers of the monotheistic way of Abraham. There was a group of believers who were living in Mecca in the early days who were followers of the message of Prophet Ibrahim (as) and all the messengers who came after Ibrahim (as); they are classified under the term "Hanifs." When Abu Talib read the marriage ceremony of the Prophet (pbuh) to Lady Khadija, he mentioned very clearly within his sermon that, "I am the follower of one God and the follower of the Prophets of God, especially the Prophets who descended from the line of Prophet Ibrahim (as)." Therefore Abu Talib and Fatima bint Asad were both Abrahamic in terms of their belief.

This is also seen in the words of Fatima bint Asad during the time when she used to circumambulate the Ka'aba. There were two types of people who circumambulated the Ka'aba at that time. There were those who believed in one God but started making images for that God in the form of idols; and then there was a group who believed in one God and would not associate any images with that God. When Fatima bint Asad used to circumambulated the Ka'aba she recited a supplication that is still with us until today. She said, "O Allah! In the name of Your Majesty, and in the name of Your Power, and in the name of the Prophets You sent from the line of Ibrahim (as), help me in this period with the pangs of labor and the pangs of childbirth and make it easy for me."

The narrations are clear, both in the books of the Imamis and in other schools in Islam. For example, if one studies the works of Imam Hakim an-Nisaburi in his book al-Mustadrak ala'l-Sahihayn, or Mas'udi in his book, Muruj al-Dhahab, all of them state that when Fatima bint Asad said these words near the Ka'aba, the Ka'aba opened up for her and she entered it. She stayed within it for three days, an honor that Islamic history has only reserved for Imam Ali b. Abi Talib (as).

You will find that there are some other historical references to other people being born in the Ka'aba but this was a group of people who tried to diminish the significance of Imam Ali b. Abi Talib (as). The fact remains that the only man to receive the honor of being born in the Ka'aba is Imam Ali (as). When his mother emerged from the Ka'aba on the fourth day, the first person to welcome her was the Prophet (pbuh). He welcomed her and took Ali from her hands, and from that day, the Prophet (pbuh) embraced Ali throughout his childhood; he would chew food before he placed it in the mouth of Ali; and Imam Ali himself narrates that, "I would follow the Prophet in those early days like a child of the she camel would follow its mother...I used to see the light of revelation and I would hear the words of Prophethood...When the religion consisted of only three people, it was always me and Khadija alongside the Prophet."

In other words, from an early age Abu Talib turned his sons and his children towards the religion of Islam; Imam Ali b. Abi Talib (as) had three elder brothers. His oldest brother was Talib, hence their father's name was Abu Talib. Talib died at the age of fifty-five; the second eldest brother was 'Aqil. He died at the age of ninety-three; then the third eldest was Ja'far who died at the age of forty; and finally the Imam. The Prophet (pbuh) was thirty when the Imam was born. Imam Ali also had two sisters - one was named Fakhita (Um Hani) and the other was named Jumana. Thus, Abu Talib and Fatima bint Asad had six children.

Due to the extreme difficulty many Arabs were facing at the time, the Prophet (pbuh) came to Abu Talib and said, "Let my uncles Hamza and Abbas and I take responsibility for your children." Abu Talib asked, "Whom would you like to care for?" He said, "Let me bring up Ali."

Thus the Prophet (pbuh) wanted to bring up the young Imam in the way that Abu Talib had brought him up. It was only ten years later when Imam Ali was ten that Prophet Muhammad (pbuh) announced his prophethood. In those early days there were only a few reverts, like Ammar b. Yasir, Bilal and Abu Dharr al-Ghiffari. Abu Dharr belonged to the tribe of Banu Ghiffar. His tribe used to worship idols. But whenever Abu Dharr would reflect, he would ask himself, "How can I worship an idol which can neither benefit me nor harm me? How can I worship an idol that cannot protect itself?" The people of Bani Ghiffar were highway thieves; nobody could mess with them. In our language today they would be known as gangsters. One day Abu Dharr saw one of the members of his tribe bringing some milk to the idol. Then after a while he saw a fox come towards the milk; the fox had a nice sip of the milk and then urinated on the idol. Abu Dharr saw this and said to himself, "If this idol cannot protect itself from the urine of a fox, then how is it going to protect Abu Dharr al-Ghiffari?"

Thus he decided to go and look for the man he had heard of by the name of "Muhammad." But finding him was a dilemma, as the message had still not spread widely in the first three years of Islam. He went to Mecca and circumambulated around the Ka'aba, trying to look for the man who was known as "as-Sadiq" and "al-Amin," but he did not want to tell anyone that he was looking for him because the Meccans had become very hostile towards anyone spreading rumors about a new religion. Abu Dharr suddenly saw a young boy of about twelve or thirteen years of age. The boy looked at Abu Dharr and said, "You look confused. Who are you looking for?" Abu Dharr said, "I don't think you know who he is. It's okay." The boy said, "Don't worry. Tell me, I might know him." "I'm looking for Muhammad, the son of Abdullah." "I think I know him. Let me lead you to him." "What is your name?" "I am Ali, son of Abu Talib."

Thus they walked together and reached the Prophet (pbuh) and within a few moments, on witnessing the intellect of the Prophet (pbuh), Abu Dharr became a Muslim. The Prophet (pbuh) said to him, "Abu Dharr, I plead with you, do not go and tell the people about Islam. I know you Banu Ghiffaris are a passionate people, but keep it quiet." Abu Dharr said, "Do not worry. I will keep it as quiet as I can."

A few minutes later Abu Dharr stood near the Ka'aba and said, "O people! Those of you who have not heard of Islam, let me tell you. There is only one God and Muhammad is the messenger of God." The people began to attack him. Abbas, the uncle of the Prophet (pbuh), intervened. When Abu Dharr reached the Prophet (pbuh), the Prophet (pbuh) said, "I told you to not tell anybody." He said, "I'm sorry, O Prophet, but you know I felt so passionately about it. I will not talk about it again." The Prophet (pbuh) said, "Very well."

A few minutes later there was another announcement on the Ka'aba, "O people! If you did not hear me properly before, then know that I am Abu Dharr al-Ghiffari, and that there is only one God and that Muhammad is His Messenger." Again they came to attack him and Abbas again intervened. Abbas whispered into the ears of one of the people saying, "You know who this man is?" "Yes, Abu Dharr." "You know which tribe?" "Who?" "Bani Ghiffar." "Bani Ghiffar? The highway thieves?" "Yes."

As soon as they heard this they knew that they musn't mess with this tribe otherwise they would lose their caravans in retaliation. So they let him go. Thus it was the young Ali who brought Abu Dharr to the Prophet .

A Momentous Incident in the Life of the Imam

From a young age Imam Ali b. Abi Talib (as) had the maturity to assist in carrying the message of the religion. That is why when Da'wat Dhul 'Ashira ocurred after Allah revealed the verse in Sura 26, verse 214, "Invite and warn your nearest relatives," the Prophet (pbuh) told the young Ali, "I want you to do something for me." "What is it, O Prophet?" "I want you to prepare a meal for me." "Which meal?" "Get a sheep, one kilo of wheat and three kilos of yogurt. I want you to make a feast and I want you to invite our uncles." The Prophet (pbuh) and Imam Ali were cousins and so they both had the same set of uncles. When they came that day, a momentous incident occurred which is vital in studying the biography of Imam Ali b. Abi Talib (as).

When they arrived at his house, the Prophet (pbuh) said to them, "Welcome to my house. I have glad tidings to give you about the message." Abu Lahab did not listen to him. But the second time they came, the Prophet (pbuh) said to them, "You know that I am truthful and you know that I am trustworthy and you know that I have not lied to any of you. I have come to bring you a message of goodness, to worship only one God and not associate partners with Him, and that there is a Day of Judgment where you will be accountable for all your acts, and that there is no difference between mAl and female, or between black and white." Abu Lahab looked at him and said, "O Muhammad, what is this sorcery that you are trying to bewitch us with?" The Prophet (pbuh) said, "Whoever amongst you accepts me as his Prophet will be my caliph and the successor after me."

From a young age Ali was already instructed with that message that he was to be the successor of the Prophet (pbuh) because Ali, at the age of thirteen, raised his hands and said, "O Prophet of God, I will listen to your message and I am the first to accept your words."

Abu Lahab turned around to Abu Talib and said, "Abu Talib, it looks like one day your son will have to lead you!" He tried to mock him. In the books of our Sunni brothers it says that Abu Talib came to Ali and said to him, "Ali, are you sure you want to accept this message? Are you ready for it?"

Ali, full of maturity at that young age, replied by saying, "O my father, Allah did not ask me when He created me, therefore I do not need to ask anyone when I am submitting back to Allah (swt)."

Thus it is written in their books as well that Ali (as) had the maturity to understand the message of our Prophet (pbuh) at that young age. Not only did he have the maturity, but the Prophet (pbuh) also mentioned on that day, "Whoever accepts this message is my successor and the caliph after me."

Thus, from that young age, the Prophet (pbuh) would constantly give him duties in order to allow him to mature and develop in the religion. At the age of twenty-four, when the whole of Mecca had decided to combat the message of the Prophet (pbuh), the Prophet (pbuh) came to Ali (as) and said, "Ali, they have decided that they want to kill me; a number of them are going to come together and kill me, so would you do a task for me?" Ali said, "O Prophet of God, what is the task?" The Prophet (pbuh) said, "I want you to sleep in my bed. Are you ready to sacrifice your soul for the message of the religion of Islam?" He said, "O Prophet, will you be safe?" The Prophet (pbuh) said, "Yes, I will."

He said, "Then my soul is dedicated to your soul and my spirit is dedicated to your spirit." Then he went into prostration and said three times, "Shukran lillah! Shukran lillah! Shukran lillah! All thanks is to Allah!"

That night when the enemies came to attack, they saw Ali sleeping in the bed of the Prophet (pbuh). After that the Prophet (pbuh) had said to him, "Ali, I want you to perform a task. There are a number of my enemies who have deposited their trusts with me. I find no one better in this religion but you to return the trusts back to them."

Hanzala, the son of Abu Sufyan, heard that Ali had remained behind and was giving everyone their trusts back. Hanzala, the oldest son of Abu Sufyan, wanted to create some trouble. He told Umayr b. Wa'il, who was a poor man, to do something for him. He bribed him with 350 grams of gold and a particular necklace which Umayr's wife used to admire when she would see it on Hind's neck. Hind was Hanzala's mother. Umayr's wife had always wanted to wear that necklace even if it was only for a day. It was a very precious necklace that was made with 35 grams of gold. Thus Hanzala promised Umayr that if he did the job for him he could keep that necklace for life.

Umayr b. Wa'il was related to the tribe of Banu Thaqif (the tribe of Hajjaj b. Yusuf and Mukhtar al-Thaqafi). He told Umayr, "I want you to go to Ali, the representative of Muhammad, who is near the Ka'aba right now, and tell him that you entrusted 250 grams gold with the Prophet (pbuh) and that you want it back." Hanzala wanted to defame the Prophet (pbuh) who was beginning to win the hearts of the people as they were being handed their trusts back. If Imam Ali (as) said that he did not have Umayr's trust, they could claim that the Prophet (pbuh) had returned all the small items but took away the more valuable ones. This would help to create some doubt in the people's minds about the Prophet (pbuh) and if Imam Ali did not deny it, he might give them the gold in order to save the Prophet (pbuh)'s reputation.

Thus Umayr agreed to do it but said, "Ali will not believe me. He will first ask me for a witness." Hanzala said, "I will provide the witnesses. Write the name of these witnesses down: Abu Jahal, Akrama b. Abu Jahal, Utbah, Abu Sufyan and myself. Now you have the name of all five witnesses." Umayr was now satisfied and went to Imam Ali (as), who, by now, had returned all the belongings of the people. He was about to leave when Umayr approached him and said, "O son of Abu Talib! Where are you going?" Imam said, "I had a responsibility to do which I have done, and now I am going home." Umayr said, "But I have come to get my amana. I had left 80 mithqal (grams) of gold and a special amana in a bag. Please return it back to me." Obviously, Imam Ali knew something was suspicious, so he smiled and said, "Really? You gave 80 mithqal gold and a special amana?" Umayr said, "Yes."

Everyone was still present there as they were opening their bags and checking their items. Imam Ali addressed them and said, "This brother of mine has come to claim his trust. Please remain seated so I can solve this problem." Then Imam addressed Umayr and said, "Okay, tell me who are your witnesses?" Umayr took the five names Hanzala had given him. Now Imam Ali asked Umayr in front of everyone, "Okay, tell me, when did you give this amana to my Prophet?" Umayr said, "It was at sunrise." Imam asked, "So when the Prophet took the amana, what did he do with it?" Umayr said, "As he was leaving for the haram, he took the amana and put it in his pocket." Imam Ali said, "Okay, now call your first witness. Who is it?" He said, "Akrama b. Abu Jahal."

Some youths went and called Akrama and he came to the scene. By this time everyone present became very interested in the whole case. When Akrama came, Umayr was told to sit quietly without uttering a word. Now Imam asked Akrama, "Umayr has stated that he had given an amana to my Prophet, are you a witness to that?" Akrama said, "Yes I am." Imam said, "Okay, so tell me, what time was this amana given?" Now Akrama was in a predicament. After some thinking, he said, "It was early in the morning." Imam said, "Okay, then what did my Prophet do with it?" He said, "Well, because he was returning from the haram, he took it and went to his house." Imam said, "Okay, now sit down." He looked at Umayr and said, "Who is your second witness?" Umayr said, "Abu Jahal."

Now Abu Jahal was called to the scene. Imam said, "O Hisham, Umayr is saying that you are a witness to the amanas that he gave the Prophet.

Tell me, what time was it when the amana was given?" Abu Jahal said, "I do not know anything. Do not involve me in this! I am not a witness to anything." Imam looked at Umayr and said, "Who is your third witness?" He said, "Utbah."

Utbah was a senior leader of the Qureish. He was called and asked the same thing. He said, "It was afternoon and the Prophet was going towards Khadija's house and so he told his slave to go and put the amana in his aunt's (Fatima bint Asad's) house." Imam Ali said to Umayr, "Now who is your next witness?" He said, "Abu Sufyan." Abu Sufyan was called and asked the same question. He said, "It was the time of Asr and the Prophet was sitting in the haram at the time. He took the amana and kept it with him." Imam Ali asked Umayr, "Now who is your fifth witness?" He said, "Hanzala b. Abu Sufyan." Hanzala said, "It was nighttime and the Prophet gave the amana to his slave and sent it to Khadija's house."

By now all the people heard the testimonies and the contradiction between all their statements. The witnesses themselves were getting extremely embarrassed listening to the contradictory statements. Umayr b. Wa'il Thaqafi was so embarrassed during this whole process that he said, "Oh Ali, forgive me. I made a big mistake. These people bribed me and told me to do this."

Thus the Prophet (pbuh) had already gone towards Medina and left Ali (as) with the responsibility. Then he had to take the "Fawatim" (the "Fatimas" of the Banu Hashim) to Medina with him; he took Lady Fatima, the Prophet's daughter; his mother, Fatima bint Asad; and Fatima, the daughter of Hamza, and they all went towards Medina.

Many people fail to acknowledge how unsafe the journey was for Imam Ali b. Abi Talib (as). Many people think that only the Prophet and Abu Bakr had an unsafe journey. They do not realize that the enemies of Islam had set their eyes on Ali when the Qureish could not catch up with the Prophet (pbuh). It was in that journey that they realized that they had a warrior on their hands. The Prophet (pbuh) was waiting for Imam Ali in the city of Quba, as he did not want to enter Medina without him. So when Imam Ali b. Abi Talib (as) reached Medina, his body was bloddy and full of injuries. The Qureish had ambushed him on the way and he fought them on his own and protected the ladies. It was in that journey that he showed his valor and bravery.

Honors Bestowed on Imam Ali (as) During the life of the Prophet

The moment they reached Medina, the Prophet (pbuh) did two things to honor Imam Ali's position. The first thing was the pact of brotherhood the Prophet (pbuh) made between the Ansar and the Muhajireen. The Muhajirs were the migrants who had left Mecca to go towards Medina and the Ansar were the people of Medina. The Prophet (pbuh) did not want any tension between the two groups so he made each Ansar a partner and brother of each Muhajir. For example, Abu Bakr was paired with Kharija b. Zohair al-Khazraji; Umar was given to Eital b. Malik; Uthman was made a partner of Aws b. Thabit. The people asked, "O Prophet, who is your brother?" He said, "For me it is only Ali b. Abi Talib; Ali is to me like Harun was to Musa, except that there is no Prophet after me."

There were some houses that shared a common wall with the mosque. People had built doors in their houses which opened to the mosque for their convenience. Allah ordered that all doors should be sealed off except for that of the Prophet and Imam Ali. This was another honor given to him by Allah.

His Battles

Imam Ali (as), at the age of twenty-four, in his first battle for Islam at Badr, then Uhud, Khandaq and Khaybar, showed a distinction like no other on the battlefield. In Islamic history, many individuals have been said to be great warriors but there is not a single warrior in Islamic history that came near the dust of Ali b. Abi Talib (as). He had a distinction in the battlefield. At Badr, he destroyed half of the opposition alone. At Uhud, The Prophet was alone on the mountain; Ali, Miqdad, Ammar, Abu Dujana Ansari and a lady called al-Harithiyya were the ones who helped him. It was on that day that the famous cry could be heard, "There is no youth but Ali and no sword but Dhulfikar!"

At Khandaq and Khaybar, he displayed a spiritual side to him, which showed that he had a balance of opposite qualities, and thus made him a complete human being. Warriors are normally reckless; and not only are they reckless but they tend to be arrogant as well. These two combinations usually are an integral part of a warrior's personality; they are either reckless or arrogant. One hardly finds any ethics in warriors and it is very rare to find any spirituality in them. When Imam Ali b. Abi Talib (as) finished the Battle of Khandaq and Khaybar, he did two things after those battles, which are beautifully described in Rumi's famous lines when he said about the Imam, "In bravery, you are the Lion of your Lord, but in generosity, who knows who you are!"

At Khandaq, Amr b. Abd Wudd, who was the goliath of the enemy, challenged the Muslims to come and fight him. It was a crucial moment in the battle when he jumped over the large ditch and began poking the tents of the Muslims challenging them to fight. None of the Muslims dared to answer his call because they knew anyone who fought Amr never survived.

The Prophet (pbuh) said, "Who will fight that man? I will guarantee paradise for him." Imam Ali b. Abi Talib (as) immediately stood up to fight him. The Prophet (pbuh) smiled and said, "Now watch as the epitome of Truth will fight the epitome of Kufr!"

Imam (as) proceeded to the battlefield. When Amr saw this young boy he felt insulted as he was used to fighting grown men. He then saw the Imam (as) a bit closer and recognized him. He said, "I know you. I knew your father Abu Talib well, so I do not want to kill you. Go back."

Imam Ali (as) replied, "But I will kill you because you are an enemy of Allah!" When they began the war, Amr knew that he would win because Amr was known for wrestling with lions. Midway through the war the people noticed that dust had gathered between the two as they were engaging in combat. Ali walked away, paused, then came back and struck Amr. He then emerged and said, "God is Great!"

The people were confused and asked Ali upon his return, "What was that moment in which you paused?" This is a moment in Imam Ali b. Abi Talib (as)'s life which is a lesson for all of us. If a man angers you, remain patient. Only get angry when Allah's purpose is being served. When Ali came back, they asked him, "Why did you walk away?"

He said, "As I was about to strike Amr b. Abd Wudd, he spat on me; if I had struck him then I would have struck him for my own ego, but I never strike a human because of my ego. So I walked away; I returned back to the battle and I struck him in service of God." Thus with one stroke Imam (as) dislodged him from the earth and walked away leaving his body. Amr b. Abd Wudd's sister was sitting among the opposition. She was having a meal and she thought her brother would come back victorious. Someone came and said to her, "We have some sad news for you." he said, "What is it?" They said, "Your brother has been killed." She said, "My brother has been killed? My brother, who wrestles with lions? Which lion killed my brother?" They said to her, "A young man by the name of Ali b. Abi Talib."

Later, as she went to see her brother's body, she was crying on her way. The narrations state that when she came near his body, she sat by it and then she suddenly got up and smiled. Then she called out to everyone and said, "I am honored that the son of Abu Talib killed my brother! Before my brother begins a war, he asks the person he is fighting, 'If you kill me, do not take my shield because it belongs to my great-grandfathers. Let it at least stay with my family.' I look at my brother's body now and I see that his shield is still on his body and it makes me understand that the son of Abu Talib fights for no one but his Lord, because if the son of Abu Talib was fighting for his ego, then he would have been like the rest of Muhammad's army who would have stolen my brother's shield. But the son of Abu Talib is different from the rest of them." In those days people wore their most valuable armour to battle, and if they died their armour would be taken as spoils of war by the one who killed them. Precious armour used to be worth a lot in the olden days. Only Imam Ali b. Abi Talib (as) was noble enough not to care about worldly possessions on the battlefield. Whatever he did was solely for the will and pleasure of Allah!

Then, at the Battle of Khaybar, Imam Ali b. Abi Talib (as) lifted a gate which none could lift. Here we are not concerned with what he lifted, but rather with what allows one to be so powerful. After Khaybar he came back from the battle and began to cry. He was asked, "O son of Abu Talib! Why do you cry? You have just lifted the gate others could not lift!"

He replied, "I cannot bear to see the Jewish soldiers with a rope around their hands. Loosen their rope. Are they not human beings?" Then he returned home and his wife Fatima (as) offered him some bread. He was known for his piety, and that he would only eat dry bread, because he would say, "How can I eat soft bread when there are poor in the Muslim world?" He tried to break the bread, but the bread did not break. They said, "O son of Abu Talib! You lifted a gate which forty men together could not lift, and you cannot break a piece of bread?" He said, "The gate

I lifted for Allah; the bread I am trying to break is for Ali. I lifted the gate of Khaybar, not with my physical strength, but with the strength of my Ruh! If I can understand my soul, then I can understand my Lord; and the moment I can understand my Lord, everything is easy before me."

In the Battle of Hunayn as well, were it not for Ali remaining behind, this religion would have been destroyed. The greatest performance of Imam Ali b. Abi Talib (as) was at Hunayn, and not at Badr, Uhud, Khaybar or Khandaq. Imam Zayn ul-Abideen (as) said in Syria, "I am the son of the one who fought at Badr and Hunayn!" Imam Ali b. Abi Talib (as), at Hunayn, was left alone against the opposition and finished them off.

After the Death of the Prophet (pbuh)

The Prophet (pbuh) was sixty-three years old when he died. Imam Ali b. Abi Talib (as) was thirty-three years old at the time. The Prophet (pbuh) had told the people, "This is my successor; be loyal to him; do not deceive him or be cunning to him or attack him; he is not just my son-in-law, he is appointed by Allah to look after my message," but the people ended up taking away the leadership of Imam Ali b. Abi Talib (as). They took his leadership, and they attacked his wife and killed her, and he was left with four orphans in his house. Yet did Imam Ali b. Abi Talib (as) allow his ego to get to him? Imam Ali b. Abi Talib (as) said, "The religion of Islam is greater than me causing disunity. I will remain silent, but when I see injustice, I will speak out against it."

When the Prophet (pbuh) died, Imam Ali b. Abi Talib (as) was thirty-three, and he became the fourth caliph at the age of fifty-eight. Some people ask, did Ali b. Abi Talib do anything for Islam in those twenty-five years? Even though Imam Ali b. Abi Talib (as) was not the caliph chosen at Saqifa, he was still the caliph for Ammar, Bilal, Salman, Abu Dharr and so on. Therefore, when Imam Ali b. Abi Talib (as) saw any injustice during that time, he would speak out; he would not just remain silent. He taught us an ethical lesson: Muslims! When you see injustice or tyranny of any type, be it big or small, never remain silent against injustice.

One day a lady came to Umar b. Khattab, the second caliph, and said, "I have committed adultery." Umar asked, "Were there witnesses?" She said, "Yes, there were witnesses and I am willing to be punished." Umar said, "Very well," and told his men to punish her. She said, "But do you mind if Ali b. Abi Talib makes the decision?" Umar said, "Why?" She said, "Because I believe that Ali b. Abi Talib is the most just human living on this earth. I know that he was brought up in the lap of the Prophet. So who else can teach justice but Muhammad?"

Umar called Imam Ali b. Abi Talib (as) and told him to pass the judgment on her. When Imam Ali b. Abi Talib (as) came, he asked her, "What is your crime?" She said, "I committed adultery." Imam said, "What were the circumstances?" She said, "I had no food for my children and I went to ask for help from one of the rich men of the area. He said to me, 'If you want food, you have to commit adultery with me.' I told him, 'O man, fear God. Do not say such words.' I pleaded the second time but the third time I gave in." Imam Ali said to her, "Very well, you are free to leave." She said, "What do you mean?" He said, "Chapter 5, verse 3." She said, "What do you mean?" She looked at Umar inquiringly and said, "What does he mean?" Umar too asked the Imam, "What do you mean?" Imam said, "Chapter 5, verse 3 says, 'Those who are compelled to sin while they are in a state of hunger, Allah forgives their sin.'" (This lady was compelled to sin but she was in a state of hunger. Allah forgives those in a state of hunger because the shame is on the state not on the people. The state should not allow a lady to be in such a situation.) It was at times like these that Umar was heard saying, "If it were not for Ali, Umar would have perished!"

Thus Imam Ali always came to help when he was summoned. There was an instance when Umar was going to fight the Romans. The army was leaving and Imam Ali stopped him from going even though he was all dressed to leave. Imam Ali said, "You are the caliph of the time if you go forward and your army gets killed they will know you have no more reinforcements as you will already be there. Stay behind. It is better for you." This guidance was to save Islam. It was the role of these representatives to ensure that Islam did not lose its position in its infancy.

When Uthman, the third caliph, appointed his family members, the Bani Ummayah, to different positions of authority, Imam Ali would speak out and would not remain silent.

His Knowledge

In those twenty-five years when he was not the caliph he would come forward and say, "Saluni Saluni, qabla an tafqiduni! (Ask me! Ask me! whatever you wish to ask me before you do not find me!) I know the ways of the heavens much more than I do the ways of the earth!" It was a challenge. The non-Muslims would come to Medina and ask, "Where is Ali b. Abi Talib?" The people would say, "Why?" They would say, "We hear that he is the successor to the Prophet; we want to ask him questions that none can answer. If he can answer them, then we will follow him."

One Jewish man came to Imam Ali b. Abi Talib (as) and said to him, "You claim to be the successor of Muhammad?" Imam said, "Yes." "I am going to ask you a mathematical question which no human can answer and it is written in the religious scriptures; and only the successor of Muhammad can answer this." "Go ahead." "Which number, if you divide it by any number between one and ten, remains a whole number?" "Two thousand five hundred and twenty." "Sorry?" "Two thousand five hundred and twenty." "How did you get that?" "The number of days in the week multiplied by the number of days in the year." The man looked puzzled and said, "Okay, in the Arabian calendar there are three hundred and sixty days in the year and there are seven days in the week." Imam said, "So multiply three hundred and sixty by seven. What do you get?" He said, "2520." Imam said, "Divide 2520 by 1. What do you get?" He said, "2520." Imam said, "By two?" He said, "1260." Imam said, "By three?" He said, "840." "By four?" "630." "By five?" "504." "By six?" "420." "By seven?" "360." "By eight?" "315." "By nine?" "280." "By ten?" "252." The Jew said, "Truly, this is Ali b. Abi Talib." (2520 divided by any number between one and ten is the only number in the world that comes out whole.)

Thus people would keep approaching him to ask for knowledge until he became the caliph.

His Life as a Caliph

The tragedy in this religion is that the Muslims did not utilise Imam Ali b. Abi Talib (as) like they could have. During his four years as a caliph, there were three civil wars fought against him. In each of those wars the dignity that he displayed in them is a message for each Muslim today; that even when another Muslim acts rudely towards you, if you are a follower of Ali b. Abi Talib, act tolerantly towards them. There may be Muslims today who look towards the Imamis and are disrespectful towards them, who may call them the people of innovation, who may call them the people of shirk. One must not reply by falling to their level; one must maintain one's dignity like the Imam maintained his dignity.

At Jamal, he saw that the lady fighting him was the wife of the Prophet; others around him said, "Show disrespect." He said, "Never!" When he came towards Malik al-Ashtar, he said, "Malik, do you see her sitting on the camel?" Malik said, "Yes." Imam said, "I want you to go and cut the feet of the camel." Then he told another companion, "When she falls, I want you to hold her body." Malik went and cut the feet of the camel. As soon as she fell the other companion held her body. She turned around and said to the man, "How dare you touch the body of the wife of the Prophet when you are not mahram to me!"

The man replied, "I am your brother Muhammad, the son of Abu Bakr, holding you." He was the only man in Ali's army who was mahram to her. Ali could have lowered his dignity, as well as hers, by sending anyone, but no. The son of Abu Talib is above all of this, this level of low dignity and ego. Then he sent her back with respect towards Medina, as she was the wife of the Prophet. She turned around and said to him, "You are the killer of the beloved ones!"

He replied, "If I am the killer of the beloved ones, then I would have killed people like Marwan and Abdullah b. Zubair right now, but I do not want disunity in the Muslim Ummah." Thus the School of Ahlulbayt (as) should never open the door for disunity.

So first they fought him as the caliph in the Battle of Jamal; then in Siffin when they fought him, Mu'awiya took control of the water. Imam told his soldiers, "Ask Mu'awiya to allow us to drink water. We are thirsty." Mu'awiya said, "I will never give them any water." Imam told the soldiers to go and win the water back. The soldiers won the water back and the water was then in the possession of Ali. Now the Muslims were told that the soldiers of Mu'awiya were thirsty. They came to the soldiers of Ali and said, "Please give us water." Imam looked at his soldiers and said, "Do you think we should give them water?" The soldiers said, "No, do not give it to them; they do not deserve it as they did not give us water." Imam said, "No. I cannot bear to see a horse thirsty, let alone a human being."

In the Battle of Nahrawan, the Khawarij, who had once been soldiers in his army, came to fight him. He was in one-on-one combat with one of them. During the combat, the Dhulfikar captured the sword of the opponent and Imam had two swords now. That soldier looked at the Imam and said, "What are you going to do? Are you going to finish me?" Imam said, "What would you like?" He said, "I hear Ali b. Abi Talib never rejects a request from a person." Imam said, "Ask me." He said, "I want the swords." Imam said, "Take them." The man said, "I want to join your path." Imam said, "No. Say, 'I want to join the path of Allah for justice'; do not look at me. Every drop of my existence is for Allah (swt)!" That is why adopting the akhlaq of Ali b. Abi Talib is what makes one a follower of Ali b. Abi Talib.

After the Battle of Nahrawan, he was walking from the battlefield and saw a lady. He came near her and saw her boiling some water and stirring it. He said to her, "O lady, what's wrong? I see you stirring some water." She said, "May God curse the son of Abu Talib!" He said, "Why do you say this?" She said, "At Nahrawan he killed my brothers, my sons and my husband; he comes back alive and they came back dead. May God curse him. If I were to meet him one day, I would tell him how much I hate him." He said, "How are you now?" She said, "Look at me. I have orphan children and no one to help."

After that day, every morning Imam would carry the wheat and make her bread. One day this lady's daughter returned home to see her mother. When she entered the house, she saw the Imam leaving. They exchanged greetings and the Imam left. She recognized the Imam and was mesmerized. She turned around and told her mother, "Mother, did you see who walked in?" The mother said, "I do not know. He is a very generous and humble man but I do not know his name." She said, "That was Ali b. Abi Talib." The mother said, "That's Ali?" She said, "Yes." The mother said, "I have been cursing him every morning to his face!" She ran back to the Imam and said, "O son of Abu Talib! Forgive me! I did not know your true character." Imam said, "O lady, forgive me if I ever hurt you in the name of Allah (swt)."

We must assess our actions and question how we can call ourselves followers of Ali if our actions do not resemble his actions.

During his caliphate nobody loved him as much as the non-Muslims of his time. The Muslims were the ones fighting him whereas the Christians and Jews loved him and mourned him. Imam Ali has a famous line in his letter to Malik al-Ashtar, which Kofi Annan of the United Nations said "is the greatest letter of government ever written by a human being." Imam Ali told Malik in that letter, "Know that people are of two types; they are either your brother in faith or your equal in humanity."

In another line, which should be cemented on the walls of our mosques, Imam said, "Know O Muslims! Our enemy is not the Christians or the Jews; our enemy is our own ignorance!"

When he walked passed a church, his companion said to him, "I wonder how much polytheism is being done by the people in the church?" Imam said, "I wonder how much monotheism is being practiced." One looked at the cup half empty; Ali would look at the cup half full.

When he would walk in the streets, he would see an old Christian begging. Imam would ask, "Why is this Christian begging? When he was young he would work and look after us and now he is old, no one looks after him? I will not move from my position until one of you promises to sponsor this Christian."

There was a Jewish man who cried when he heard that Ali (as) had died. They asked him why he was crying. He said, "I was walking towards Kufa to my home. I met a man and we started talking and I told him I'm Jewish and he said he was Muslim. We kept on talking and walking. I remembered that at the beginning of the conversation he had said that he was going to Kufa; but now as we were walking, we went past Kufa and were going towards my house. So I turned around to him and said, 'O man, you said you are going towards Kufa; why are you still walking with me?' The man said, 'Because in Islam we are taught that the right of the person who travels with us is that we do not leave them until they give us permission. You never gave me permission, so I kept on walking to your house.' I said, 'Go ahead. I give you permission. Today I have learnt about your religion through your morals.'"

The narrations state that as soon as Ali left, his Jewish friend approached him and said, "How did you form a relationship with him?" The Jew said, "What do you mean?" He said, "Do you know who that was?" The Jew said, "No. He was just one of the Muslims who lives in part of the empire." He said, "That is the head of the empire!" The Jew said, "He was Ali b. Abi Talib?" He said, "Yes." The Jew said, "The caliph of the whole Muslim empire?" He said, "Yes, but why did he come to this Jewish area?" The Jew said, "Would you believe, he said that the rights in Islam of a traveller is that you have to wait for their permission before they let you go."

These were the morals of Imam Ali b. Abi Talib (as) until the day he died. After b. Muljim struck him, one may ask, which human being says, "Give water to my killer, he is thirsty?" Which human being says, "Feed my killer what you are going to feed me?" Which human being says, "Give shelter to my killer in the way you have given shelter to me?"

Imam Ali b. Abi Talib (as) is the human being who is an example for each and every one of us in our lives. His legacy can be seen in the fact that Malik al-Ashtar died for Ali; Hujr b. Adi died for Ali; Muhammad b. Abi Bakr died for Ali; Qanbar died for Ali; Kumayl died for Ali; Maytham al-Tammar died for Ali; there is not a single human being (except for the Prophet) for whom companions gave up their lives like Ali.

Rajiv Gandhi said, "I would never enter a cabinet meeting in my government without giving a new minister Ali's letter to Malik al-Ashtar." Kofi Annan said, "That letter to Malik al-Ashtar is the greatest letter anyone has ever written."

The famous American philosopher, Ralph Emerson, said, "No human can understand the essence of humanity like Ali b. Abi Talib. Look at the mixture in one human being; in one minute he is a warrior, the next minute he is a leader; the next minute he is a man of knowledge and the next minute he is a man of philosophy. Have you seen a human being this rounded? Look at his words. Which human says, 'O mankind! You came as a drop of semen and you leave as a piece of dust; you do not now when you came and you do not know when you are going, so why do you walk around like you know everything?' Which human would say, 'Mankind know yourself, then you will know your Lord.' Which human would look at the peacock and say, 'The peacock is the clearest sign of an arrogant creation that is insecure because the peacock makes you look at its feathers because it is insecure about its skinny legs.' Which human being has understood the essence of worship [so well] that he says, 'God, I do not worship you because of my fear of hell because that's the worship of a slave; and I do not worship you because of my love of heaven because that's the worship of a business man; I worship you because you are worthy of worship. That's the worship of a free man.'?"

Look at the duas like Kumayl and Mashlul which are spoken from the tongue of Imam Ali b. Abi Talib (as). A befitting line is a line from one of the Sikh poets, Kinor Singh, who says, "O Ali! You belong to every faith, every age and all people. We will never let anyone take your honor and we will never let anyone claim you as their own because Ali b. Abi Talib belongs to every human being!"

Lecture 3

Imam Hassan b. Ali al-Mujtaba (as)

Imam al-Hassan (as) was born on the 15th of Ramadan in the 3rd year after Hijra, and died in the month of Safar in the 50th year after Hijra; he is a man from whose life many a lesson may be learnt and many examples may be derived and a man whose life has to be examined in depth, for his life affects each and every one of our lives today. Unfortunately, however, he continues to be a man whose depiction is extremely negative, both in Muslim and as well as in non-Muslim circles. Arguably, the most misunderstood of the Imams of Aal Muhammad is this Imam, in the idea that until today, he is not been given the credit that he deserves for the amount of sacrifices and acts of bravery and wisdom that he performed in his life.

Some Misconceptions about Imam al-Hassan (as)

Until today many people question the bravery of Imam al-Hassan (as); many question the wisdom of his decisions; many question his lifestyle; and you find that, in the academic world as well as in the Muslim world, there are many who portray him in a very negative light. For example, Willi Frischauer, in his book on the Aga Khans, speaks of Imam al-Hassan (as) as a man who spent his entire life marrying and divorcing. They used to call him "the habitual divorcee." Similarly, Mir Ali, in his book, The Spirit of Islam, talks about how Imam al-Hassan (as) was a man who was fond of the easy and quiet life. He was not interested in the religion of Islam; he was interested only in marrying women and divorcing them.

This negative portrayal of Imam al-Hassan (as) exists until today. One of the other negative depictions about him was that they placed Imam al-Hassan (as) alongside personalities who did not build the religion of Islam, but rather sought to destroy it. A documentary has been made where people talk about Imam al-Hassan (as) and Mu'awiya as the great restorers of the religion of Islam who brought unity to the religion. It is really sad that Imam al-Hassan (as) is compared with personalities whose only aim was to build a power base and a kingdom, not a caliphate in the religion of Islam.

Therefore you find that one of the accusations that exists until today about Imam al-Hassan (as) was that he sold his caliphate for seven million dirhams. There is a book that discusses this, that he gave two million to Imam Hussein (as), he kept five million for himself and allowed Mu'awiya to continue ruling. All of these accusations are not surprising because Imam al-Hassan (as)'s grandfather is accused of similar things even today. Even today people accuse the Prophet (pbuh) of being "a man who loved women," and a man who signed treaties more than showing bravery. Therefore, when you analyze the biography of Imam al-Hassan (as), you will find many similarities to his grandfather, the Holy Prophet (pbuh).

Let us examine his life and see what myths were created about Imam al-Hassan (as) and how we can refute these myths because, unfortunately, in our communities many of us know more about Imam Hussein (as) than about Imam al- Hassan (as). This is very unfortunate because Imam Hussein (as) himself used to look up to Imam al-Hassan (as). Moreover, some of the people actually believe that Imam Hussein (as) was braver than Imam al-Hassan (as). What they do not realize is that, if you swap their positions, they both would have acted in exactly the same way.

His Birth

Imam al-Hassan (as) was born on the 15th of Ramadan in the 3rd year after Hijra. His parents were married the year before. Thus he was the first child in the household of the family of the Prophet (pbuh). Being the first child in the family brought delight to the household of the Prophet (pbuh), especially the Prophet. With Imam Hussein (as), there was more sadness in the reaction of the Prophet. The ahadith tell us that when Imam Hussein (as) was born, the Prophet (pbuh)'s steps were very heavy as he walked to the house of his daughter; but with the birth of Imam al-Hassan (as) he was overjoyed.

When he came to the house of his daughter and held the child there was an immediate connection between the two. The narrations tell us that Imam Ali b. Abi Talib (as) was asked, "What are you going to name this boy?" The Imam gave an interesting reply, which requires some reflection. He said, "The naming of my son is with the Prophet." Then when the Prophet was asked, "What are you going to name your grandson?" He replied, "The naming of my grandson is with Allah (swt)."

This is a point to be noted because when Allah (swt) names a child, that is an indication that this person will be guided by Allah (swt). For example, when I believe in the rightly-guided caliphs, I also know that many of the rightly-guided caliphs names were given to them by their Mushrik fathers, isn't that true? Yet we call them "rightly-guided." However, can we come to this conclusion that someone named by his Mushrik father is rightly-guided, but the one who Allah (swt) names, we are unsure whether to call him rightly-guided or not.

Today in the world, when you ask people, "How many rightly-guided caliphs are there?" They mention four names. Then you ask them, "How about Imam al-Hassan (as)?" They say, "We are not sure about Imam al-Hassan (as). Him and Mu'awiya are on the same level but we are not sure which one of them is right."

Our reply to them is that when the Prophet says, "I await Jibra'il's command before I name him," isn't this an indication that Imam al-Hassan (as) is guided by Allah (swt)? Thus the Prophet then tells his family that, "Jibra'il has just come to me and has said to name him Hassan."

The name Hassan was never given to anyone before him. There was a mountain in Arabia called the "Hassan Mountain." But there was never a human being by the name of Hassan. Therefore, the first person to be given this name was Imam al-Hassan (as).

Later on in Islamic history there were tyrants who would pride themselves on sacrificing anyone who had this name. One person narrates that, "I went to Damascus to see one of my cousins. I noticed that in Damascus no one was called 'Hassan' or 'Hussein.' I was disappointed. I entered my friend's house and heard my friend call out to his two sons, 'Hassan and Hussein come here!' I said to him, 'Mashallah, you have named your sons Hassan and Hussein after the grandsons of the Prophet!' He said to me, 'What do you mean [by saying] mashallah?' I said, 'It is an honor that you have named your sons these names!' He said, 'No, I named them this so that when I get angry I can send my curse on Hassan and Hussein!'" The hatred towards the Ahlulbayt had reached to such a level that people were embarrassed to keep these names for their children.

Imam al-Hassan (as)'s Relationship with the Prophet (pbuh)

There was no relationship as beautiful as the relationship of Imam al-Hassan (as) and Imam Hussein (as) with the Prophet; to the extent that the Prophet used them as an intermediary for giving children their rights in the religion. The Arabs used to be embarrassed to show affection to their children. According to them, a man was not very masculine if he showed affection to a child, for example, by hugging or kissing a child. They were proud of their children but to kiss them or show any kind of affection was unheard of in Arabian society. The Prophet would outwardly express his love for Imam al-Hassan (as), not only out of love for him, but also so that others would learn by seeing his example.

For example, whenever he would walk past the house of his daughter, he would stop outside and say, "O family of the Prophet! Where is the flower of my heart al-Hassan?" Hearing this Imam al-Hassan (as) would run out of the house and the Prophet would hug him in front of all his companions and say, "I love him and Allah loves the one who loves him."

On another occasion, the Prophet would walk around by putting Imam al-Hassan (as) on his shoulders or on his back. The companions would see the Prophet (pbuh) doing this and they would say to Imam al-Hassan (as), "O son, how blessed you are because of the steed you are riding!" The Prophet would reply, "No. How blessed am I because of the rider!" All of these acts and sayings were indications of the status of Imam al-Hassan.

Once the Prophet (pbuh) was in sujood when Imam al-Hassan (as) came and rode on his back; the Prophet (pbuh) would then lengthen his sujood while Imam al-Hassan (as) was on his back.

The Prophet (pbuh) would refer to Imam al-Hassan (as) saying, "This is the master of the youth of paradise; this is the flower of my life."

One day one of the Arabs by the name of Agra (meaning, "the bold-headed one") said to the Prophet, "O Prophet, I saw you kiss al-Hassan (as) today." Prophet (pbuh) said, "Yes." Agra said, "I have ten sons and I have never kissed any of them." The Prophet (pbuh) asked, "Why?" Agra said, "O Prophet, they are my sons, why would I kiss them? I want them to be men." The Prophet (pbuh) said, "Whoever does not have mercy on his children will not receive mercy from Allah (swt)."

Therefore, the Prophet was one of the first influences on the life of Imam al-Hassan (as).

Imam al-Hassan (as)'s Relationship with his Mother

The second influence on Imam al-Hassan (as)'s life was the spirituality of his mother, Fatima (as). The origin of every lesson that Imam al-Hassan (as) learnt in his life was from his mother. That is why Imam Hassan al-Askari (as) has a phenomenal line where he said, "We, the Imams, are a Hujjah (proof) over the people and Fatima is a Hujjah over us!"

Imam al-Hassan (as) showed us that a mother with spirituality could build a household. Napoleon used to say, "Give me good mothers and I will give you a strong nation!" On many occasions Imam al-Hassan (as) would talk about the lessons he learnt from his mother.

No Imam had the spirituality that Imam al-Hassan (as) had during hajj. Imam al-Hassan (as) went for hajj twenty-five times on foot. He learnt this love for worship from his mother. Imam al-Hassan (as) narrates, "In the middle of the night, when I was a child, I would wake up and see my mother reciting Salat ul-Layl; I would go and sit next to her while she would be supplicating, and I would listen to her dua. I would hear her say, 'Ya Allah, forgive the members of the community and then forgive us; Ya Allah, bless the members of the community and then bless us; Ya Allah, be generous to the members of the community and be generous to us.' I would ask my mother, 'Mother, in the middle of the night I see you praying for everybody else, but not for your household?' To which she would reply, 'O my son Hassan, first the neighbors then the household.'"

One of the conditions of a dua being accepted is that first we have to pray for our friends and then pray for ourselves. One day a person came to the Prophet and said, "O Prophet, my dua is not being accepted." Prophet (pbuh) said, "Do you pray for others first, then yourself?" He said, "No." The Prophet (pbuh) said, "Pray for others, then for yourself." So the person prayed in front of the Prophet and said, "Ya Allah! Bless me, bless Muhammad and do not bless anyone else." Prophet (pbuh) said, "No, no. I mean pray for everybody and then for yourself." One has to remove this selfishness from oneself.

Imam al-Hassan (as) narrates, "In the middle of the night, when the world was asleep, I would see my mother Fatima supplicate for others. Then in the daytime I would see my mother answering the questions of religion for the women of Arabia."

This is a mother who had spirituality and performed services for Allah. Today there is a lack of spirituality in most mothers, while there is a greater concern for the image, schooling and degree of a child so that it can add to her own image in the community. A mother needs to be a role model in spirituality for her daughter and son.

Imam al-Hassan (as) said, "My mother would cook, clean, and nurture all of us." He narrates an incident, which is one of the many incidents he witnessed in his house. Imam al-Hassan (as) was very young when he was observing his mother's actions. He was only eight years old when his mother died. So one can imagine how young he must have been noticing all the incidents.

Once a lady came to Fatima (as) and said, "O my lady Fatima, my mother is ill. I have come to ask questions on her behalf; I want you to answer them." Fatima (as) asked, "What are your questions?" She said, "They are questions concerning prayer." Fatima (as) said, "Go ahead and ask." That lady asked Fatima (as) many, many questions until at the end she said, "O Lady of light, I may have troubled you too much with my questions. Forgive me. Maybe it is better that I do not ask anymore." Fatima (as) said, "If a person was asked to carry something from the ground to the roof of a building for a thousand dinars, would they say that they are tired?" The lady said, "No." Fatima (as) said, "When I answer your questions, Allah has promised a reward of pearls between the heaven and the earth. Why would I be tired when it is a service to Allah (swt)?" Thus Imam al-Hassan witnessed his mother's acts of kindness and generosity .

Imam al-Hassan (as)'s Relationship with his Father

Imam Ali b. Abi Talib (as) had a major impact on the life of Imam al-Hassan (as). Imam al-Hassan (as) observed the sacrifices his parents made as a couple. A child always observes and absorbs the relationship of his parents. Is it a healthy relationship? Is the conversation between them softly spoken? Are there constant arguments and shouting at home? Many children are psychologically damaged when they see their parents fighting all the time.

Imam al-Hassan (as) said, "I would see my mother and father in harmony and unison with each other." They were the most beautiful combination of individuals in a marriage.

Imam al-Hassan (as) narrates, "One night when Hussein and myself were ill, my parents were worried about us and they asked the Prophet, 'O Prophet, what is it that we should do? Hassan and Hussein are ill.'

The Prophet said, 'Make a vow that if they get better, you will fast for three days.' The first night I saw that, as we were about to break our fast, someone knocked at our door. I saw my mother and father speak to each other saying, 'Whoever it is, and whatever they need, we will give it to them.' I saw my father answer the door. The person said, 'O family of the Prophet! I am an orphan.' The next night the same thing happened and a man said, 'I am a traveller,' and on the third night a man said, 'I am a captive'; and on all three nights I saw my parents give away their share of the food and go to sleep without having any food."

One cannot count the sacrifices this family has made, whether it was in terms of food, wealth or their own lives. It was then that the verse of Surah al-Dahr (76:8) was revealed, wherein Allah talks of a group of people who give out of the love for Allah and expect nothing in return from the people. Thus Imam al-Hassan (as) saw that the sacrifices of his parents were done from their hearts.

Imam al-Hassan (as)'s first grand occasion in Islam was when his grandfather the Prophet took him on the occasion of Mubahila, when he went to meet the Christians of Najran. Imam al-Hassan (as) was six years old and Imam Hussein (as) was five years old. These Christians were amazed. They could not believe that the Prophet had brought a five and a six year old to an event where Allah was going to send down a curse on the disbelievers. This event took place a year and a half before the Prophet died, and was exactly one year before the day of Ghadir. When the Prophet went to Mubahila, many companions thought that he would take them with him. But when the Prophet took his family, he said, "When it comes to sacrificing for this religion on a day like Mubahila or any day after Mubahila, these are the five all of you have to look up to." The Prophet (pbuh) had taken Imam al-Hassan (as) and Imam Hussein (as) as his sons when the Quran stated, "Bring your sons…"

Thus Imam al-Hassan (as) experienced years of glory in the first eight years of his life. Then all of a sudden the trials of life began to hit him. His grandfather the Prophet died. The narrations tell us that when the Prophet (pbuh) was dying and when Imam Ali b. Abi Talib (as) came to remove Imam al-Hassan (as) from his grandfather's side, the Prophet said, "No, no. Let me smell more of him and let him smell more of me." Then only a few months later, Imam al-Hassan (as) saw his mother Fatima (as) being hurt by the companions and eventually die in front of him. Those images stayed with him for years. He was only eight years old at the time. All the books of hadith narrate that when the companions banged on the door, Fatima (as) said, "This is the house of the daughter of the Prophet!" To which the reply was, "So what! We will come and burn the house!" The books of hadith clearly state whom Fatima (as) was angry with when she died. After the death of his mother, a lot of responsibility came upon Imam al-Hassan (as) to act as a role model and a father figure for his younger brother Hussein and two younger sisters, Zaynab and Kulthum.

One of the biggest myths created about Imam al-Hassan (as) is that some people say, "Imam al-Hassan (as) was not as strong as Imam Hussein (as); he did not have Imam Hussein's bravery. Imam al-Hassan (as) was someone who was fond of the easy life; he enjoyed staying away from the battlefield."

On the contrary, in the Battle of Jamal and Siffin there was no one as important as Imam al-Hassan (as) on the battlefield. Before the Battle of Jamal, Imam al-Hassan (as) gave a powerful speech to the Muslims, which motivated them to come and fight alongside Imam Ali b. Abi Talib (as).

When Abu Musa al-Ashari was in Kufa, he was telling the people not to go and fight with Imam Ali b. Abi Talib (as) and he was urging them to remain in Kufa. Imam Ali b. Abi Talib (as) told Imam al-Hassan (as), "Hassan, go with Ammar b. Yasir and tell them who I am."

Imam al-Hassan (as) gave a powerful speech where he told the people of Kufa, "Have you forgotten the day of Ghadir when my father was chosen? Did you forget what my father gave the religion of Islam when he was younger at Badr, Uhud, Khandaq, Khaybar and Hunayn? And now there are people who are coming out to fight my father and you are sitting here?"

He rallied the troops on the day of Jamal as well. On the day of Jamal, Imam al-Hassan (as), Malik al-Ashtar, Muhammad b. Abi Bakr, Muhammad b. Hanafiyya and many others were standing on the front lines on the battlefield. Imam Ali b. Abi Talib (as) told Muhammad b. Hanafiyya, his son from Khawla bint Ja'far, "O Muhammad, you see those soldiers? Even if those arrows are coming towards you, remain firm like the mountains."

Muhammad b. Hanafiyya was a valiant warrior; he went out and then shortly returned to Imam Ali b. Abi Talib (as) and said, "Father, I cannot continue." Imam asked, "Why?" He said, "Because the arrows are sharp and they are showering on us." Imam looked at him and said, "That is the difference between all sons and the sons of Fatima Zahra." He asked, "Why?" Imam said, "Look at Hassan. If I let him out on that battlefield, he will annihilate the army." When Imam Ali b. Abi Talib (as) says this about someone you can rest assured that Imam Ali b. Abi Talib (as) knows a soldier. But during the battle Imam Ali b. Abi Talib (as) kept calling Imam al-Hassan (as) back, and when Imam al-Hassan (as) would ask, "Father, what is it?"

Imam Ali b. Abi Talib (as) would say, "Hassan, stay back. You are the Imam after me." Imam knew that his son was always in the middle of the battlefield and he was so brave that nobody wanted to be near him.

Even in the Battle of Siffin, Imam al-Hassan (as) had a major effect in the battle, to the extent that Ubaydullah b. Umar b. Khattab tried to bribe Imam al-Hassan (as) at Siffin. The enemies used to say, "If you can break Ali, Hassan and Malik al-Ashtar, you can win."

Ubaydullah came to Imam al-Hassan (as) on behalf of Mu'awiya and said, "Hassan, listen. The Arabs hate your father because he killed many of their fathers when he was younger. Take this envelope and join our side. We will look after you in a way no one will." Imam al-Hassan (as) said, "A man like me would join a man like you? A man like me would leave a father like my father? You will die shortly," and it was only shortly after that that Ubaydullah died.

At Siffin, when Imam Ali b. Abi Talib (as) confronted Sulayman al-Khuza'i, Imam said to him, "Sulayman, I expected you to be loyal to us." Sulayman said, "Imam, forgive me, but I am here now." Imam said, "But I thought you would be alongside me." Sulayman went to Imam al-Hassan (as) at Siffin and said, "Hassan, look at the way your father talks to me. Why is he so angry with me?"

Imam al-Hassan (as) said, "When my father loves someone he feels disappointed when he does not see his loyalty. Calm down and do not be angry." Imam al-Hassan (as) would have this calming influence in the Battle of Siffin that people would look up to him when the times got tough. On the battlefield, when they would see Imam al-Hassan (as) standing somewhere, they would go and stand alongside him for comfort. When the Battle of Siffin ended, Imam al-Hassan (as) was very disappointed. He looked at the people at Siffin, where he saw a personality like his father on one side and Mu'awiya on the other; the people left the man who had sacrificed everything for the religion and joined a man whose father wanted to destroy the religion.

During the arbitration at Siffin, Imam al-Hassan (as) looked at Abu Musa al-Ashari and then looked at the people and said, "You choose Abu Musa al-Ashari? If Umar b. Khattab thought Abu Musa to be any good he would have included him in the Shura; and Abu Musa wants to choose Abdullah b. Umar? If Abdullah b. Umar was worthy then his father would have elected him; and as for you Khawarij who say that there should not be any arbitration - bravery is not only shown with the sword, sometimes you have to be brave with your tongue as well. Did the Prophet not use Sad b. Maz with his arbitration with the Banu Quraiza? Then why are you talking about no arbitration?" But the Khawarij unfortunately left the side of Imam Ali b. Abi Talib (as) and in the 40th year after Hijra Imam al-Hassan (as) saw his father struck in the mosque of Kufa by a member of the Khawarij, Abdur Rahman b. Muljim.

Imam al-Hassan (as) was deeply affected by his father's death for a number of reasons: The first reason was the natural sentimental value a son has with his father; and can one imagine what it would be like to have a father like Ali b. Abi Talib? It is impossible for anyone to come close to Ali b. Abi Talib in terms of his warmth, his generosity and his justice;

none could come near the son of Abu Talib. Also, one must remember that Fatima (as) died when her children were very young, so it was Imam Ali b. Abi Talib (as) who had brought up Imam al-Hassan (as), Imam Hussein (as), Lady Zaynab and Lady Umm Kulthum.

The second reason was that he saw his father say to him, "If Abdur Rahman b. Muljim is thirsty, then make sure you give him water; and if he needs food, give him some food; and if his one strike ends up killing me, then you too must strike him just once. Do not mutilate his body because the Prophet has said, 'Do not even mutilate the body of a dog with rabies.'" How difficult it must have been for Imam al-Hassan (as) to live after the death of a father like this.

Imam al-Hassan (as) said, "When I went to bury my father, on my way back I saw a man crying. I looked at him and asked, 'O man, what is wrong?' He said, 'For every night in this holy month there used to be a man who would come and feed me; but for three nights he hasn't come. I do not know who the man was. I am crying because I was used to him coming to feed me.' I began to cry as I said to him, 'That was my father Ali b. Abi Talib.' He looked towards me and said, 'Where has he been for these three nights?' I said, 'Ibn Muljim struck him and I have just come after burying him now.'"

Imam al-Hassan (as)'s Treaty with Mu'awiya

After the martyrdom of Imam Ali b. Abi Talib (as), Imam al-Hassan (as), at the age of thirty-seven, had to take over the responsibility of Imamate. When he stood up in Kufa, he told the people, "O people! Last night the best of Allah's creation after the Prophet has died. A man who was a man of piety, a man of justice and honor! Now I take over the position of succeeding my father."

It is very surprising to hear the Muslim Ummah say that there are only four rightly-guided caliphs. Are they implying that Imam al-Hassan (as) was not rightly-guided? When Imam al-Hassan (as) came to power, Mu'awiya, who had already fought Imam Ali (as), was in control of four countries: Palestine, Lebanon, Jordan and Syria. In those days "Sham" did not mean modern-day Syria. "Sham" in those days included four countries.

After the death of Imam Ali b. Abi Talib (as), Mu'awiya began an onslaught against Imam al-Hassan (as). Mu'awiya was sending spy after spy instructing them, "Find out! What is he saying? What is he doing?" When Imam al-Hassan (as) caught these spies, he said, "What is it that he wants? Does he want a war? Let's have a war. Does he know whose son I am?"

But there was one problem. His father just had three wars and his soldiers did not want to fight anymore. That was the problem he faced; and that is the problem many did not understand. Jamal, Siffin and Nahrawan were three wars which were fought in four years. Imam al-Hassan (as) wanted to finish Mu'awiya but when he went to the mosque of Kufa and said, "O soldiers! Get ready! Let us go out and fight Mu'awiya," many of them turned around and said, "We are tired of fighting!" He said, "But there is injustice and oppression; what do you mean you are tired? We all have to stand up." Adi al-Hatim, the son of Hatim al-Ta'i, stood up and said to the people, "What's wrong with you all? Is this not the grandson of the Prophet who is telling you to come out and fight?"

Despite the situation, Imam al-Hassan (as) tried to mobilize twenty thousand soldiers whereas Mu'awiya had seventy-six thousand. Even then Imam al-Hassan (as) did not give up. But the second problem he faced was that the soldiers who did turn up to fight were being bribed by Mu'awiya. For a million dinars they were willing to switch sides and change their loyalties. One can now appreciate the unflinching seventy-two that Imam Hussein (as) had at Karbala; but even seventy-two was not a large number. It is hard to find true faithful followers in life.

Thus, if Imam al-Hassan (as) had more soldiers, he would have gone ahead and fought; his own cousin Ubaydullah b. Abbas had eight thousand soldiers under his command. When Imam al-Hassan (as) sent them to the front lines, Mu'awiya sent one million dinars to bribe them and they immediately switched sides. Mu'awiya had a massive government that included Syria, Lebanon, Jordan and Palestine. He was promising soldiers that he would marry his daughters and nieces to them, which meant instant power; to others he was promising land, wealth and money; to others he was offering important positions and posts. Soon Imam al-Hassan (as) ended up with only eight thousand soldiers which was nothing compared to the huge Syrian army.

Even then Imam al-Hassan (as) was saying to his soldiers, "Let's fight; if you all are ready to fight, I will proceed."

But then Mu'awiya planned another conspiracy; he spread a rumor amongst Imam al-Hassan (as)'s people that Imam al-Hassan (as) did not want to fight whereas Imam al-Hassan (as) actually wanted to fight; he had conveyed to his soldiers that he had the confidence, that if he was given that battlefield, even if there were ten times more soldiers than his, he could finish them, as he had soldiers like Adi b. Hatim, Hujr b. Adi al-Kindi and Ammar b. Hamakal Khuza'i alongside him.

But Mu'awiya's rumor spread, and the Khawarij (who had defected to Imam Ali) were present at the time. The Khawarij were furious and said to Imam al-Hassan (as), "We hear that you want peace." They came and stabbed Imam al-Hassan (as) in his thigh. This made Imam al-Hassan (as) realize that if I have soldiers who are going to stab me in the back, while Mu'awiya wants to stab me in the front, whom can I trust? So now when Imam al-Hassan (as)'s loyal soldiers said to him, "Let's fight, even if there is a few of us left," Imam al-Hassan (as) evaluated the circumstances and said, "No. I swear that if we fight there will not be a single follower of Ali left living on this earth."

So he did what his grandfather the Prophet did at Hudaybiyya. Most of the time the Imams based their decisions on what their grandfather did in his life. When his soldiers asked him, "So then what are you going to do?" He said, "I will do what my grandfather did at Hudaybiyya; we will sign a treaty but through the treaty we will expose the other side."

If Mu'awiya and Imam al-Hassan (as) would have fought, and Mu'awiya would have killed Imam al-Hassan (as), people would have still said as they say today, "Sayyedna Mu'awiya and Sayyedna Hassan; there was just a quarrel between them." Imam al-Hassan (as) did something else instead.

When the Prophet (pbuh) had signed the treaty, some of his companions objected and said, "Why? Let's kill them." The Prophet (pbuh) said, "If we fight, people will still not know who is right and who is wrong; instead we will make a peace treaty stating our conditions. When the other side breaks it then people will know who is on the right and who is on the wrong."

So when the people asked Imam al-Hassan (as), "What are you basing your decision on by signing a peace treaty with Mu'awiya?" He said, "My grandfather did the same at Hudaybiyya." Thus Imam al-Hassan (as) signed the treaty because the terms would expose Mu'awiya's behavior. Mu'awiya and Yazid were two different people. Yazid was publicly and privately irreligious whereas Mu'awiya was publicly unbelievably religious. Imam Hussein (as) had to fight Yazid because of Yazid's blatant moral corruption; whereas Imam al-Hassan (as) had to be clever with Mu'awiya. He set the following terms:

1. "Handing over authority to Mu'awiyah provided that he should act according to the Book of Allah, the Sunnah of His Apostle."

2. "The authority should be for al-Hassan after him (Mu'awiyah).If an accident happened to him (al-Hassan), the authority should be for his brother al-Hussein. Mu'awiyah has no right to entrust anybody (else) to it."

3. "He (Mu'awiyah) should abandon cursing the Commander of the faithful (Ali) as well as the practice of using personal prayer (Qunut) against him (al-Hassan) in Salat (the prescribed ritual prayers), and that he should not mention the name of All except in good manner."

4. "He (Mu'awiyah) should keep excluded what is 'in the treasury of Kufa, that is five million (dirhams). So, handing over the authority does not include it (the sum of this money). Mu'awiyah should send al-Hassan one million dirham per year, he should prefer banu Hashirn in giving and gifts to banu Abd ash-Shams, and should divide one million (dirham) among the sons of those who were killed helping the Commander of the faithful (Ali) in the Battle of the Camel and the Battle of Siffeen and should spend that from the taxes of Dar Abjard."

5. "The people should be safe wherever they are in the earth of Allah; in Sham (Syria), Iraq, Hijaz, Yemen, etc. He should give security to the black and the red alike. He (Mu'awiyah) should bear their slips, should not follow some of them for the bygone, nor should he punish the Iraqis foe hostility."

6. "The companions of Ali should be given security wherever they are; that he (Mu'awiyah) should not expose them to any evil; that they should be given security over their lives, their properties and women and children; and that he should give them their rights.

7. "He (Mu'awiyah) should not seek a calamity secretly or openly for al-¬Hassan or his brother al-Hussein, nor for anyone from the progeny of Ahle Bait of the Apostle of Allah, nor should he frighten them in any country or territories."

Mu'awiya did not honor any of these terms:

1. For sixty years, every single Friday prayer began with the cursing of Imam Ali b. Abi Talib (as).
2. Salat ul-Juma'a was prayed on a Wednesday. According to Islamic jurisdiction, the leader of the prayer has to stand while giving the khutba on Friday, but Mu'awiya would sit while giving the khutba. These were just of the innumerable changes he made in the sunnah of the Prophet (pbuh).
3. Mu'awiya killed Hujr b. Adi al-Kindi, Ammar bil Hamak al-Khuza'i, Rushayd al-Hajari and many other Shi'as.
4. He did not return any blood money.
5. He appointed his son Yazid as his successor.

So what did Imam al-Hassan (as) achieve from that peace treaty?

Imam al-Hassan (as) achieved two things: The first was that he exposed Mu'awiya's character in front of everyone. Now people could see clearly his true nature. Despite knowing his real character can any Muslim bless or pray for a man who curses the fourth caliph? Can Mu'awiya and Ali both be referred to with the phrase "Radi Allah 'anhu (May Allah be pleased with him)?"

Also, by signing the treaty, Imam al-Hassan (as) made sure that the followers of Aal Muhammad's lives would be saved because, had Imam al-Hassan (as) not used the wisdom of his grandfather in signing that treaty, there would not be a single follower of Aal Muhammad today. Mu'awiya would have annihilated them. But Imam al-Hassan (as) saw that the best option was to sign the treaty with Mu'awiya, which eventually led to the tenth of Muharram.

Answers to Some Accusations Against Imam al-Hassan (as)

To those who say Imam al-Hassan (as) was not brave, we say, if Imam al-Hassan (as) had his way, and if he had his brother's companions, he would have finished Mu'awiya right away.

Some people created a myth about Imam al-Hassan (as)'s personal life. They said that all Imam al-Hassan (as) did was get married and divorced.

The first to make up this myth was Abul Hassan al-Mada'ini. He said, "Imam al-Hassan married and divorced seventy women in his life." If you study the life of Abul Hassan, you will realize that nobody loved the Bani Ummayah like Abul Hassan al-Mada'ini. So it is not surprising to read a statement like this from such a personality. Another person by the name of Shablanji, in his book, Nur ul-Absar, wrote, "Imam al-Hassan married ninety women and divorced all ninety of them."

Arguably, Abu Talib al-Makki made the worst statement about him. He wrote a book called Quwwat ul-Qulub, which is available until today; it is a fourth century book. He wrote, "Imam al-Hassan married three hundred women and divorced all of them."

One needs to ask the question whether that is even possible mathematically. Can someone marry and divorce three hundred times in a span of fourteen years, including the period of "iddah" and the "revocables?" They say he married three hundred women between his father's caliphate until his death. Imam Ali b. Abi Talib (as) became the caliph in 36 AH and Imam al-Hassan (as) died in 50 AH. That is a span of fourteen years. Imam al-Hassan (as) was already married to three women: Khawla al-Fazariyya, Umm Ishaq b. Talha, and Ja'da, who eventually killed him. In this fourteen-year period, he was supposed to have married three hundred women. If we suppose that he married a fourth and kept divorcing and divorcing, and we also keep in mind the iddah period and the revocable period during which the woman can return to the man, with all the calculations it still comes to fifty-six wives. So where did the number three hundred come from?

Also, when you study the life of Abu Talib al-Makki, the hadith specialists say that in the last days of his life he went insane to the extent that he would look up to the skies and say, "O people, beware of Him because He causes all the trouble in my life." Would anyone take the words of someone like that seriously? Yet he made such statements about Imam al-Hassan (as) and people believed him.

The rumor of Imam al-Hassan (as)'s many marriages was started by his cousin, al-Mansur al-Dawaniqi, the Abbasid caliph. During his caliphate, all of the sayyeds from Imam al-Hassan (as)'s children were actively campaigning against the Banu Abbas. For example, Muhammad Nafs al-Zakiyya, Hassan al-Muthanna, Abdullah b. Yahya b. Hassan and Hussein b. Ali al-Khayr were all grandsons and great-grandsons of Imam al-Hassan (as) and they were all fighting the Banu Abbas. So the caliph decided to attack them by destroying the character of their great grandfather. He started a campaign against the character of Imam al-Hassan (as). The effects of that propaganda can be seen until today. Recently a television show aired an interview with a so-called religious scholar who was asked, "How great is Imam al-Hassan?" He replied, "He is good, but he cannot be compared to Mu'awiya." The man asked, "Why?" The scholar replied, "Because Mu'awiya was not foolish enough to divorce the way Imam al-Hassan would frequently divorce."

There is one hadith of the Prophet which speaks volumes about the character of Imam al-Hassan (as) and is enough to destroy all these myths. The Prophet (pbuh) said, "My sons Hassan and Hussein are Imams whether they are sitting or standing; whoever fights them fights me and whoever fights me fights Allah (swt); whoever angers them angers me and whoever angers me angers Allah." "Standing" refers to Imam Hussein (as) at Karbala and "sitting" refers to Imam al-Hassan (as). Here "Imam" refers to being the Imam of the soul and a source of guidance for the human being.

The Character of Imam al-Hassan (as)

Despite all the accusations and criticisms that Imam al-Hassan (as) had to face, he maintained the highest manners. They used to call him a man of morals, a man as noble as the Prophet. People used to ask the Prophet (pbuh), "What has Hassan inherited from you?" He said, "My manners and my nobility."

One day as Imam al-Hassan (as) was walking, a man approached him saying, "May God curse you and may God curse your father Ali b. Abi Talib!" Imam al-Hassan (as) said, "O man, you seem like a stranger in Medina; if you do not have a house, come and live in my house. If you do not have food, let me give you food. If you do not have clothes, let me give you clothes. O man, you are welcome to my house. Maybe you have been given some wrong information about me and my father." The man stared at him and said, "No, no. I have never seen morals like your morals. I abused your father and you talk to me so politely? Truly, Allah knows where to place His message."

Imam al-Hassan (as) was also known to be generous. On one occasion a man narrates that, "I entered Medina and I was hungry. I saw this man walking, so I said to him, 'Excuse me, do you mind if I come and eat some food at your house? I do not have anything to eat.' The man said, 'You are more than welcome, but I have a son who lives down there. Why don't you go to him?' I said, 'Well, now that I have seen you, I prefer to eat at your house.' I entered his house to eat with him, but all this man was eating was dry bread. I tried to break this bread and I could not break it. I said to him, 'Excuse me, where was your son's house again?' He said, 'It is the one there.' I went to his son's house and had a brilliant meal there.'" It was Imam al-Hassan (as)'s house. Imam al-Hassan (as) asked the man, "Who sent you here?" He said, "I do not know. It was a man who lives down the road from you." Imam asked, "What did the house look like?" The man described the house to the Imam. Imam asked, "What did he look like?" The man gave a description to the Imam. Then Imam asked, "What was he eating?" The man said, "He had dry bread." Imam said, "So why did he send you here?" The man said, "He said to me, 'You will not find anyone as generous as my son!'" Imam al-Hassan (as) said, "What a father I have!"

Imam Ali b. Abi Talib (as) used to say, "Nobody embodies knowledge like my son Hassan; if you want my knowledge, ask him any question."

One day a group of Romans came to Mu'awiya and said to him, "You claim to be the caliph of God?" He said, "Yes. I am Amir al-Mu'minin." "We have some questions to ask you." "What are they?" "What is the distance between the heavens and the earth? What is the distance between right and wrong? What is a neutral gender? Which existence came without a mother and a father? Which ten things are such that one is harder than another?" "I have no clue what you're talking about. Go to Hassan and ask him." The Romans went to Imam al-Hassan (as) and said to him, "We have some questions to ask you." Imam said, "Go ahead." "What is the distance between the heavens and the earth?" "The cry of an oppressed person in dua." "What is the distance between right and wrong?" "Four fingers between the ears and the eyes; what you hear with your ears must be verified by your eyes." "What is a neutral gender?" "If you cannot tell the gender of a child, wait for seminal emission; if there is no seminal emission, wait for the urine; depending on the shape of the urine you will know if it is a mAl or a female; if it is still unknown after that, it will be known as a neutral gender." "Which existence came without a mother or a father?" "Animals and humans; Adam, Eve, the sheep in the story of

Ibrahim, the snake in the story of Musa, the crow who showed Qabil how to bury the dead, and the camel of Prophet Saleh (as)." "Which ten things are such that one is harder than the other?" "Stone is hard; iron breaks the stone; fire melts the iron; water extinguishes fire; the clouds carry water, the wind blows the clouds; an angel controls the wind; the angel of death overpowers the angel who controls the wind; death overpowers the angel of death; and Allah overpowers death because He is the Living that does not die."

All these Romans came towards the religion of Islam. In terms of his generosity, his knowledge and his morals, there was none like al-Hassan b. Ali. He had left a legacy behind whereby at Karbala he had more sons to give away than Imam Hussein (as). One of his sons was Abdullah. Sayyeda Zaynab narrates that, "I saw Hussein lying on the ground with arrows surrounding his body and Umar b. Sa'd said to Harmala, 'Shoot an arrow at his chest!' As he was about to shoot, I saw the young son of Hassan run out and shout, 'How dare you strike my uncle! First strike me!' He sat near his uncle and put his hand out and said, 'My uncle, I will never allow them to kill you while I am alive!'" The other son was Qasim.

There are some very absurd narrations about how Imam al-Hassan (as) died. One historian, Donaldson, wrote that Imam al-Hassan (as) died of tuberculosis; another said he died when a stick fell on his foot; yet another said he was stabbed. On the contrary, Mu'awiya said to Ja'da, the wife of Imam al-Hassan (as), "If you poison Hassan, I will let you marry Yazid." Thus she poisoned Imam al-Hassan (as) and then said to Mu'awiya, "Now let me marry Yazid," to which he said, "You just poisoned the grandson of the man who brought this religion. Do you think I am going to allow you to marry my son?"

Lecture 5

Imam Hussein b. Ali (as)

Imam Hussein (as) was born on the 3rd of Sha'ban in the 4th year after Hijra, and died on the 10th of Muharram in the 61st year after Hijra, at the age of fifty-seven. He is revered by many as the greatest martyr in Islamic history, and is also seen by many as an ideal exemplar in terms of his leadership, generosity, bravery and humility. He is a man from whose life many a lesson may be learnt and many principles may be derived. He was a man whose acts and standpoints in life have affected both Muslims and non-Muslims until today. Unfortunately, however, this personality has been understudied because when you look at the majority of our knowledge concerning his life, it only relates to the last year of his life - when he left Medina to go to Mecca; when he left Mecca to go towards Kufa, and when he stopped at an area called Karbala. That is about as much knowledge people have about this holy personality's life.

It is shameful that a person whom the Prophet (pbuh) described as "the master of the youth of Paradise," and for whom the Prophet (pbuh) said, "Hussein is from me and I am from Hussein; Allah loves the one who loves Hussein," that we only know about the last days of his life. How many hadith can one narrate from the reference of Imam Hussein (as)? How many stories of Imam Hussein (as) do we know about? Many Muslims will tell you that, barring the events of the tenth of Muharram, their knowledge is quite limited.

Thus this biography is an examination of Imam Hussein (as) from the day he was born until the day he was martyred in order to see the number of important lessons that we can learn from his life, not only in understanding his relationships but also in understanding the principles that have affected non-Muslims as much as it has affected Muslims.

His Birth

Imam Hussein (as) was the second child born to one of the most beautiful marriages within the religion of Islam. Imam Ali b. Abi Talib (as) had married Fatima (as) and they had four children. Lady Fatima (as) had miscarried her fifth child, Mohsin. Their four children were Imam al-Hassan (as), Imam Hussein (as), Lady Zaynab and Umm Kulthum.

Lady Fatima (as) had known that she was pregnant with Imam Hussein (as) fifty-two days after she gave birth to Imam al-Hassan (as) and the narrations tell us that there were mixed feelings surrounding the birth of Imam Hussein (as). Normally when a child is about to be born in a family there is a sense of joy and pride surrounding the entire family; it is very rare to see a grandfather who is sad. Yet many of the reports indicate that, surrounding the birth of Imam Hussein (as), there was a sense of awareness that this child would have an ending that is full of sadness.

The first to comment on this was Umm ul-Fadl, the wife of Abbas, who was the uncle of the Prophet (pbuh). Umm ul-Fadl came to the Prophet (pbuh) and said, "O Prophet! I saw a strange dream last night." He said, "What did you see?" She said, "I saw a piece of your flesh in my lap and I wondered, 'What is this?'" The Prophet (pbuh) said to her, "Glad tidings! Fatima will give birth and the boy will be in your hands."

When Lady Fatima (as) gave birth to Imam Hussein (as) on the 3rd of Sha'ban, the narrations tell us that the Prophet walked with heavy steps to the house of Lady Fatima (as). But when Imam al-Hassan (as) was born, the Prophet walked briskly to her house. The Prophet then called Asma and said, "Asma, where is my Hussein?"

She brought Imam Hussein (as), and as soon as he took Imam Hussein (as) in his arms, he began to cry. Asma said, "O Prophet of God, why do you cry? This is a newborn child; surely this is meant to bring joy?" He said, "This child will be slain by an unjust group of people and may Allah not grant them intercession for what they did; but do not tell Fatima, for Fatima has just come out of labor and I do not want her to hear this news."

Therefore, from the beginning, Imam Hussein (as)'s grandfather had a major connection with him. This highlights to us a very important point: a child learns as much from the grandfather as they do from the father, especially if both are living in the same house. The narrations tell us that the importance of the grandfather is like the father because the child picks things up from the grandfather as much as he picks things up from the father. Thus, the first thing the Prophet did in showing his affection for this child was that he performed a series of ceremonies which would become lessons for us when a child is born in our family.

The first thing he did when Imam Hussein (as) was in his lap was that he recited the adhan in his right ear and iqamah in his left. The Prophet (pbuh) said that, "This moves away the whispers of Satan from the child," as in Surah al-Nas, Allah says, "Say: I seek refuge from the whisperings of Satan."

Then seven days later the Prophet (pbuh) performed the "aqiqa" ceremony. He said, "A sheep has to be slaughtered and the meat of that sheep has to be given away to the poor; and a leg of mutton is to be given away to the midwife because of her help in the child's birth."

Then when the Prophet (pbuh) shaved the head of Imam Hussein (as), the weight of the hair in silver was given out to the poor. That has become the sunnah that remains with us until today.

After that, the Prophet (pbuh) recited a dua where he prayed, "Ya Allah! Remove the envy of the people from Hussein like the way Ibrahim prayed to you to remove the envy from Ishaq and Isma'il." Not everyone is happy when you tell him or her about the birth of a child in your house. There are some who may be childless and there might be emotions of envy within them; there may be others who have had one child but you have had your second; thus not everyone is happy for your happiness. One must always read the prayers for protection from negative energies.

When the Prophet (pbuh) came to the naming of Imam Hussein (as), there are three different narrations about it; two of them have been rejected and one is accepted. One report states that, "When Imam al-Hassan (as) was born Imam Ali b. Abi Talib (as) wanted to name him

'Harb.' 'Harb' means war. So the Prophet came to him and said, "No Ali, change his name from Harb to Hassan." Then when Imam Hussein (as) was born Imam Ali b. Abi Talib (as) said, "Now I want to name him 'Harb.' the Prophet said to change his name from Harb to Hussein. Then the narration continues that when Mohsin was born Imam Ali b. Abi Talib (as) named him Harb, but again he told Imam Ali b. Abi Talib (as) to change his name to Mohsin."

Why do we reject this hadith? Firstly, Mohsin was never born; he was the miscarried child of Fatima (as). Secondly, when the Prophet tells Imam Ali b. Abi Talib (as) once not to do anything, he does not repeat it thrice. Thirdly, is there no better name for Imam Ali b. Abi Talib (as) to name his child than Harb? These were the names of the time of Jahiliyya. In Jahiliyya they used to name their sons "Satan," and "Dhalim," meaning "oppressor."

A second narration states that Imam Ali b. Abi Talib (as) wanted to name him Hamza or Ja'far. But the Prophet said no. The third narration that is unanimously accepted by all scholars is that the Prophet decided that the name would be "Hussein."

Imam Hussein (as)'s Relationship with his Grandfather

The attachment between the Prophet and Imam Hussein (as) was a wonderful attachment. Sometimes a grandfather can be the worst role model for a child and sometimes a grandfather can be the best role model for a child. How many times do we see on television that the grandfather is drunk or abusive or wasted and has bad language? The Prophet taught us that the child observes your behavior; for example, if you are rude, angry, unpleasant, stubborn or difficult to approach, the child picks up on your mannerisms, whereas if you are the embodiment of warmth and humility, the child grows up to be a warm and humble child. Today in Muslim communities we have some grumpy grandparents. They are nagging all day, "Where's the food? Where's the tea? Bring me this. Bring me that."

The Prophet was the perfect embodiment of warmth and manners. The Prophet (pbuh) used to lengthen his sujood if Imam Hussein (as) was on his back. When he would see Imam Hussein (as), he would hug and kiss and embrace him.

One day one of the Arabs by the name of Agra (meaning, "the bold-headed one") saw the Prophet embracing Imam Hussein (as). He said to the Prophet, "Muhammad! Do you actually kiss your children?" The Prophet (pbuh) said, "Yes, why?" Agra said, "I have ten sons and I have never kissed any of them." "Why?," the Prophet (pbuh) asked. Agra said, "O Prophet, it is a sign of masculinity; they are my sons, why would I kiss them? I want them to be men." The Prophet (pbuh) said, "Whoever does not have mercy on his children will not receive mercy from Allah (swt)."

Imam Hussein (as) would see his grandfather humble and respectful with everyone; after all it was said about his grandfather, "Innaka 'ala khuluqin 'Adhim!" He had the highest morals.

One day Imam Hussein (as) was standing next to his elder brother seeing a man performing the wudu'. They notice that the man was doing wudu' completely wrong. He was washing his hands first, then his face, then his feet and then the head. Today when some Muslims see their fellow Muslims not performing their prayers properly, they will mock and criticize him. Imam al-Hassan (as) and Imam Hussein (as) came to the man and said, "O Sheikh! You are older than us. Do you mind observing our wudu' and tell us which one of us is doing it right and which one is doing it wrong?" The man said, "O grandsons of the Prophet, it would be my honor. Go ahead and perform the wudu'." After they performed the wudu', towards the end, he looked at them and said, "It is not you who are performing it wrong. It is me who is performing it wrong."

Their approach was so mature at such a young age because they had been observing their grandfather all along. If the grandfather in a house has the highest akhlaq, then the grandchildren will as well.

Imam Hussein (as) was only five years old when one of the greatest and most important events in Islamic History took place. This was the event of Mubahila. The Prophet (pbuh) took the young Hussein and Hassan alongside him to confront the Christians. Who takes a five and a six year old to the ambassadors of a Christian country? The Christians of Najran came to visit the Prophet (pbuh) and had a dialogue with him. He gave them an argument and they were not convinced by it. The Prophet (pbuh) said to them, "Very well. If you dispute with me over the knowledge I have given you, then we will bring our sons and you bring yours; we will bring our women and you bring your women; we will bring ourselves and you bring your selves." Among the Christian envoys there was nobody under the age of forty. All of them were elders. The Prophet was asked to take his sons, women and a man like himself. The man who was like himself was Imam Ali b. Abi Talib (as); the woman was Lady Fatima (as); as for the sons, he took Hassan and Hussein, when one was only five and the other was only six.

What was he showing us? He was showing us that youths have to be at the front of this religion and not at the back. When we go to meet people from other religions, if our youth are mature then they will lead this religion forward; but if our youth have to wait to go for hajj and then get married, then become religious, it means you have got a religion that is not fulfilling its purpose. Thus the Prophet (pbuh) put Imam al-Hassan (as) and Imam Hussein (as) in the front. When these Christians came, they were amazed that Muhammad had trust in a five and a six year old. The Prophet was showing us that if you give young men responsibility from a young age then they will blossom and mature earlier; if you do not trust them then they will have an inferiority complex that they are not trustworthy individuals. The Christians saw this and said, "We will not enter into a Mubahila with these five because of the amount of light that shines from their faces. If they told the mountain to move, the mountain would move from its position."

Therefore Imam Hussein (as) was very close and attached to his grandfather in those early years. When the Prophet was dying, Imam Hussein (as) came and laid down on his chest. When Imam Ali b. Abi Talib (as) wanted to remove him, the Prophet said, "No, their grandfather is dying. Let me have more of them and let them have more of me."

Imam Hussein (as)'s Relationship with his Father

When the Prophet died, Imam Hussein (as) was only seven years old at the time; and only a few months later his mother Lady Fatima (as) passed away. Imagine the double blow that affects the young Hussein? As a seven year old his grandfather died and then his mother died. From that day he built an attachment with his father like no other attachment. Nobody was as close to Amir al-Mu'mineen as Imam Hussein (as). When the fourth Imam was asked, "What is your name?" He said, "I am Ali b. Hussein." They said, "We see your father named all his sons Ali." Imam replied, "If my father had a thousand sons, he would name them all after his father."

Imam Hussein (as)'s attachment to his father was phenomenal, as one can imagine, because his father was fathering four orphans and Imam Hussein (as) was only seven years old. Wherever his father would go, Imam Hussein (as) would be alongside him; whatever sermon his father would give, Imam Hussein (as) would listen; whatever piece of knowledge his father would give others, Imam Hussein (as) would take it in.

One of the most famous duas in Islamic history was a dua Imam Hussein (as) learnt from Imam Ali b. Abi Talib (as) called Dua Mashlul. "Mashlul" means "the one who is paralyzed" or "one who is stricken with a severe illness." Imam Hussein (as) narrates that, "I was with my father. We were doing the tawaf of the Ka'aba. All of a sudden we laid our eyes on someone who was holding onto the Ka'aba and crying bitterly. I said to my father, 'Father, I have never seen anyone cry like this.' My father said, 'Hussein, my dear son, go and see what's wrong.'I went to this young man who was holding onto the Ka'aba and I said to him, 'Young man, what's wrong with you?' He said, 'I was a person who was rude and disobedient to my father.' I asked, 'What did you do?'

He said, 'On many occasions I was rude to him. When he would ask me for something I would rudely answer back and there was an occasion where I pushed my father away from me. My father said, "Wallah! I will never forgive you! And I am going to read a dua against you for what you have done!" From the day he recited a supplication against me, I have been paralyzed. You see how my hands are holding the Ka'aba and my legs do not even move? The lower part of my body has no movement. I beg of you, help me.'

I went back to my father, the leader of my life, the person from whom I take the best examples from and I said to him, 'O my father Amir al-Momineen, what shall we do?' He said, 'Hussein, is the young man sincere?' I said, 'Yes, my father. I saw tears coming from his eyes.' My father said, 'Let him recite this dua.' I asked, 'What's the dua?' He said, 'Dua Mashlul. Whenever a person is ill or in grief or in a bad situation, let him recite Dua Mashlul after Salat ul-Isha and you will see that the illness will be removed.'

I went to that person and told him, 'Tonight, after Salat ul-Isha, recite the following dua.' I began to recite the dua for him and the person repeated it after me. The next day I saw this person walking near the Ka'aba. I looked at him and said, 'How come you are walking?'

He said, 'Wallah, in the name of the Prophet (pbuh) whom God chose as His final messenger, and who is your grandfather, last night he came in my dreams and he said to me, 'Come towards me, young man, as you have recited Dua Mashlul.' He touched me on the area where I was paralyzed; as soon as I woke up that entire area had been cured.'"

His Marriages and his Children

Imam Hussein (as) was thirty-six years old when Imam Ali b. Abi Talib (as) died. Imam Hussein (as) married seven women and he chose many of his wives on the basis of his father. [Imam Ali b. Abi Talib (as) had married nine women; Lady Fatima (as), Amama, the niece of Fatima (as), Khawla bint Ja'far, Fatima bint Hizam al-Qilabiyya, also known as Umm ul-Banin, Asma bint Umais, Layla, Unsayee bint Thaqafiyya, Sahba and Mahya, the daughter of Umra b. Qais.]

All Imam Hussein (as)'s marriages were monumental. He married Layla, the daughter of Abi Murra, who was the son of Urwa b. Mas'ud al-Thaqafi. Thus Layla's grandfather was Urwa. Urwa was the mu'min of Al Yasin at the time of the Prophet. Layla's maternal grandfather was Abu Sufyan. Her mother Maymuna was the daughter of Abu Sufyan, which made Mu'awiya her uncle and Yazid her first cousin. As a result, Ali Akbar's great grandfather was Abu Sufyan. Thus Layla gave Imam Hussein (as) a son like Ali Akbar, the eldest of Imam Hussein (as)'s sons. The historians are unanimous that the oldest son of Imam Hussein (as) was Ali Akbar. However, there are a few who say he was younger than Imam Zayn ul-Abideen (as).

Then Imam Hussein (as) married Rubab. Rubab's father was originally a Christian. He converted, and then Imam Ali b. Abi Talib (as) married Rubab's elder sister Mahiyat. Imam al-Hassan (as) married the next sister Hayyat and Imam Hussein (as) married Rubab.

He also married a lady called Shahzanan. In Arabic Shahzanan means "Sayyedat un-Nisa." When Imam Hussein (as) married her, Imam Ali b. Abi Talib (as) said to change her name to Shahrbanu, as there was only one Sayyedat un-Nisa and that was Lady Fatima (as). Lady Shahrbanu gave Imam Hussein (as) Zayn ul-Abideen (as).

Umm Ishaq b. Talha was initially the wife of Imam al-Hassan (as). When Imam al-Hassan (as) died, he had written in his will, "O Hussein, marry my wife. She is a good woman. Do not leave her as a widow with no one to protect her."

Then there are two of his other wives about whom the history books differ regarding their names.

During this period Imam Hussein (as) had several children: he had seven sons and four daughters. From his sons, Ali Akbar was the eldest; then there was Ali Zayn ul-Abideen and Ali Asghar. In many traditions Ali Asghar is seen as a sixth month old baby. However there is no evidence in the history books where a reference has been made as to Ali Asghar being a sixth month old baby. The sixth month old baby was actually named Abdullah al-Radhi. That is why in the Iraqi, Iranian and Lebanese communities the sixth month old son is referred to as Abdullah. The use of the name Ali Asghar is more of an Indo-Pak trend. In the history books Ali Asghar is the son of Imam Hussein (as), but he was seven years old, and according to some narrations, he was twelve years old on the tenth of Muharram.

Imam Hussein (as) had four daughters: Ruqayya, who died in Sham; Sukayna, who lived to be old. Some history books say that she was a poet and a singer but that reference is to another Sukayna who was the daughter of Khalid b. Zubeiriyya. Then there was Fatima, who married Imam al-Hassan (as)'s son, Hassan. Imam Hussein (as) used to say, "No lady looks like my mother Fatima like my daughter Fatima." Then he had a fourth daughter by the name of Zaynab. Therefore, this period before Karbala was the period of the marriages of Imam Hussein (as) and he had his children during that time.

Imam Hussein (as)'s Personality Outside the Event of Karbala

Imam Hussein (as) witnessed a very turbulent period in Islamic history where many of the great companions of Imam al-Hassan (as) and Imam Ali b. Abi Talib (as) were killed in front of his eyes. His brother Imam al-Hassan (as) was poisoned, and Hujr b. Adi, Amr b. Hamaq, Rushayd al-Hajari were all killed; for Aba Abdullah to maintain his patience in that period was difficult.

Imam Hussein (as) had displayed every great attribute of his personality before the event of Karbala, but on the Day of Ashura they all came together. For example, in Karbala we all hear that Imam Hussein (as) was generous. But Imam Hussein (as)'s generosity was apparent years before Karbala. When the Prophet was about to die, he told the companions to leave Medina with the army under the leadership of eighteen-year-old Usama. The companions, however, did not join Usama. Usama b. Zayd was at Ghadir when he saw the Prophet say, "Man kuntu Mawla fa hadha Ali Mawla."

After the Prophet died, the companions came to Usama and asked, "Was Ali b. Abi Talib chosen by the Prophet or no?" He said, "Do not ask me. I do not want to get involved in these things." At the Battle of Jamal, they asked Usama, "Usama, who is right, Ali or them?" He said, "I do not know. I'm not sure. I do not want to get involved." At Siffin again he was approached and asked, "Who is right, Ali or Mu'awiya?" He said, "I do not know. Maybe they are both good." This is a lesson for all of us that when you see injustice, do not say, "I prefer not to get involved." Get involved and support the truth because you may be the cause of dissension in history because of your silence. In the end, we do not remember the words of our enemies; we remember the silence of our friends.

When Usama was dying, he had a sixty thousand dinar debt on his shoulders. The only person he could think of who could pay it back for him was Imam Hussein (as). He was pleading, "Please bring Hussein." So Imam Hussein (as) came and saw Usama lying on the bed. He said to him, "Usama, what's wrong?" He said, "Hussein, please forgive me. Your father was chosen on the day of Ghadir. I saw it with my own eyes. At Jamal too, in my heart I knew he was right because I had heard the Prophet say, 'Ali is with the truth and the truth is with Ali'; and at Siffin I said, 'I don't know who is right,' but I know that Ali b. Abi Talib is in the heavens whereas Mu'awiya is on the earth. Hussein, I'm in trouble." Imam Hussein (as) said, "What is it?" He said, "I have a sixty thousand dinar debt. Please help me." Imam Hussein (as) said, "Usama, do not worry. You are remorseful for your stand. May Allah forgive you." He turned around and told the person to please come and collect sixty thousand dinar for Usama.

Similarly, when the third caliph, Uthman, was alone in his house and the Muslims were attacking him, Imam al-Hassan (as) and Imam Hussein (as) stood by the door of Uthman to protect him so that the Muslims would not be disunited. They could very well have said, "Uthman mistreated Abu Dharr and Abdullah b. Mas'ud and took our father's leadership!" Instead, they did not want disunity to occur between the Muslims and stood at his door to protect him. They were the ones who gave water to him while the Muslims were preventing it; and the saddest thing is that later these Muslims were the one who blamed Imam Ali b. Abi Talib (as) for the cause of Uthman's death whereas Imam Ali b. Abi Talib (as) had sent his sons to protect him despite their political differences.

There are many great hadiths that have been quoted from Imam Hussein (as). Imam Hussein (as) said, "I heard from my grandfather the Prophet that, 'The best quality of a Muslim is that he speaks little about a topic that does not concern him.'" How many Muslims make it their business to get involved in every issue?

On another occasion he said, "I heard my father Amir al-Mu'mineen say, 'I am surprised at the human being who refrains from food due to fear of illness but does not refrain from sin even though he knows about hellfire.'"

Once a young man came to Imam Hussein (as) and said, "O son of the Prophet, I cannot stop sinning and I am just going to have to continue. What do I do? Give me some advice." Imam Hussein (as) said, "Keep sinning." He said, "Sorry?" Imam Hussein (as) said, "Keep sinning." He said, "Imam Hussein, I came to you for advice and you tell me keep sinning?" Imam said, "Yes, keep sinning, but under five conditions: Sin, but sin in the place where Allah cannot see you." He said, "But Aba Abdullah, Allah can see me everywhere." Imam said, "Okay. The second condition is sin, but do not sin on God's earth. Go and build your own earth and sin there. Sin, but do not use Allah's sustenance as energy to sin. Sin, but when the angel of death comes to take your soul away, do not say, 'Not yet!' Sin, but when you are being punished in the fire of hell, do not say, 'I should not be here, get me out!' If you can fulfill these five conditions, continue sinning." The man said, "Ya Aba Abdullah! I'm never going to sin after this."

Once Imam Hussein (as) asked a teacher, Abu Abdur Rahman al-Salami, to teach his son how to recite the Quran. When that teacher finished teaching, Imam Hussein (as) saw his son recite, "Bismillah hir Rahman nir Rahim." Upon hearing this, Imam gifted the teacher with many valuables such as pearls and clothes. People came to Imam and said, "Aba Abdullah, all this person did was to teach your son how to recite, 'Bismillah hir

Rahman nir Rahim,' and you give him this much hadiya?" Imam said, "Whatever I gave him would never be enough because this person taught my son how to mention Allah's name."

Imam Hussein (as) gave his biggest self-sacrifice before the event of Karbala, and which was in fact related to Karbala. After Imam Ali b. Abi Talib (as) died, a man by the name of Assam b. Mustalaq, who was from Syria, came up to Imam Hussein (as) and said, "What is your name?" Imam said, "Hussein." The man said, "Son of?" Imam said, "Son of Ali b. Abi Talib." He said, "May Allah curse you and curse your father, Ali." Imam said, "Is the wind of this area hurting you or maybe you have had a disagreement with your wife? Is there a shelter for you to stay in or has no one provided you with clothing? Please come and stay in my house if you are a stranger in this area. That person began to cry. He said, "Aba Abdullah, I cursed your father in front of you and this is the way you reply to me by making your house available for me?" Imam said, "We are the family of the Prophet and this is how we treat people because our grandfather the Prophet came to perfect the morals of mankind."

In the Battle of Nahrawan, the soldiers who were caught by Imam Ali b. Abi Talib (as) were standing there. One of the soldiers who was fighting Imam Ali b. Abi Talib (as) on that day was captured and had a rope around his hands. Imam Hussein (as) walked past him and saw that soldier. That soldier saw him and said, "Hussein, I beg you. Please remove this rope from around my hand because the rope is causing nervousness in me." Imam Hussein (as) went back to his father and said, "O my father, I would like a favor from you." Imam Ali b. Abi Talib (as) said, "What is it?" Imam Hussein (as) said, "That person over there. Do you see him?" Imam Ali b. Abi Talib (as) said, "Yes, I see him." Imam Hussein (as) said, "He said to me that the rope is tight around his hand, even though you would never do that, but it seems to be hurting him and he asked me to remove it. O my father, do you allow me to do so?" Imam Ali b. Abi Talib (as) looked at his son and said, "Aba Abdullah, go ahead. But why do you want to do this?" Imam Hussein (as) said, "Father, when someone asks through me how can I reject him? I do not want to disappoint the person." Imam Hussein (as) went back to the person and said, "Give me your hands."

Then he removed the ropes from the hands of Shimr b. Dhil-Joshan. What mercy did this man show to the Imam when he sat on his chest on the afternoon of Karbala?

Thus Imam Hussein (as) did not only display these attributes of mercy and kindness and generosity and wisdom on the lands of Karbala, but he was displaying them throughout his life, years before the event of Ashura. Karbala was when he manifested all these attributes together on one day, such as generosity, knowledge, humility, forgiveness, care, honor and dignity. So much so that Hurr b. Yazid al-Riyahi, who was a commander of the opposition and who had blocked water from the children of Hussein, the forgiving heart of Aba Abdullah forgave him.

Which man who is thirsty, but before he drinks the water says to his horse, "You drink. I cannot bear to see you thirsty?" Today Muslim countries have no respect for animal rights whereas the master of Islam displayed respect towards his animals. Which man lies on the ground with his killer on his chest and he says to his killer, "If you give me water, I will intercede for you on the Day of Judgment?"

When you study the biography of Imam Hussein (as), you realize it is not just Muslims who have been affected by this colossal figure. When Gandhi went on his salt march with seventy-two people and he was asked, "Why have you taken seventy-two people?" He said, "Because Hussein took seventy-two and Hussein's seventy-two were eternal. I want my seventy-two to be eternal too. I learned from Hussein how to achieve victory while being oppressed."

Charles Dickens said, "If Hussein had fought to quench his worldly desires…then I do not understand why his sister, wife and children accompanied him. It stands to reason therefore that he sacrificed purely for Islam."

Nehru said, "Imam Hussein's sacrifice is for all groups and communities, an example of the path of righteousness."

Antoine Bara, the famous Lebanese Christian said, "No battle in the modern and past history of mankind has earned more sympathy and admiration, as well as provided more lessons, than the martyrdom of Hussein in the Battle of Karbala."

All of these people show us that Hussein continues to live in the hearts of every human being and that is why it is said, "The martyrdom of Hussein causes a surge of heat in the heart of the believer that will never subside!"

Lecture 6

Imam Ali b. Hussein (as)

Imam Ali b. Hussein (as) was born on the 5th of Sha'ban in the 38th year after Hijra and died on the 25th of Muharram in the 95th year after Hijra. He is revered by many as one of the greatest leaders in Islamic history and as an ideal exemplar when it comes to piety, worship, spirituality and humility in virtually every school in the religion of Islam. Imam Ali b. Hussein (as) is seen as a colossus when it comes to spirituality. Today every school in the religion of Islam takes their spiritual knowledge from Imam Ali b. Hussein (as).

Unfortunately, his life has not received significant study. Many schools within the religion of Islam have limited their knowledge of Imam Ali b. Hussein (as) to simply studying or talking about the emotional aspects of his character in the context of Karbala and the tragedy of the tenth of Muharram. It is very rare for people to dissect the biography of Imam Ali b. Hussein (as) outside of what happened at Karbala. Normally when you hear of this man, you hear about him being sad and crying after Karbala. There isn't much of an analysis of Imam Ali b. Hussein (as) as a great spiritual reformer, or Imam Ali b. Hussein (as) as the man who changed the direction of the religion of Islam when the religion was at its lowest ebb. Therefore, here we will seek to examine a personality who himself is seen as such a colossus, that even his great grandfather, the Prophet (pbuh), had mentioned his name even before he was born.

His parents and His Relationship with Them

As we stated previously, the Imam was born on the 5th of Sha'ban in the 38th year after Hijra. His father was, of course, Hussein b. Ali (as). His mother was named Shahzanan, the daughter of the last of the kings of Persia, although her name was referred to as Sayyedat un-Nisa in Arabic. (Later she was referred to as "Shahrbanu" because "Sayyedat un-Nisa" was the title of Lady Fatima (as)). When Imam Hussein (as) married her, his father Amir al-Mu'mineen had of course known she had come originally from Persia. When Jabir b. Horaith had conquered Khorasan, one of the women from Khorasan who had converted to the religion of Islam was Shahzanan.

The narrations tell us that Imam Ali (as) chose her to marry Imam Hussein (as). We find that this was the beginning of the mixing of the Arabs and the Persians. Before that, no such thing had really happened. The Arabs used to detest the Persians and the Persians did not like the Arabs. So this marriage of Imam Hussein (as) to Shahzanan was a marriage that began a cross-cultural link. It is as if Imam Hussein (as) was highlighting that there is no problem in the religion of Islam to marry a woman from a different culture. Today you find that many Muslims find this a sticking point and therefore the youth must discuss this with their parents when they want to marry someone from a different culture whereas their Imams, the leaders of this religion, over four or five of them married a woman from a different culture.

When Imam Hussein (as) married, he could have easily married someone from Medina, or someone from his background. But it is as if he was enacting the verse of the Quran which says, in chapter 49, verse 13, "O mankind! Verily, We have created you from a mAl and a female, and made you into nations and tribes, that you may get to know each other; Verily the most honored of you with God is the one who is most conscious of God's presence. Verily God is All-Knowing, the All-Aware." Thus Imam Hussein (as) could have easily married someone from his city or village. On the contrary, he married this Persian woman and she became the mother of an Imam. This began the marriage of Arabs to Persians, so much so that the Umayyad caliph Abdul Malik b. Marwan himself married a Persian woman.

One day Abdul Malik went to propose to one of the daughters of 'Aqil al-Murri for his son. Abdul Malik b. Marwan went to 'Aqil al-Murri's house and said to him, "I would like one of my sons to marry one of your daughters." 'Aqil replied with the most racist Arabic statement possible. He looked at Abdul Malik and said, "Spare me the hujanah!" Abdul Malik looked at him and said, "What do you mean, hujanah?" He said, "Your sons are half-Persians and my daughters will only marry full-blooded Arabs."

Thus you find that the racist tendency was still there. Imam Hussein (as) noticed that, "If I marry a Persian, first I am showing that there is no difference in the eyes of God except with taqwa (piety). Secondly, it will allow for a cross-cultural exchange where, not only families could cross culture, but literature could cross culture as well." You'll find that many of the later Umayyads or Abbasids started marrying Persians and they even started employing Persians because of this marriage trend. For example, Marwan II, the last Umayyad caliph's mother, was half-Kurdish and half-Persian; the treasurers and secretaries of Banu Abbas, like Abu Salal al-Khallal, Yaqub b. Dawud and Il Muryani were all Persian; the Barmaki family was Persian and Aj Sahel was Persian. This influenced the world of literature as well; Arabs started to read Persian literature and Persians began to read Arab literature. For example, Ahmad b. Yahya Baladhuri translated Kisra (Khosrau)'s words of wisdom, and so on and so forth.

Thus Imam Ali b. Hussein (as)'s mother was Persian, and his father was an Arab and it would be the first marriage of Ahlulbayt where an Imam of Aal Muhammad would marry someone who was not an Arab. The sad news for Imam Ali b. Hussein (as) was that his mother died a few days after giving birth to him. Therefore the only man who brought him up in his life was his father Imam Hussein (as). However, the other wife of Imam Hussein (as) was a mother figure to him and his wet nurse too was like a mother to him.

His manners towards these ladies who replaced his mother would make you think that they were his real mothers. For example, one of the most famous stories of Imam Ali b. Hussein (as) was that when he would sit to eat dinner with his stepmother, he would be sitting down and his stepmother would be sitting down too. Then he would stay there looking at the food, and then he would look at his stepmother. She would look at him and say, "What's wrong? Why are you looking at me?" He would say, "I am scared to put out my hand towards some food which you had your eyes on." (At home sometimes when we eat with our mothers we do not even wait for them to come from the kitchen. Before you know it, the dinner is done and you have gone to watch television and your mother has not even started eating.)

But our Imam, even with his stepmother, was so careful and wanted to see if she was looking at some food, and would not put his hand there until she took, and the moment she took, then he would take.

Imam Hussein (as) loved his son so much, he was not only his second eldest son, but in addition to that, Imam Hussein (as) saw the light of revelation on the face of Imam Ali b. Hussein (as). In what way? Imam Hussein (as) narrates, "I once saw Ali b. Hussein when he was young and ill. I said to him, 'My son, do you want me to get you a doctor?' He said, 'Father, Allah (swt) will look after me, I'm sure.' Then I said to him, 'You remind me of Prophet Ibrahim, that when Prophet Ibrahim was in the fire and the angel Jibra'il said, 'Do you want any help?' Prophet Ibrahim said, 'Only my Lord will help me.' Likewise you have the same mannerisms of Prophet Ibrahim."

Imagine, when you have an attachment to your father like this, how then do you feel on the day your father needs you the most but you cannot be there for him?

Imam Ali b. Hussein (as)'s Experience at Karbala

At Karbala he was twenty-two years old. You ask any son and he will tell you that you want to be by your father's side at every moment of your life, isn't it? Your father is the great attachment in your life. He is your life. He is what you look up to. He is your source of pride and warmth and comfort. Those of you who have been to your father's funeral when he passed away, don't you just wish he could return to life? But sometimes the only sense of solace is that you looked after your father, and that you treated him well until the day he died, and that when he needed you, you were there for him.

Only Allah knows how Imam Ali b. Hussein (as) recovered after the tenth of Muharram. Some people ask, "When did he become ill?"

He did not become ill on the tenth of Muharram. He became ill on the journey towards Karbala. On the journey towards Karbala, he picked up an illness that he could not recover from. When the tenth of Muharram arrived, he noticed that his father was now on his final legs; his brother Ali al-Akbar had died, and his sixth month old brother, Abdullah, had died, and his cousin Qasim had passed away, and all of the companions had passed away. Narrations tell us that on the tenth of Muharram, just before Imam Hussein (as) was about to leave, Imam Ali b. Hussein (as) woke up from unconsciousness, and said, "O People! Get me a sword and get me a stick." They looked at him and said, "Why?" He said, "I want a stick so I can stand up and a sword so I can defend my father in his final moments." One can imagine that, to Imam Ali b. Hussein (as), his father Imam Hussein (as) was everything to him because his mother had died shortly after he was born. The narrations say that his father said to him, "O Zayn ul-Abideen! You are God's proof over His creatures after I die. You must remain patient in this period." The next time he saw a horse return it was with his father's body on top of it.

Many people ask, "Who performed the ghusl of Imam Hussein (as)?" It was Imam Ali b. Hussein (as) who performed the burial rites, three nights after the tenth of Muharram. When Imam Ali b. Hussein (as) returned to Karbala, the narrations say to us, that the wives of Bani Asad were embarrassed by their husbands because their husbands did not help Imam Hussein (as) at Karbala. So these women told their husbands, "If you are not going to be alongside the Prophet's grandson, then at least go and bury the body of the grandson of the Prophet." Thus the men of Bani Asad went to Karbala after the tenth of Muharram. They wanted to bury the bodies of Imam Hussein (as) and his companions but there was one problem. How do you know which body belongs to which head? The heads have gone, and all you see are bodies; you do not know whom to bury where. Then they said, "From a distance we saw Imam Ali b. Hussein." At the time they did not recognize him. They said, "We saw a man wearing black. He came towards us, we looked at him, and he said to us, 'What are you doing here?' We said, 'Oh, we have just come to look at the place.' He said, 'No. Tell me honestly what are you doing here?' We said, 'We have come to bury the body of Aba Abdullah.'

Then Imam Ali b. Hussein (as) said to them, "Go and dig three different graves." They went to dig the graves and came back to him and said, "What shall we do now?" He said, "The first grave is for the companions of my father. Bury them all in one grave; the second grave is for the family members; and the third grave is for Habib b. Mudhahir. My father said he should have a grave for himself." Then he said to them, "I am now going to bury a body which only I and those who are with me can bury." They asked him, "Whose body is it?" He said, "I am going to bury my father."

He had not seen the state of his father's body because he, along with his family, had been taken away from Karbala as prisoners. Now he started to walk towards the body of Aba Abdullah. When he got near the body of Imam Hussein (as), he noticed there were fingers on the ground. (Imam Hussein (as) had a ring on his finger and someone had chopped off his fingers to take his ring). Then when he got near his father's body, he wanted to kiss his father's neck but he saw the body was without a neck, and the body that was covered with arrows. He then took out a prayer mat, and when he was asked what he was doing with the mat, he said, "So I can collect the different pieces of my father's body."

Then after that, the narrations say that he said to them, "I am going to the Furat (Euphrates). There is a body that lies there." When he went towards that body he narrates, "When I lifted the right side, the left side fell to the ground. Then when I lifted the left side, the right side fell on the ground." Then he called out, "Ya Qamar Bani Hashim! Abul Fadl al-Abbas!"

He ended up burying all the bodies and returned to Kufa and then proceeded towards Syria. When they would ask him later, "O Ali b. Hussein! What was the most difficult part for you? Was it Karbala? Was it Kufa? Was it Sham?" He would reply, "Ash-Sham! Ash-Sham! Ash-Sham!" Then he would say, "If you only saw the way they treated us in Sham."

The first day when they entered Sham, Sahel b. Sa'ad al-Sa'adi, a companion of the Prophet (pbuh), came towards Imam Ali b. Hussein (as). Sahel said, "I saw everybody merrymaking. Everyone was joyous and happy, so I asked someone, 'Is this a day of Eid?'" They said, "No. Do not be surprised if the heavens turn on us and the earth sucks us out." Sahel said, "What is it?" The reply was, "These are the descendants of the Prophet of God and they have been killed, and these are their prisoners."

Sahel b. Sa'ad al-Sa'adi narrates, "I saw Imam Ali b. Hussein with chains around his body. I came to him and I said, 'O Imam Ali b. Hussein! I am Sahel b. Sa'ad al-Sa'adi, the companion of your great grandfather, the Prophet.' He looked at me and said, 'O Sahel, I beg of you one thing.

Please go and buy a piece of cloth for me.'"

Sahel thought to himself, if I go and buy a piece of cloth it must mean that Imam Ali b. Hussein wants to cover his body. He narrates, "I brought the piece of cloth to Imam Ali b. Hussein and I saw him put the piece of cloth between the chain and his neck, and he said to me, 'O Sahel! The chain has been cutting through my neck since Karbala.'"

Then after that Imam Ali b. Hussein (as) narrates, "Wallah! We were walking and a man came to me and said, 'Curse on you! And curse on your people!'" Imam Ali b. Hussein (as) looked at him and said, "Do you know who we are?" The man said, "I do not, but I have been told you are a group of rebels; so curse on you!" Imam Ali b. Hussein (as) said to him, "O Man, have you read the verse in the Quran, 'Qul la asalakum 'alayhi ajran illal muwaddata fil qurba?'" He said, "Yes, I have." Imam Ali b. Hussein (as) then said, "Have you read the verse in the Quran, 'Wa a'lamu annama ghanimtum min shai'in fa anna llillah khumusahu wa li'-l-rasul wa li-dhi'l-qurba?'" He said, "Yes, I have." Imam Ali b. Hussein (as) said, "Have you read the verse in the Quran, 'Innama yurid Allah li yudhiba 'ankum al-rijs Ahl al-bayt wa yutahhirakum tathira?'" He said, "Yes, I have." Imam Ali b. Hussein (as) said, "Do you know who those verses refer to?" He said, "Yes, they refer to Aal Muhammad." Imam Ali b. Hussein (as) said, "Then who are we?" The man looked at him and said, "Who are you?" Imam Ali b. Hussein (as) said, "I am from Aal Muhammad. That is my father's head you see on the spear." He said, "Who?" Imam Ali b. Hussein (as) said, "Hussein b. Ali." He said, "They have killed Hussein b. Ali?" He said, "Yes."

Imagine, those people did not know who was killed. The narrations say that when Imam Ali b. Hussein (as) was taken through the bazar of Sham, known as "Jama' al-Umawi" today, Lady Zaynab said that, "There were people throwing boiling water on the head of my nephew and they were poking him with spears as they were walking through the bazar, and then we arrived at Yazid's palace."

Then Imam Ali b. Hussein (as) had to see Yazid flick the lips of Imam Hussein (as) with a stick. But the khutba (sermon) that Imam Ali b. Hussein (as) gave in Syria was mesmerizing. He was only twenty-two years old; it is a message to our twenty-two year olds. Have you ever given a lecture like your master Zayn ul-Abideen? At the age of twenty-two he stood in front of Yazid and he gave a khutba which shook Yazid's empire.

Yazid permitted all the people to come to his palace, so the hall of his palace became full of people who came and congratulated him on the false victory. He was pleased and happy, because the world yielded to him, and the kingdom belonged to him only. So he ordered the orator to ascend the pulpit and to defame al-Husayn and his father, Imam Ali, the Commander of the Faithful, peace be on him. The orator ascended the pulpit and went too far in slandering the pure family (of the Prophet), and then he lauded in a false way Yazid and his father Mu'a`wiya. Thus, Imam Zayn al-Abidin, peace be on him, interrupted him, saying: "Woe unto you, orator! You have traded the pleasure of the creature for the wrath of the Creator, so take your place in the fire (of Hell)."

Then the Imam turned to Yazid and asked him, saying: "Do you permit me to ascend this pulpit to deliver a speech that will please Allah, the Almighty, and that will bring good rewards for these people?"

The attendants were astonished at this sick man, who interrupted the orator and the governor while he was a captive. Yazid refused, but the people begged him. He said to them: "If he ascends the pulpit, he will not descend (from it) till he exposes me and the family of Abi Sufyan."

The people asked him: "What will this sick man do?" The people did not know the Imam. They thought that he was like the other people, but the tyrant, Yazid, knew him, so he said to them: "These are people who have been spoon-fed with knowledge."

They kept pressuring him till he agreed. So the Imam ascended the pulpit and delivered the most wonderful speech in history in eloquence. He made the people weep. The people were confused because the Imam's speech controlled their hearts and feelings. The following is some of what he said: "O people, we were granted six things and favored with seven: We were granted knowledge, clemency, leniency, fluency, courage, and love for us in the hearts of the believers. We were favored by the fact that from among us came the chosen Prophet, Mohammed, may Allah bless him and his family, al-Siddiq (the very truthful one), al-Tayyar (the one who flies in the heaven), the Lion of Allah and of the Prophet, may Allah bless him and his family, the mistress of the women of the world Fatima the chaste, and both lords of the youths of Heaven from among this nation"

Having introduced his family, the Ima`m continued his speech explaining their outstanding merits, saying: "Whoever recognizes me knows me, and whoever does not recognize, let me tell him who I am and to what family I belong: I am the son of Mecca and Mina; I am the son of Zamzam and al-Safa; I am the son of the one who carried Zakat in the ends of the mantle; I am the son of the best man who ever put on a loincloth and clothes; I am the son of the best man who ever put on sandals and walked barefooted; I am the son of the best man who ever made tawaf (the procession round the Kaaba) and Saee (ceremony of running seven times between Safa and Marwa); I am the son of the best man who ever offered the hajj and pronounced talbiya (Here I am at your service); I am the son of the one who was transported on the buraaq in the air; I am the son of the one who was made to travel from the Sacred Mosque to the Remote Mosque, so glory belongs to Him Who made (His Servant) travel; I am the son of the one who was taken by Gabriel to sidrat al-muntaha ; I am the son of the one who drew near (his Lord) and suspended, so he was the measure of two bows or closer still; I am the son of the one who led the angels of the heavens in prayer; I am the son of the one to whom the Almighty revealed what He revealed; I am the son of Mohammed al-Mustafa ; I am the son of 'Ali al-Murtada` ; I am the son of the one who fought against the creatures till they said: There is no god but Allah. I am the son of the one who struck (the enemies) with two swords before Allah's Apostle, may Allah bless him and his family, and stabbed (them) with two spears, emigrated twice, pledged allegiance twice (to the Prophet), prayed in the two qiblas, and fought (against the unbelievers) at Badr and Hunayn and never disbelieved in Allah not even as much as the twinkling of an eye. I am the son of the best of the believers, the heir of the prophets, the destroyer of the unbelievers, the Commander of the Muslims, the light of the mujahidin, the ornament of the worshippers, the crown of the weepers, the most patient of the patient, and the best of the steadfast from among the family of Yasin, and the Messenger of the Lord of the world's inhabitants. I am the son of the one who was backed by Gabriel, supported by Mikael. I am the son of the one who defended the Muslims, killed the oath breakers of allegiance and the unjust and the renegades, struggled against his tiring enemies, the most excellent one of those who walked (to war) from among Quraysh, the first to respond to Allah from among the believers, the prior to all the previous ones, the breaker of the aggressors, the destroyer of the atheists, an arrow from among the shooting-places of Allah against the hypocrites, the tongue of the wisdom of worshippers, the supporter of the religion of Allah, the protector of the affair of Allah, the garden of the wisdom of Allah, the container of the knowledge of Allah, tolerant, generous, benevolent, pure, Abtahi, satisfied, easily satisfied, intrepid, gallant, patient, fasting, refined, steadfast, courageous, honored, the severer of the backbones, the scatterer of the allies, the calmest of them, the best of them in giving free rein (to his horse), the boldest of them in tongue, the firmest of them in determination, the most powerful of them, a lion, brave, pouring rain, the one who destroyed them at the battles and dispersed them in the wind, the lion of al-Hija`z, the possessor of the miracle, the ram of Iraq, the Ima`m through the text and worthiness, Makki, Madani, Abtahi, Tuhami, Khayani, 'Uqbi, Badri, Uhdi, Shajari, Muha`jiri, the Lord of the Arabs, the Lion of war, the inheritor of al-Mash'arayn, the father of the two grandsons (of the Prophet) al-Hasan and al-Husayn, the one who manifested miracles, the one who scattered the phalanxes, the piercing meteor, the following light, the victorious Lion of Allah, the request of every seeker, the victorious over every victorious, such is my grandfather, 'Ali b. Abi Talib. I am the son of Fatima, the chaste. I am the son of the mistress of women. I am the son of the purified, virgin (lady). I am the son of the part of the Messenger, may Allah bless him and his family.1 I am the son of the one who was covered with blood. I am the son of the one who was slaughtered at Karbala. I am the son of the one for whom the Jinns wept in the dark and for whom the birds in the air cried."

The Imam continued saying 'I am....' until the people wailed.

Yazid thought that a discord would occur, for the Imam made a cultural revolt through his speech when he introduced himself to the Syrians and made them know what they did not know, so Yazid ordered the muadhin to say the adhan and he said: "Allahu Akbar!"

The Imam turned to him and said: "You have made great the Great One who cannot be measured and cannot be perceived by senses, there is nothing greater than Allah."

The muadhdhin said: "Ashhadu an la ilaha illa Alla`h!" 'Ali b. al-Husayn said: "My hair, my skin, my flesh, my blood, my brain, and my bones bear witness that there is no god but Allah."

The muadhdhin said: "Ashhadu anna Mohammedan rasool Allah!" The Ima`m turned to Yazid and asked him: "Yazid, is Mohammed your grandfather or mine? If you say that he is yours, then you are a liar, and if you say that he is mine, then why did you kill his family?"

Because of this khutba of the Imam Zayn ul-Abideen (as) and the khutba of Lady Zaynab, Yazid had to allow Imam Ali b. Hussein (as) to leave. That is why, on the fortieth day after Ashura, they returned to Karbala.

Unlike the general misconception, it was not a year but forty days after Ashura that they returned to Karbala. It can be proved logically, historically and mathematically that it was forty days. Historically, it is very clear within the narrations. The journey of the Ahlulbayt from Karbala to Kufa to Sham and finally the return to Karbala geographically is very clear that it took forty days. If Yazid had kept them for a year in prison after the khutba of Imam Ali b. Hussein (as), then what effect did the khutba have? Their khutba was so powerful, that Yazid had to get rid of them. Their khutba shook Yazid's palace.

One may ask, "How can you do that journey in forty days?" Well, if Imam Hussein (as) left Mecca on the 9th of Dhul Hijja, and arrived in Karbala on the 2nd of Muharram, and it took Imam Hussein (as) twenty-two days to travel from Saudi Arabia to Iraq, so what is wrong with the forty day round journey?

When they returned back to Iraq on the fortieth, Jabir b. Abdullah al-Ansari was the first visitor to the grave of Imam Hussein (as). He came with Ati'a al-Aufi. Jabir was blind at the time and he asked Ati'a, "Ati'a, what do you see?" Ati'a said, "I see from far away some people are coming." Jabir said, "If it is b. Ziyad, then tell me, and if it is Imam Ali b. Hussein, also tell me." Ati'a said, "It is Imam Ali b. Hussein."

When Jabir was taken to Imam Ali b. Hussein (as), Jabir wanted to ask Imam Ali b. Hussein (as) what happened at Karbala; Imam Ali b. Hussein (as) proceeded by telling Jabir, "O Jabir, you do not know what they did to us in Karbala, nor at Kufa, nor at Sham."

His Life after Karbala and Reformation of Society

The question now arises that, since Imam Ali b. Hussein (as) lived for thirty-five years after Karbala, what did Imam Ali b. Hussein (as) do in those thirty-five years to reform the society he was living in?

Imam Ali b. Hussein (as) recognized that the people who were at the helm of the Islamic empire were the same people who killed his father. In their prayer they would say, "Ashhadu anna Muhammad ar-the Prophet," yet after their prayer they went and killed the grandson of the Prophet.

Imam Ali b. Hussein (as) therefore began a reform system of the whole Islamic empire where, in thirty-five years, he gave Islam life after it was in a state of death. When Yazid was in power, Islam was dead. Imam Ali b. Hussein (as), through his actions, gave Islam life again. After Karbala, Imam Ali b. Hussein (as) was wondering, how do I give life to these people again? Especially after they had killed Imam Hussein (as), he wondered, what's the best way to reform society?

The first thing he did was that he kept on purchasing more servants in his house and teaching them the origins of the teachings of Ahlulbayt. He knew that the Arab mind was so closed that, even if you struck it with a hammer, it would not open. So the best option was to bring these servants into the house and culture them with the teachings of his grandfather. Slowly the change would be seen. By the end of his life, his servants were more religious than most of the Muslims who were born Muslims. Have you noticed how a convert is sometimes more religious than the one who is born into the religion? Thus Imam Ali b. Hussein (as) bought these servants and taught them the manners and the principles of Ahlulbayt in his house.

Once Imam Ali b. Hussein (as) called for one of his servants to come. Once he called, there was no reply; a second time there was no reply; a third time there was no reply; the servant came after he called the fourth time. Imam said, "I called you three times, did you not hear me?" The servant said, "No, I heard you very well." Imam said, "So why didn't you reply?" The servant said, "I wanted to taste the flavor of the mercy of Ali b. Hussein." Imam said, "What do you mean?" The servant said, "For all other masters we had, if we did not come to their first call, they would hit us, yet when Ali b. Hussein calls three times and you do not come, and after the fourth time when you come, he looks at you with humility, it is not a master-slave relationship but the relationship of a friends.

On another occasion one of his servants was pouring soup. The entire soup fell over Imam Ali b. Hussein (as). Some of us are the rudest to our servants when they make a mistake in our house, aren't we? Some of us may swear, some of us may sack them. Whereas Imam Ali b. Hussein (as) shows us that that is a fellow human, he is not your trust, he is the trust of Allah (swt). When that servant poured the hot soup on the robe of the Imam, Imam Ali b. Hussein (as) knew that these people were not as privileged as others, so he treated them with humility.

The servant looked in the face of Imam Ali b. Hussein (as) and said, "...wa'l kadimin al-ghaydh...those who restrain their anger..." Imam replied, "I have restrained my anger..." The servant then continued, "... wal 'afeena 'an an-nas - and those who forgive mankind..." Imam said, "I have forgiven..." The servant said, "...wallah yuhibb al-mohsineen - Allah loves the righteous." Imam said, "You are free for the sake of Allah (swt)."

Do you know what is beautiful about this? Not the Imam's behavior, but that a servant knows as much Quran as the Imam. Ask yourself, have you discussed the Ahlulbayt with your servants at home? Or are they just doing work? Imam Ali b. Hussein (as) would bring the person close to Allah and Ahlulbayt.

Saeed b. Mussayyab narrates a phenomenal story. He says, "We were with Zayn ul-Abideen one day. The area we were in had suffered a drought. There was no rain coming down at all. Imam Ali b. Hussein (as) said to all of us, 'Everyone get together in dua; raise your hands all of you together and Allah will send rain down.' All of Zayn ul-Abideen's servants and his friend's servants came. I looked at all of them who were reciting dua with tears flowing. But there was still no sign of rain. Then some of them left, except one servant of Zayn ul-Abideen, a black servant. I looked at him from far away. Everyone had stopped reciting dua except this black servant. As soon as the black servant began reciting dua, within a few minutes the rain started pouring down on us. I went to Zayn ul-Abideen later and said, 'Imam, do you mind if I purchase one of the servants from you?' Imam said, 'Why purchase? I will give him to you?' I told the Imam there was a specific one I wanted. Imam asked, 'Which one? Have a look at the ones who are in my house, they are not my servants, they are like my students. Choose.'" He looked at them and said, "He is not here." Imam said, "There is only one more of them and he is outside." Saeed narrates, "I went outside and I saw him in front of me. I said, 'Imam, that's the one,' and Imam said, 'Why?' I said, 'Imam that's the one; when he recited dua, the rain came pouring down.'" Imam said, "Take him." When that servant was leaving, he turned to Imam Ali b. Hussein (as) and said, "Why is it that he wants me to go with him?" Imam said, "Because he saw your dua, and he wants you to be alongside him because he knows you are a man of piety."

This servant left Imam Ali b. Hussein (as). Saeed b. Mussayyab said, "I saw him walking, and then I saw him stop at a place and I heard him say, 'Ya Allah! Now that my secret between me and You has been divulged, I prefer You to take away my life now because I do not want to act insincere with the gift you have given me.'"(If some of us had that gift, we would abuse it).

These servants were told to go to every house in Medina and tell them about the Ahlulbayt. The servants would then go out and tell the people about Ahlulbayt. When they would come back, Imam Ali b. Hussein (as) would ask them, "How are things going?" They would say, "Not too well." Imam Ali b. Hussein (as) would ask, "Why?" They would say, "We are speaking with the elders but they are not listening." Imam Ali b. Hussein (as) would say, 'Leave the elders, go to the youth and tell them about the Prophet, Imam Hassan and Hussein; their hearts are more willing to accept it."

The second way in which he reformed society was that he wrote his magnificent book of supplications, Saheefa as-Sajjadiyah. There is no book of supplications like this one. The Imam would always say, "Dua is the weapon of the believer and it is the light of the heavens and the earth."

Once Imam Hassan was asked, "What is the difference between heaven and earth?" Imam replied, "The difference between the skies and the earth is the cry of an oppressed person [engaging] in dua." Saheefa as-Sajjadiyah is the greatest book of supplications written by a human being. Someone may ask the question, "Why did he write a book on dua?"

The answer is that dua is what opens up our relationship with God. Imam Ali b. Hussein (as) felt that when the Arabs had killed his father they had lost all relationship with God in their life. There was no more God in their life. They were thinking of a world of "I" and not of "we." So he wrote a dua for your mother; a dua for your father; a dua for someone who is ill; a dua for the companions of the Prophet; a dua for jihad; a dua for absolutely every stage in your life. Fifty-one duas, and the shame is that there are lovers of Imam Ali b. Hussein (as) who have never read even one dua in the Saheefa as-Sajjadiyah.

Even the Pope, had the Saheefa as-Sajjadiyah in his library. When he was asked by one of our Muslim brothers, who had the opportunity to visit the Vatican, he said, "I do not see a book of Psalms of Dawud like this book of psalms." In this book, amongst the most beautiful duas he has collected is the dua Makaram al-Akhlaq. This is a phenomenal dua. In this dua there are three lines in which he talks about relations with the family members. He felt the people had lost their relationship with their families, and that they were wiling to kill their own family members.

In that book he wrote, "...Ya Allah! Change the hatred of my cousins into love for me; and change their insolence into devotion; and change their difficulties into ease." Imam Ali b. Hussein (as) saw that "silat ul-rahm" was being broken in society, brothers did not talk to each other; sisters hated each other; in-laws hated each other; thus he wrote this dua so that the morals between the people would return. In these three lines he tried to rectify the akhlaq of the people.

Imam Ali b. Hussein (as) had a cousin who had fallen in some debt. That cousin kept on saying, "Where is Zayn ul-Abideen? Why does he not lend me some money?" And Imam Ali b. Hussein (as) wouldn't come to him. That cousin began to abuse Imam Ali b. Hussein (as) day and night in front of the people. When Imam Ali b. Hussein (as) died that cousin met Imam al-Baqir (as). He said to him, "There was a man who used to wear a hood, and in the middle of the night he would come and give me food. But I have not seen that man for a few nights? Who is it?"

Imam al-Baqir (as) said, "That was my father, the cousin whom you used to abuse. You used to abuse him in the morning and in the evening he brought you food." Imam Ali b. Hussein (as) was the embodiment of his duas. When he would say something in his dua, he would act on it after reading the dua.

The third way he reformed society was that he wrote the Risalat ul-Huquq, or The Treatise on Rights. He wrote on the right of God; the right of yourself; the right of your mother; the right of your father; the right of your brother; the right of your sister; the right of your teacher; the right of your stomach; the right of your eyes; the right of your hands; the right of your private parts; the right of fasting; the right of prayer; the right of the non-Muslim; the right of the Muezzin; the right of every single right you can imagine. Today we have the United Nations declaration of human rights, don't we? Does this declaration tell me about the right of God? Or the right of my soul? Or the right of my eye? Or the right of my hand? Or the right of my mother?

One thousand four hundred years before the UN prepared the declaration of human rights, our Imam wrote the Risalat ul-Huquq, the treaties of the rights of the human being. For example, in the rights of the father Imam Ali b. Hussein (as) wrote, "Know that the right of your father is that he is your root and you are his branch; and were it not for him, you would never be. So whenever you see anything in yourself that impresses you, know that it is because of your father's blessings that you achieved it."

Another way in which he changed the society around him was through his prayer. The three most famous names of Imam Ali b. Hussein (as) are:

1. "As-Sajjad" - the one who used to always be in sujood (prostration). When people used to come to him and say, "Your worship is so great," he would say, "My worship is not half as great as my grandfather Ali b. Abi Talib."

2. "Zayn ul-Abideen" - the adornment of the worshippers. The Prophet (pbuh) gave this name to him. When Imam Hussein (as) was born, the Prophet (pbuh) had Imam Hussein (as) in his lap. He looked at Jabir b. Abdullah al-Ansari and said, "O Jabir! This Hussein will have a son called Ali. On the Day of Judgment there will be a call which will say, 'Where is Zayn ul-Abideen?' and his son Ali will come forward and say, 'Ana Zayn ul-Abideen.'"

3. "Dhul Thafanath" - "Thafanath" are called "callouses" in English. Some of the skin of the camel gets peeled off or hangs out because it grazes its knee so much on the ground. The Imam used to perform prostrations so much that the skin of his forehead would peel off. That skin which peeled off his forehead when it would stick out would look like the skin sticking out of the knee of the camel. So they called him, "Dhul Thafanath." This name highlights how disciplined he was in his worship. He was the one who said the famous line, "If mankind knew how much reward they were getting in prostration, they would never lift their head (from prostration)." Imam al-Baqir (as) used to say, "My father would cut off the skin from his forehead twice a year. Because of the amount of sujood he did, the skin would be hanging out of his forehead."

Someone asked, "Why did he focus on prayer so much?" If a person is disciplined in their prayer, they will be disciplined everywhere else in their life. And so Imam focused on his prayer.

Through all of this, for thirty-five years after Karbala, he spread the message through his servants, through his books and through his companions. We must never forget the companions of Imam Ali b. Hussein (as). The first of them was Abu Hamza ath-Thumali. He is famous for the

Dua of Abu Hamza ath-Thumali that Imam taught him, and it is read by many in the month of Ramadan. "...and why should I not cry when you place me in the grave. And I see the darkness of the grave and the narrowness of the grave and I see Munkar and Nakir coming towards me in the grave asking me questions..." The same Abu Hamza ath-Thumali was one the greatest companions of Imam Ali b. Hussein (as).

Saeed b. Jubair was another great companion who was killed by Hajjaj b. Yusuf al-Thaqafi because of the greatness of his prayers. Qanber too died in the time of Imam Ali b. Hussein (as). Kumayl also was killed in the time of Imam Ali b. Hussein (as). He too is famous for the dua, Dua Kumayl, which is read by many on Thursday nights. All of them were killed by Hajjaj b. Yusuf.

Do you know how much Hajjaj b. Yusuf and Hisham b. Isma'il used to bully Imam Ali b. Hussein (as)? There is one story that highlights the final way he changed the society around him. The Imam's akhlaq was phenomenal. When Hisham b. Isma'il was the governor of Medina and Imam Ali b. Hussein (as) would leave his house, Hisham used to tell the children to go and pelt things at Imam Ali b. Hussein (as). He would barrage Imam Ali b. Hussein (as) when he walked on the street. Hisham's maternal uncle was Abdul Malik. When Abdul Malik b. Marwan was replaced by Walid, Walid appointed Umar b. Abdul Aziz as governor of Medina. Umar b. Abdul Aziz sacked Hisham. When he sacked him, he caught Hisham and chained him to a wall. Then he called out to the people and said, "O people! Whoever Hisham b. Isma'il has been bad to, come and take your revenge from Hisham." The companions came to Imam Ali b. Hussein (as) and said to him, "Do you know who got caught today?" Imam said, "Who?" They said, "Hisham b. Isma'il. He is now chained. What shall we do to him now that he is chained?" Imam said, "What are you thinking of doing?" They said, "Can we take revenge?" Imam said, "I will tell you what we should do. Go up to him and say, 'O Hisham! If you are hungry then Zayn ul-Abideen will feed you, and if you are thirsty then I will quench your thirst, and if you have a loan, I will pay the loan for you. Ask yourself, 'Would you do this to someone who has tortured you?''' The way he inspired people was through his morals.

Taoos al-Yamani narrates, "I was near the Ka'aba when I saw a man holding on to the Ka'aba crying and crying and crying. I thought, who is this man? Surely he has committed a lot of sin for him to cry that much.

I got near him and saw that it was Zayn ul-Abideen. I looked at him and I was listening to his dua and I heard him say, 'O Allah! If you removed your rope from me then whose rope will I hold onto? O Allah! You always increase my life, but what if I increase in sinning against you?' I thought if Zayn ul-Abideen talks like this then what do I say? I said to him, 'O Imam, you cry? You? And we are the sinners?' Imam turned around to me and said, 'O Taoos, it does not matter if you are an Ethiopian slave or you are a son of Qureish, all of us will be made answerable on the Day of Judgment.'"

Someone asked, "Why do the Ahlulbayt talk like that? Is it because they are sinners?" No. They are teaching us that if we talk like this to Allah, then how must you talk to Allah?

When Hisham b. Abdul Malik was sitting near the Ka'aba, he unsuccessfully tried to get to the Hajr ul-Aswad. Then he saw a man walking towards the Hajr ul-Aswad. When he saw this man walking, he saw the entire crowd parting, giving way for him. The man kissed the Hajr ul-Aswad and returned. Hisham arrogantly turned to Farazdaq, the famous poet, and said, "Farazdaq, who is that man?"

Farazdaq said his famous lines of poetry for which he was later imprisoned. He said, "He is someone whose footsteps are known by every place; and he is someone who is known by the house in Mecca and the place that is visited the most frequently by the sanctuary. He is the son of the best of all of the men of God, a man who is upright and chaste and unstained and righteous. He is Ali b. Hussein, whose grandfather is the Prophet and whose mother is Fatima. He who claims to recognize Allah, recognizes his primacy and superiority above all men because nations came to this religion because of his family. When he goes towards the Ka'aba, it is as if the Ka'aba is grasping to hold him!"

When Hisham b. Abdul Malik heard this he said, "How dare you talk like this about anyone else!" and he imprisoned him. When Imam Ali b. Hussein (as) found out that Farazdaq was imprisoned, Imam Ali b. Hussein (as) went and paid for him to be released. Farazdaq said, "Imam, you do not have to pay for me. All I did was speak the truth. There is none like Ali b. ul-Hussein walking on the face of this earth!"

One of the famous Iranian scholars says, "In my dream I saw Farazdaq and I asked him how is your position now? He replied, "Because of my lines of poetry for Zayn ul-Abideen, Allah has honored me to be where I am today."

Therefore, every angle of Imam Ali b. Hussein (as)'s life was an example for us and without a doubt he would never forget what happened on the tenth of Muharram. Imagine how hard those thirty-five years must have been after Karbala. If he saw a sheep being slaughtered, he would say to the butcher, "O Butcher! When you slaughter a sheep, do you give it water?" He said, "Yes, O Zayn ul-Abideen, every creation of Allah deserves water before it dies." Imam would look at him and say, "They killed my father without giving him any water." On another occasion he saw a man who used to dig graves. He said to him, "O man, when I die will you bury me?" The man said, "Of course. I will never leave you alone." He said, "My father was left alone with no one to bury him."

On a third occasion he saw a man calling out, "I am ghareeb! I am a stranger, help me!" Imam came to him and said, "Do you have food?" He said, "Yes, I do." Imam asked, "Do you have clothes?" He said, "Yes, I do." Imam said, "O man, if you were to die, would your family bury you?" He said, "Yes." Imam said, "Then do not call yourself a ghareeb. A ghareeb is one who lay alone on the ground in Karbala with no one to bury him for three nights ."

Imam al-Baqir (as) narrates that, "When I was with my father in his final moments, my father was lying on the bed. The poison of Walid had surrounded his body." It was thirty-five years after Karbala. Imam al-Baqir (as) said, "I came to my father; the poison was circulating in his body. I came to him, and as a son should do to a father, I embraced my father along his chest. My father began to cry in a way I had never seen him cry. I said to him, 'O my Father, why do you cry? In a moment you will see the Prophet, in a moment you will see Fatima Zahra, in a moment you will see Ali b. Abi Talib, in a moment you will see Hassan and in a moment you will see Hussein. My father, why do you cry?' Imam Ali b. Hussein (as) said, 'O my son, I cry because when I am dying you are on my chest whereas when my father was dying, do you know who sat on the chest of my father when he lay on the ground?'"

Those images remained with him until the day he passed away and that is why Abu Hamza ath-Thumali would say to him, "O Imam Zayn ul-Abideen, why do you cry? Karbala was so many years ago."

He replied, "O Abu Hamza! Nabi Yaqub cried so much for Nabi Yusuf even though Yusuf was alive. I saw seventeen, eighteen members of my family killed in front of me, and you expect me not to cry for them?"

Lecture 7

Imam Muhammad b. Ali al-Baqir (as)

Imam Muhammad b. Ali al-Baqir (as) was born on the 1st of Rajab in the 57th year after Hijra and died on the 7th of Dhul Hijja in the 114th year after Hijra. He is seen as a colossus of Islamic knowledge and a beacon of light when it comes to each and every one of the Islamic sciences. He is a man from whose life many lessons may be learnt, especially in the fields of jurisprudence, theology and ethics; and many examples may be derived from this man who was responsible for the spread and the dissemination of many of the teachings of the Prophet (pbuh). Unfortunately, Imam Muhammad al-Baqir (as)'s life has not been studied in the way it should be because many people do not know what his role was amongst the Imams of the Ahlulbayt, and many have not appreciated the amount of knowledge that he disseminated in his life.

If you were to ask many people to tell you about the life of Imam Muhammad al-Baqir (as), you will find that they are more able to tell you about his son Imam as-Sadiq (as) and are not able to elaborate on his own role, or on his own transformation of the sciences of the religion of Islam. Arzina Lalani's recent work sheds some light on his legacy. When you dissect his life, you realize that the solidifying and the crystallization of the School of Ahlulbayt occurred in the lifetime of Imam Muhammad al-Baqir (as).

His Birth

His mother was Fatima, the daughter of Imam al-Hassan (as), and his father was Imam Zayn ul-Abideen (as), the son of Imam al-Hussein (as). His grandfather from one side was Imam al-Hassan (as) and his grandfather from the other side was Imam al-Hussein (as).

His mother Fatima, the daughter of Imam al-Hassan (as) was one of the most pious and devout wives of any of the Imams of Ahlulbayt. The narrations tell us that there was no equivalent to Fatima bint Hassan (as) when it came to her beauty. Imam al-Hassan (as) had given his daughter Fatima an apt title. Her title was "Sideeqa." This title was of course the title of Fatima Zahra (as) and it was a title that continued with Fatima, the daughter of Imam al-Hassan (as). On many occasions Imam Muhammad al-Baqir (as) would say, "My mother Fatima, her title was 'Sideeqa,' she was truthful in every aspect of her life." The mother of Imam Muhammad al-Baqir (as) was known for her truthfulness in her words, her behavior, her trusts and her religious aspects; there was nobody like her in the whole of Medina who was known for their truthful nature. Her title was "Umm Abdullah."' Fatima gave Imam Zayn ul-Abideen (as) two sons: Muhammad al-Baqir and Abdullah al-Bahir. Abdullah, the brother of Imam Muhammad al-Baqir (as) was called "Abdullah al-Bahir" because of his beauty. They used to say, "Of the sons of Zayn ul-Abideen, no one is as beautiful as Abdullah al-Bahir."

Now someone may ask the question, what about Zayd, the son of Imam Zayn ul-Abideen (as)? Who did he come from? He came from the wife of Imam Zayn ul-Abideen (as) who was from Sindh, in the Indo-Pak subcontinent. In other words, from the wives of Imam Zayn ul-Abideen (as), Fatima bint Hassan gave him Muhammad al-Baqir and Abdullah al-Bahir.

His Childhood Experiences

Imam Muhammad al-Baqir (as) was born in extremely difficult circumstances. He was born in the 57th year after Hijra, towards the end of the caliphate of Mu'awiya b. Abu Sufyan. Mu'awiya had reached a stage where he had complete dominance over the Islamic empire. Nobody could come near his dominance. The narrations tell us that he had killed many of the companions of Amir al-Mu'mineen (as) and many of the companions of Imam al-Hassan (as) as well. He had killed people like Hujr b. Adi al-Kindi, Rushaid al-Hajari, Amr b. Hamaq al-Khuza'i. He had also put many great companions under a lot of pressure like Maytham at-Tammar and Habib b. Mudhahir and Mukhtar al-Thaqafi.

Many people thought that when Mu'awiya died he would give the leadership back to Imam al-Hussein (as). Why? Because Mu'awiya had signed a treaty with Imam al-Hassan (as) which stated that the leadership would be given back to the Ahlulbayt. However, Mu'awiya appointed Yazid to become his successor. As we know, Mu'awiya had told Yazid, "Beware of four people: Abdur Rahman b. Abu Bakr and Abdullah Omar and Abdullah b. Zubair and Hussein b. Ali." Yazid made sure that a couple of them were politically quiet, while another one secluded himself, and as we know Imam Hussein (as) rose on the plains of Karbala with his famous lines, "A man like me does not pledge allegiance to a man like him."

When Imam Hussein (as) was killed on the tenth of Muharram, Imam Muhammad al-Baqir (as) was three and a half years old and was at Karbala at that time. Normally as a child you want your experiences at that young age to be experiences of warmth and comfort and happiness. You do not want to be in an environment at the age of three and a half where you witness something like the event of Karbala. But Imam Muhammad al-Baqir (as), at the age of three and a half, was sitting in the tent of his father, Imam Zayn ul-Abideen (as), at the end of the tenth of Muharram. You can imagine for someone at that age, he may not necessarily have seen what was happening outside, but the first thing he saw was his dad very ill on the bed. The second thing he saw was his aunt Zaynab running from one tent to another as the tents were burning. Imam Muhammad al-Baqir (as) too had to run because the horses were galloping across the children of Ahlulbayt. Therefore Imam Muhammad al-Baqir (as), at that age, had to witness Karbala in front of him and had to witness the oppression that came after Karbala. They had chained him next to Ruqayya and Sukayna bint Hussein. Imam Muhammad al-Baqir (as) and the other children of Ahlulbayt were all chained together and taken from Karbala to Kufa and from Kufa to Sham.

In Sham Imam Muhammad al-Baqir (as) said his first words of knowledge in front of Yazid. Up until that stage nobody had really asked who this young man was. They referred to him as Muhammad b. Ali, and they thought that he was just like any other Muhammad. At that time he did not have any titles as he was only three and a half. While Yazid was sitting down on his throne, he looked at Sukayna and Ruqayya and he looked at Lady Zaynab and Umm Kulthum and Rubab. He then said, "I think the best thing to do with all of you is that we will sell some of you off as slave women, and the rest of you, we will kill you one by one." The place became silent.

All of a sudden somebody spoke and said, "O Yazid! When Pharaoh was in power and he caught Musa and Harun, Pharaoh at least asked his people, 'What should we do to them?' and his people said, 'Let them go and live far away,' whereas you Yazid have no respect for the family of the man who brought this religion." The people looked around and Yazid said, "Who said that?" It was the three and a half year old Imam Muhammad al-Baqir (as). Yazid said, "How old is this kid?" They said, "He is three years old." He asked, "What is his name?" They said, "Muhammad b. Ali b. Hussein." He said, "Which Ali b. Hussein? We killed Ali b. Hussein." They said, "No, that is Ali al-Akbar. This is Ali Zayn ul-Abideen." He said, "That three year old speaks like that to me?"

He wanted to do something but he thought it would be an act of cowardice if he slapped a three year old. So he left him alone. Many of the people realized that this young boy was not an ordinary child because to be able to answer a caliph with knowledge like that is extraordinary. It was not extraordinary because he was three years old but mainly because how does one have knowledge of Pharaoh, Musa and Harun at that age? Who would be able to say at that moment, "Pharaoh said to Musa and Harun…" Normally you need to learn these stories over a number of years before you have that kind of knowledge. Imam Muhammad al-Baqir (as) at the age of three was already speaking like that to Yazid.

When Yazid released them, they left for Karbala and then they returned to Medina. Imam Muhammad al-Baqir (as) lived under his father Imam Zayn ul-Abideen (as) for a few years in Medina. The narrations tell us that there was a man waiting in Medina to give him salams from the Prophet.

The Significance of His Name "al-Baqir"

There was a man living in Medina at the time called Jabir b. Abdullah al-Ansari. Jabir was one of the oldest surviving companion of the Prophet (pbuh). He lived until the age of ninety, and some reports say until the age of ninety-three. Jabir's father Abdullah and his grandfather Amr were the most generous and richest men in Medina. They used to have a mansion where Masjid ul-Qiblatayn is today. Jabir's father, Abdullah al-Ansari, was known for his generosity, to the extent that he gave away so much money that he fell into debt. He was the man who said to the people of Medina, "O people of Medina! I hear that there is a Prophet who announced his prophethood in Mecca, but the people of Mecca do not want him. So let us, the people of Medina, go to him and welcome him to our land."

That is why when the Prophet (pbuh) came to Medina, one of the most hospitable people to the Prophet (pbuh) was Abdullah al-Ansari, the father of Jabir. In the Battle of Badr, Jabir, who was only nineteen at the time, came up to his father and said, "Father, I want to fight today." His father said, "No." Jabir said, "Why?" He said, "You have nine older sisters; you have to look after them in case I die." So Jabir went to the Prophet (pbuh) and said, "O Prophet, I want to fight with you in the Battle of Badr, but my father isn't allowing me." The Prophet (pbuh) looked at him and said, "Why?" He said, "Because I have nine sisters." The Prophet (pbuh) said, "Jabir, you must look after them." So then Jabir said, "O Prophet (pbuh), then what role can I have in the Battle of Badr?" The Prophet (pbuh) replied, "Jabir, carry the water for the soldiers; it is a form of showing love for Allah in this battle."

Then in the Battle of Uhud, Jabir's father got killed. Hind, the mother of Mu'awiya, mutilated two bodies in the Battle of Uhud; that of Hamza and Jabir's father. They cut their bodies to pieces. Jabir was so close to the Ahlulbayt that hadith al-Kisa is narrated by Jabir b. Abdullah al-Ansari. Jabir was a companion of the Prophet (pbuh), Imam Ali (as), Imam al-Hassan (as), Imam Hussein (as) and Imam Zayn ul-Abideen (as). The Prophet (pbuh) had said to him, "O Jabir, one day you will meet a young man whose name is my name, whose attributes are like my attributes, who has noor (light) shining from his face and who has wisdom and knowledge like none other. His name is al-Baqir. Make sure you send my salam to him."

Jabir would be sitting outside the mosque of the Prophet (pbuh) saying, "Where is al-Baqir? Where is al-Baqir?" The people would walk by Jabir and say, "Jabir's old age has gotten to him…Jabir is becoming insane… Jabir is just saying loud words!" Narrations tell us that one day Imam Zayn ul-Abideen (as) brought Muhammad b. Ali (as) and said to Jabir, "O Jabir, there is someone who wants to see you." Jabir had become blind towards the end of his life. Jabir faced the direction from where the voice of the Imam was coming. When someone is blind, his or her other senses become sharper, and so Jabir touched him and said, "I felt the footsteps of the Prophet coming towards me. Who is this?" Imam Zayn ul-Abideen (as) said, "This is Muhammad b. Ali, the one you are calling al-Baqir." Jabir took Imam Muhammad al-Baqir (as) and placed him in his lap and said, "I want to kiss your hands and your feet. Your grandfather the Prophet said to me, 'O Jabir, send my salams to Muhammad al-Baqir and know that he is al-Baqir because he will split knowledge completely.'"

"Baqir" comes from the word "baqr." When a farmer rips his farmland or rips open the soil, they call that process "baqr." As Imam Muhammad al-Baqir (as) ripped and split and scrutinized and spread knowledge, they called him "al-Baqir." Sometimes they would call him "Baqir al-Uloom," the one who splits, scrutinizes and spreads knowledge. That is a lesson for us today, that we who claim to follow Imam Muhammad al-Baqir (as), have we split knowledge open? Have we scrutinized knowledge? Have we spread our knowledge?

Some people heard Jabir refer to Imam Muhammad al-Baqir (as) as "Baqir," and so they started to make fun of Imam Muhammad al-Baqir (as) because they were jealous of him. One person was walking one day and looked at Imam Muhammad al-Baqir (as) and said, "Baqar!"

"Baqar" is different from "Baqr." Baqar means "cow," as in Surah Baqarah of the Quran. Imagine, in the face of Imam Muhammad al-Baqir (as), he called him "the cow." Imam Muhammad al-Baqir (as) looked at the person and said to him, "No, my title is al-Baqir." The person said to him, "Your mother! Her job is a cook! Nothing more!" Imam said, "That is her profession." He said, "I heard your mother was a black woman. Shame on you!" Imam said, "If you are telling the truth, may Allah forgive you, and if you are lying, may Allah forgive you as well."

Thus people would hear this name "al-Baqir," and some would try and make fun of him and call him "Baqar" or "Baqarah," whereas Imam

Muhammad al-Baqir (as) would reply to them with akhlaq. He would be patient until the day when he would disseminate his knowledge.

The Political Situation at the Time

Thus the narrations tell us that the reason he was named Baqir was because, in a period where many different schools of knowledge were emerging, people went to him when they needed to scrutinize and understand knowledge.

In his time as an Imam, Imam Muhammad al-Baqir (as) faced over five caliphs of Bani Ummayah. Some of them were the most irreligious caliphs you will ever find. In some cases, their irreligiosity actually helped the Imam to spread his message because they were more concerned with the world of women, music and luxury. Imam Muhammad al-Baqir (as) thought, while these people are busy, let me spread the knowledge of Aal Muhammad.

There were different kinds of caliphs in his time. Abdul Malik b. Marwan employed Hajjaj b. Yusuf al-Thaqafi as his governor. Hajjaj used to say, "I wish I was present on the tenth of Muharram so I could have been the man who beheaded the grandson of the Prophet." Who appoints someone like this as your governor? History books refer to Abdul Malik b. Marwan as the "great caliph of Islam."

On Eid ul-Adha while Muslims sacrificed animals, Hajjaj b. Yusuf said, "What do people do on Eid ul-Adha?" The reply was, "People sacrifice animals." Hajjaj said, "Very well, get me everyone called Ali, Hassan and Hussein so I can sacrifice them as well."

Imam Muhammad al-Baqir (as) had to also face someone like Sulayman b. Abdul Malik. When Sulayman b. Abdul Malik was told to lead the Salat ul-Jum'a, as people expected their caliphs to lead the prayers, he would look at them and say, "Are you joking? I have got two women in my room right now and you want me to come out and pray? Get someone else to lead Salat ul-Jum'a." This caliph would have two girls who would accompany him all the time. One was called Sallama and the other was called Habbaba. Sulayman b. Abdul Malik used to keep Habbaba next to him, and at the time of Salat ul- Jum'a he would sing his poetry and say, "While all of these people are going down in their prayers, I am enjoying the comforts of life with Sallama and Habbaba."

One day Allah taught them a lesson. Abdul Malik b. Marwan died because of a disease where, if he drank water, he would die. During Salat ul-Jum'a, while Sulayman b. Abdul Malik was sitting with his women, he brought a pomegranate and said to her, "Eat, eat, enjoy." While they both were eating the pomegranate, one pomegranate seed choked one of the women in her throat and she died. When he saw this, he fell on top of her, and ended up dying.

Imam Muhammad al-Baqir (as) knew there were caliphs like this and he made the most of the situation by spreading the knowledge of Aal Muhammad. Many new schools of thought began to develop during the period of Imam Muhammad al-Baqir (as). Imam Ali, Imam Hassan, and Imam Zayn ul-Abideen (as) were not able, in their own respective eras, to spread the teachings of the Prophet because they were under much pressure. Imam Muhammad al-Baqir (as) is the man who began the spread of the teachings of the Prophet in the School of the Ahlulbayt.

He used to sit in the mosque of the Prophet (pbuh) and would spread the words of the Prophet (pbuh) to everybody. People had heard Jabir say, "This man is al-Baqir," thus many people would come and ask Imam Muhammad al-Baqir (as) questions. The narrations state that lots of people started claiming, "We heard this from the Prophet...we heard that from the Prophet," and thus many schools were emerging within Islam.

For example, there was a school called the "Murje'ah" in the time of Imam Muhammad al-Baqir (as). They used to say, "You cannot say a caliph is bad due to drinking alcohol because you do not know what is in his heart."

There was another school called the "Khawarij," and they were the ones who fought Imam Ali (as) at Nahrawan. They also existed at the time of Imam Muhammad al-Baqir.

Another school was the "Mutazila," who had debates about predestination and free will and the position of the Muslim sinner in the Islamic state.

In other words, in that period of Islam, many people were confused. They did not know whom to follow.

Some of His Academic Discussions

Amongst all this confusion, most of the people decided to go and study under Imam Muhammad al-Baqir (as) in the university that he set up in Medina. That is why Imam Muhammad al-Baqir (as) and Imam Ja'far as-Sadiq (as) were called "al-Baqirayn." Sometimes people also referred to them as "as-Sadiqayn." Imam as-Sadiq (as) said, "The greatest teacher I had in my life was my father Muhammad al-Baqir." In addition to that, he would say, "I did not just learn Islamic studies from my father; we studied astronomy, cosmology, geography, philosophy and Greek mysticism and thought." Imagine. Imam Muhammad al-Baqir (as) did not just teach Islamic law, Islamic theology or Islamic ethics. Imam Muhammad al-Baqir (as) wanted to show Muslims that every science is worthy of learning in the religion of Islam. You do not just have to learn fiqh or hadith or Quran. One must be learned in every area.

People would come to Imam Muhammad al-Baqir (as) for any type of question, whether it was pertaining to the Quran, a legal issue, history, hadith or Imamate. For example, a person came to him and said, "O Imam, we have a question which we have asked many scholars but none could not answer. You are Muhammad al-Baqir! You split knowledge in half. Can you give us the answer?" Imam said, "Go ahead." "Chapter 21, verse 30, says, 'Have those disbelievers not seen how the heavens and the earth were closed and we opened them up?' What does this mean that the heavens were closed and then we opened them?" "When Allah (swt) sent Adam on the earth, there was no vegetation because there was no rain. Allah opened up the heavens, so rain would come down and the fertile land could have plants growing from it." "Thank you."

Muammar al-Laithi, a famous scholar of the time, came to Imam Muhammad al-Baqir (as) and said, "O Muhammad al-Baqir, we have a question about Islamic law." "Go ahead. What's your question?" "Do you, the Imamis, believe in mut'ah (temporary marriage)?" "Yes, we do." "But do not you think mut'ah is a type of zina?" "The Prophet would not sanction a type of zina because the Quran, in chapter 4, verse 24, clearly says, 'And (all) protected (married) ones of the women (are forbidden unto you) except those whom your right hands possess. (This is) God's written ordinance to you; And it is allowed for you, (all women) besides these that you may seek by means of your wealth taking (them) into marriage and not committing fornication. As for those whom you have enjoyed [in 'mut'ah'], give them their dowries as a fixed reward; and it shall not be a sin on you, in whatever you mutually agree (to vary) after the fixed reward; Verily God is All-Knowing, All-Wise.' There were companions in the time of the Prophet like Jabir b. Abdullah and others; if they traveled from their homes, they would look after themselves in terms of their desires, they would say, 'O Prophet, are we allowed to engage in a temporary marriage?' To which the Prophet would say, 'Yes.'" "Would you allow your women to do it? "First and foremost, if your women are virgins, then you have to seek the permission of the father (Mut'ah is not for everyone who wishes [to do it]; there is a law behind it); O Muammar, if a person who does knitting from Medina came and proposed to your daughter, would you allow your daughter to get married?" "No, I wouldn't give her to someone who knits." "But isn't it halal?" "Yes." "Therefore, if it is halal, you do not necessarily have to do it. Likewise, with us, mut'ah is halal but it does not mean mut'ah is wajib."

There is a big difference here. Just because it is halal, it does not mean everyone practices it. When you come and ask, "Would your sister do it?," it is as if you are implying that it is wajib for my sister to do it. No. It is optional. Muammar left with his head down and walked away.

Once a group of historians came to Imam Muhammad al-Baqir (as). They said, "O Muhammad b. Ali, we have a question none can answer." "What is it?" "Our question is, 'Who was the first of our ancestors to ever speak the Arabic language?'" "The first person to speak the language was Prophet Isma'il (as)." Prophet Isma'il was brought up in Mecca, thus he was the first person to ever speak that language. Another group came up to the Imam and said, "O Imam, you know Satan is the enemy of all the Prophets?" "Yes." "Did Satan ever have conversations with any of the Prophets?" "Yes." "Who?" "Satan had a conversation with Prophet Nuh (as)." "So what was the conversation between the two of them?" "Satan would come to Prophet Nuh and say to him, 'O Prophet Nuh, I am going to give you a present because you have done me a great favor.' So Prophet Nuh looked at Satan and said, 'What do you mean?' He said, 'Because you prayed to Allah to remove all those who oppressed the religion, so Allah removed them; so I did not have any work in your generation.' So then Prophet Nuh said, 'Then what is the present you are going to give me?' Satan said, 'I am going to give you three pieces of advice.' Prophet Nuh said, 'What?' Satan said, 'Remember me in three places; I am always there.'

Prophet Nuh said, 'Where?' Satan said, 'When you are angry, remember that I am always standing next to you, looking to make you more angry; (How many times when you are angry do you hear a whisper saying, "Go ahead and hit him?" - alladhi yuwaswas fi sudur al-nas - he who whispers into the hearts of mankind.) When you are about to give charity, know that I am always whispering, 'Do not give, do not give'; And when you are alone with the opposite gender, know that I am the third of the three.'"

Imagine this school in Medina where Imam Muhammad al-Baqir (as) had thousands of students under him. Another person would come to Imam Muhammad al-Baqir (as) saying, "You Imams claim you are infallible?" "Yes." "What are the proofs for it?" "Why do human beings sin?" "I do not know. You tell me." "Because of four reasons - either because of anger, or because of lust or because of envy or because of greed. Why would we need to be greedy when Allah has given us the knowledge He has given us? Why would we be envious when we are the grandchildren of the Prophet? Why would we lust over anything when Allah has honored us with the Holy Quran? And why would we get angry over anything when Allah (swt) has allowed the message of prophethood to be in our lines. Therefore, a person normally commits a sin because of lust or anger or envy or desire, Allah has given us so much that these four things never affect us in our life."

Therefore, Imam Muhammad al-Baqir (as) would disseminate knowledge and many of his students emerged from his school. People like Zurara, Hamran and Jabir b. Yazid al-Jofi would emerge and would continue to spread his words everywhere, but the caliphs of the time were unaffected. However, one caliph was affected in a good way and one was affected in a bad way. Umar b. Abdul Aziz was one of the Umayyad caliphs who was positively influenced by Imam Muhammad al-Baqir (as).

Umar b. Abdul Aziz's father in law was Abdul Malik b. Marwan. He was the great-grandson of Umar b. Khattab. Up until the time of Imam Muhammad al-Baqir (as) every Salat ul-Juma'a khutba (sermon) had to begin with "In the name of God, the Most Beneficent, the Most Merciful; May God curse..." Imam Ali (as) would be cursed in every khutba of the Friday prayer. That is why this idea seems to be a myth that Ali b. Abi Talib (as) was the fourth rightly-guided caliph in that time. That's impossible. That came later. How could he be the fourth rightly-guided caliph while the Banu Ummayah were in charge for eight years? Every week at Friday prayer Ali b. Abi Talib (as) was cursed. Who curses their own caliph?

Umar b. Abdul Aziz used to say, "Whenever my father Abdul Aziz would talk about Ali b. Abi Talib, he used to get nervous. So I used to tell my father, 'Whenever you talk about any man you are calm except Ali b. Abi Talib, why?' My father would say to me, 'If the people knew the merits of Ali b. Abi Talib, they would not have us as leaders.'" So Umar b. Abdul Aziz, because of Imam Muhammad al-Baqir (as)'s knowledge, got affected by him and also by a personal tutor. He was the Umayyad caliph who stopped the cursing of Imam Ali (as) on the pulpit.

One day when Umar b. Abdul Aziz became the caliph he said to Imam Muhammad al-Baqir (as), "O Muhammad b. Ali, you are the one on whom the Prophet sent his greetings; I want to ask you a question. What three pieces of advice do you give me now that I have become the caliph?"

Imam Muhammad al-Baqir (as) gave him three pieces of fantastic advice. He said to him, "When you celebrate or have an extravagant celebration, do not forget [what is] halal and haram (one must question the weddings and other celebrations one attends or organizes); when you become angry, do not forget halal and haram (when we get angry, sometimes cursing just becomes part of our vocabulary); and do not usurp the property of the people."

So they had a conversation and Umar asked, "Which property are you referring to?" Imam Muhammad al-Baqir (as) said, "Fadak belonged to my grandmother, Fatima. The Umayyads took Fadak away from my grandmother." Umar said, "Fadak belonged to your family and I as caliph will make sure it is given back to you."

Although we may differ from him on certain aspects, his two commands to stop the cursing of Amir al-Mu'mineen and return Fadak to Imam Muhammad al-Baqir (as) will never be forgotten.

The caliph after Umar b. Abdul Aziz was Hisham b. Abdul Malik. He absolutely despised Imam Muhammad al-Baqir (as). He was envious of him, and he was probably thinking to himself, how could this person have more knowledge than me when I am the caliph? He tried every way possible to embarrass Imam Muhammad al-Baqir (as). Hisham b. Abdul Malik would gather the most knowledgeable Christians, atheists and Muslims from outside the School of Ahlulbayt to debate Imam Muhammad al-Baqir (as).

One day Hisham b. Abdul Malik was sitting near the Ka'aba. He had Nafae' with him. This was a person who used to be the slave of Umar b. Khattab and was of the Khawarij who fought Imam Ali (as). They saw Imam Muhammad al-Baqir (as) walk towards the Ka'aba and everyone opened up the space. Nafae' said, "Who is that?" Hisham b. Abdul Malik said, "He is the prophet of the people of Iraq." Nafae' said, "What do you mean?" He said, "They call him al-Baqir. Apparently he can split knowledge and answer questions no one can answer." Nafae' said, "Leave this guy to me. Bring him. Let me show him." Nafae' called Imam and said, "Baqir, come here." Imam came. Nafae' said, "I hear the people say you are knowledgeable." "I am not of the ignorant." "Very well, answer my questions if you think you have any knowledge." "Go ahead." "What was the number of years between Jesus and Muhammad?" "In your opinion six hundred, in my opinion five hundred." Nafae' was staring at him. How does he know my opinion in this issue? (You know when the Imam takes the level of knowledge higher…)

"Muhammad, in surah 43, verse 45, God says, 'O Prophet of God, ask the prophets who came before you, did they tell the people to disbelieve in other than God?' Muhammad, how could Allah tell the Prophet to ask those who came before him? That's impossible. The prophets who came before him have gone." "No. On the night of Meraj Allah let his Prophet lead all the prophets in prayer, and when he finished his prayer, he turned around and he said to them, 'Did you ever tell your people to disbelieve in Allah?' and they said, 'No, O Prophet of God. We told them to believe in Allah and in your prophethood." "You're good. Where is God?" "Show me where He is not and I will show you where he is." "Okay, when did God come about?" "Show me when He was not and I will show you when He came."

Hisham b. Abdul Malik went crazy and said, "How can none of you answer?" So Hisham brought someone else. He said, "Come, I beg you. You're the top scholar? Debate Muhammad al-Baqir and finish him. This man is getting too popular. People say he is al-Baqir, he splits all knowledge and no one can answer him." So this scholar said, "Leave him to me. I will ask him." So he came to Imam Muhammad al-Baqir (as) and said, "I have got some questions for you. You claim to be al-Baqir? Answer my questions." "Go ahead." "But you know my questions are from the Bible and the Quran." "Go ahead." "My first question is this: In which fast in history were you allowed to eat and drink?" "Simple. The fast of

Lady Maryam, when Allah told her to remain silent. That was her fasting." "I have a second question: Tell me, when was a quarter of humanity killed?" "Simple. When Qabeel killed Habeel, a quarter of humanity died." "What increases and never decreases?" "The water of the ocean." "What decreases and never increases?" "Your life." "Which people spoke the truth yet were still called liars?" "The first verse in Surah Munafiqun: 'The Munafiqun come to you and say, 'You are the Prophet of God,' but We know that they are liars.'" (The statement is true, but the Munafiqun were still liars.) "This is a question which none can ever answer." "Which one?" "Which twins were born on the same day and died on the same day but one of them was a hundred and fifty and the other one was a fifty?" (You need to be Baqir to answer this question, true? You need to be able to split knowledge into half.) Imam said to him, "It is easy. Prophet Uzair and his brother Aziz. Prophet Uzair and his brother were together, then he asked Allah, 'How do you raise the dead and give them life?' They were both thirty years old when Allah caused one of them to die for a hundred years. When Prophet Uzair came back life due to Allah's permission, he lived for another twenty years. The elder brother was a hundred and fifty, while Uzair was only fifty years of age [when they eventually died on the same day]." He said, "I swear there is no inheritor of knowledge of the Prophet like Muhammad al-Baqir."

Hisham b. Abdul Malik brought a third person who was a Christian. Hisham said to him, "Finish Muhammad al-Baqir off." The Christian said, "I have got three questions to ask this man but first let me ask you, are you from the line of Jesus or Muhammad?" "I am from the line of Muhammad." "Are you of the scholars or of the ignorant?" " I am not of the ignorant." "Let me ask you my three questions." "Go ahead." "Which period is neither day or night?" "Just before sunrise, the color of the sky is neither day or night." "What happens in that period to the human being?" "If you are ill, Allah removes your illness at that period of time." "Okay, you say in heaven that we will eat so much and we will not excrete; how can that be?" "The embryo in the womb...it eats and eats but does not excrete." "Okay, you say in heaven we will eat and eat but there will still be so much food; how can that be?" "The candle which lights another candle but does not lose any of its source is like the food in Jannah." The Christian became a Muslim at that moment because of Imam Muhammad al-Baqir (as).

Imam Muhammad al-Baqir (as) had covered every angle of knowledge. But there is an important question. Did Imam Muhammad al-Baqir (as) only serve Islam through his knowledge? No. Imam Muhammad al-Baqir (as) also had a job. He taught us, like his grandfather Amir al-Mu'mineen, to teach Quran and give lectures but also to go out and earn a living.

Muhammad b. Munkadir narrates that, "It was in the heat of Medina, I was walking and there was no one on the streets and I saw one man on the streets plowing and plowing and plowing. I thought to myself, 'Who is this man chasing the world at this time?' I got nearer and I saw it was the grandson of the Prophet, Muhammad al-Baqir. When I came to him, I said, 'O grandson of the Prophet, you are chasing the dunya (world)? What are you doing working in this heat?'

He said to me, 'And what is wrong with me working? If I die in this state, at least I am dying in a state of worship of Allah (swt); for earning a living is a form of worshipping Allah and Allah does not like to see the hands of anyone, except the hands of a person who earns a halal living in their life, on the Day of Judgement.'"

Therefore, Imam Muhammad al-Baqir (as) used to work and earn a living because he had five sons and two daughters from his wife Umm Farwa, the daughter of Qasim, the son of Muhammad b. Abu Bakr, and from his other wife, Thaqafiyya.

There are many lectures of Imam Muhammad al-Baqir (as) where he describes the qualities of his Shi'a or the responsibilities of following him.

In one hadith he says, "Our followers are three types: one of them are those who follow us but rely and depend on others; the second are like glass, all they do is watch themselves as a reflection and nothing else; the third are like gold, the more they suffer, the more they shine."

In another hadith Imam Muhammad al-Baqir (as) said, "When Allah loves His servants He drowns them in the sea of suffering."

The Umayyad caliphs could not take it anymore and became extremely jealous of Imam Muhammad al-Baqir (as). They began to put poison into his food. Some even began to plant needles into his saddle so that if he sat on the saddle the needle would go through his thigh. Before Imam Muhammad al-Baqir (as) died, he gave a beautiful wasiya (will) to Imam as-Sadiq (as). The first thing he said to Imam as-Sadiq (as) was, "Spend the money that I have left behind to spread ilm (knowledge) because education is the essence of Islam; bury me with my robe which I used to offer my prayers because salat will speak for me on the Day of Judgement; and make sure you organize majalis at Mina every year at hajj, the majalis of my grandfather Imam Hussein (as)."

One hundred of his students graduated in reading poetry and verses commemorating Imam Hussein (as). That is why Imam Muhammad al-Baqir (as) has the famous hadith that says, "Whoever cries a tear that is the size of a wing of a fly for Imam Hussein (as), that tear can cure sins the size of an ocean." Therefore, Imam Muhammad al-Baqir (as) taught all areas of knowledge, such as theology, ethics, jurisprudence, astronomy, cosmology, physics, biology and especially the discipline of leading majalis of Imam Hussein (as).

Lecture 8

Imam Ja'far b. Muhammad as-Sadiq (as)

A Great Disservice to the Imam

Imam Ja'far b. Muhammad as-Sadiq (as) was born on the 17th of Rabi ul-Awwal in the 80th year after Hijra and died on the 25th of Shawwal in the 148th year after Hijra. He is regarded by many as the master of all jurisprudence and as a colossus in the world of Islamic law. He is revered for his knowledge, wisdom, piety and humility. He is seen as the master of all the teachers of Islamic knowledge; for when you look at many of the great scholars in Islamic history, many of them were students of Imam Ja'far as-Sadiq (as). Therefore his life requires a thorough examination, for not only does his life affect each and every one of our lives, it affects the lives of every Muslim in the world today.

The Imamis call their school of thought the "Ja'fari" school, which is named after him. Does this mean that he is greater than the other Imams? No. Rather it means that the flourishing of Islamic knowledge occurred in his time along with its crystallization. Imam Ja'far as-Sadiq (as) is just like Imam Hassan al-Askari (as), or like Imam al-Jawad (as) or like Imam Hussein (as); the difference in terms of their abilities with knowledge was that he had more freedom than anybody else to disseminate the knowledge. That is why the school today is called the "Ja'fari" madhhab.

On many occasions, if you were to read books of fiqh today, you will hear people saying, "This is the opinion of Abu Hanifa…this is the opinion of Malik b. Anas…this is the opinion of Imam ash-Shafi'i…this is the opinion of Imam Ahmed b. Hanbal…" and unfortunately you hardly ever hear, "This is the opinion of Ja'far as-Sadiq." From the time he passed away until today, a disservice has been done to Imam Ja'far as-Sadiq (as) to the extent that the greatest of works on Imam Ja'far as-Sadiq (as)'s knowledge have been written by non-Muslims rather than Muslims. If you were to look at the Islamic texts, for example, Imam al-Bukhari, in his famous Sahih al-Bukhari, in over thousands of narrations within Sahih al-Bukhari, there is not a single narration from Imam Ja'far as-Sadiq (as). There are narrations from Imran b. Hussein, Imran b. Hattan, Samara b. Jundub and Marwan b. Hakam, but not one narration from Imam Ja'far as-Sadiq (as). Even further than that, when 20th century writers like Dr. Ahmed Amin, in his book Duhal Islam, have written about jurisprudence, he writes about Abu Hanifa, Malik, Imam ash-Shafi'i and Ahmad b. Hanbal, then he says, "…and I hear that Ja'far as-Sadiq also had some legal opinions but I have never seen any of them." Even Ahmed Ati'a has a book which is a whole encyclopedia and dictionary of the religion of Islam, Qamoos al-Islami, and within that there are four hundred and twenty pages on Imam ash-Shafi'i and only seven lines on Imam Ja'far as-Sadiq (as) and at the end of those seven lines he has written, "…and there was a person called Ja'far as-Sadiq. I think they call him Sadiq because he did not lie."

So therefore you find that in Islamic history there was a disservice done to Imam Ja'far as-Sadiq (as) where they tried to cover up and overshadow his knowledge and more fame was given to his students. Why? Because they knew if people found out that he was the teacher of so many scholars, then they would focus on the teacher instead of the students. There are great works on Imam Ja'far as-Sadiq (as) in Western literature. For example, Etan Kohlberg has a fantastic work on Imam Ja'far as-Sadiq (as) that looks at the four hundred disciples of Imam Ja'far as-Sadiq (as) and the works they had produced. There is a PhD dissertation housed at the University of Strasbourg in France which has now been made into a book called Imam Ja'far as-Sadiq: The Great Muslim Scientist and Philosopher. Therefore, when we dissect Imam Ja'far as-Sadiq (as)'s biography, our aim is to be able to bring Imam Ja'far as-Sadiq (as) to the lofty position he deserves more than any one of his students.

His Childhood

Imam Ja'far as-Sadiq (as) was born in the 80th year after Hijra, on the 17th of Rabi ul-Awwal. Therefore he shares his birth with Prophet Muhammad (pbuh). Imam Ja'far as-Sadiq (as) had the honor of being born on the same day as the Prophet (pbuh). His love of knowledge and learning first began under his grandfather who is our fourth Imam. Imam Zayn ul-Abideen (as) was the teacher of Imam Ja'far as-Sadiq (as). Imam as-Sadiq (as) was fifteen years old when Imam Zayn ul-Abideen (as) died. Thus Imam Ja'far as-Sadiq (as)'s first fifteen years was under the guidance and teachings of Imam Zayn ul-Abideen (as). He saw Imam Zayn ul-Abideen (as) write Saheefa as-Sajjadiyah; he saw him write Risalat ul-Huqooq, and in this book there was one chapter which had a profound affect on Imam Ja'far as-Sadiq (as)'s love of teaching. In the Risalat ul-Huqooq, Imam Zayn ul-Abideen (as) had written about the rights of your teacher.

Imam Ja'far as-Sadiq (as) in his youth, while studying under Imam Zayn ul-Abideen (as), read the rights of the teacher. Imam Zayn ul-Abideen (as) had said, "The first right of your teacher in Islam is that you fix your eyes towards them when they are speaking; then you purify your heart for them when they are teaching; you never raise your voice above your teacher; when your teacher is answering a question, do not interrupt them; if anyone speaks ill about your teacher behind your teacher's back, you must defend your teacher."

Imam Zayn ul-Abideen (as) was, in other words, elucidating the saying of his grandfather, Amir al-Mu'mineen, when he said, "Whoever taught me one letter has become my master." In the rights of the teacher, when it says, "Fix your eyes towards them when you are speaking…," this is an important aspect to understand because sometimes when our teachers are speaking, we are looking another way, or we are speaking on our phones or texting on our Blackberries.

"Purify your heart towards them…" In learning, 30% involves our intellect while 70% involves our attitude. If we enter class and our heart does not want to listen to this teacher, then we will never learn, but when you purify your heart for your teacher, it makes a difference. "Never raise your voice above your teacher" The way some of our students speak to our teachers today is abysmal; some of them are rude and arrogant. "Do not interrupt them, and if anyone attacks your teacher behind his back, make sure you protect them"

Thus you find that a teacher can make or break the life of a human being. Socrates' students loved him so much that when he was taken to prison many were willing to sacrifice their lives for him. Umar b. Abdul Aziz removed the cursing of Ali b. Abi Talib (as) because of his teacher. Mu'awiya, son of Yazid, loved Imam Zayn ul-Abideen (as) because of his teacher. A teacher can have a great affect on the life of a human being.

Therefore Imam Ja'far as-Sadiq (as) had recognized the importance of teaching from Imam Zayn ul-Abideen (as). Then he studied under Imam Muhammad al-Baqir (as), his father, to the extent that Imam Ja'far as-Sadiq (as) would say, "When I was eleven years old, my father taught me astronomy and philosophy; he taught me Greek ethics, theology and law." All of these subjects Imam Ja'far as-Sadiq (as) managed to study under Imam Muhammad al-Baqir (as). Therefore, from a young age, Imam Ja'far as-Sadiq (as) had a love for learning. He loved the attainment of knowledge, safeguarding it, bettering himself with his knowledge and disseminating it.

The Circumstances that Helped Spread His Knowledge

There was a struggle for power in the Islamic empire. When Imam Ja'far as-Sadiq (as) was born, the Umayyads ruled the Islamic empire. It was impossible for Imam Ja'far as-Sadiq (as) to teach then because the Umayyads would not allow any of the sons of Fatima Zahra (as) to spread their knowledge that far. The people were now getting sick and tired of the hypocrisy of the Umayyads, because they would observe them and think, "You people are meant to be the representatives of God on earth, yet you are hypocrites. You tell us about religion while you do not practice any of it."

The community saw some of these Umayyad caliphs living a life which was the most un-Islamic of anyone. For example, Walid b. Abdul Malik had a girlfriend. This girl was around him all the time. One day both of them had drunk so much that he said to her, "Do you ever want to lead prayers in your life?" She said, "What do you mean?" He said, "I want you to lead prayers." She said, "But I am a woman." (Being drunk was obviously not a problem to her.) He said, "It does not matter. You go and lead these men and watch them. None of them can say anything against us." She went and led them in salat while she was drunk.

Another example occurred one day when Yazid II of the Bani Ummayah decided to get the builders to make a swimming pool for him in his house. He told them, "I do not want water in the pool; I want only alcohol in it. Put as much alcohol as you can." Thus people were getting frustrated in the time of Imam as-Sadiq (as). They saw that this family was ruling the Islamic empire but all their actions were the actions of hypocrites. The Umayyads even killed Imam as-Sadiq (as)'s uncle, Zayd.

In Yemen today, there are about nine million of our Zaydi brothers. They follow Lady Fatima (as) and her children who became jurists and led revolts to establish justice. They follow and narrate hadith from Zayd, the son of Imam Zayn ul-Abideen (as) and the brother of Imam Muhammad al-Baqir (as). Zayd saw the increased tyranny and hypocrisy of Bani Ummayah over the years. So he told the people, "Listen, O people. I know that there are many stories about the [character of] Umayyads. Let me go and see for myself." Zayd went to the palace of Hisham b. Abdul Malik and when he entered he saw Hisham sitting next to a Christian poet by the name of al-Akhtal. Zayd heard the poet curse the Prophet. Zayd stood up and said, "How dare you curse my grandfather! You claim to be the caliph and you allow this Christian poet to curse the Prophet?" Hisham b. Abdul Malik said, "Name yourself." "I am Zayd, son of Zayn ul-Abideen." "You are the son of that slave girl from Sindh, aren't you?" "And what is wrong with that?" "Zayn ul-Abideen could not find a mother for you except a slave?" "There was a Prophet of God called Isma'il, and his mother was a slave called Hajar. What is the shame in it?" "Get out of here otherwise we will finish you off and all those who support you!"

After Zayd left the palace, he decided that he would never allow a man like this to rule while he was alive. Thus Zayd caused a revolt which was the beginning of the downfall of the Umayyads. The Umayyads ruled Islam for eighty-nine years. The beginning of their downfall was Zayd. He led an army and confronted the army chief of the Umayyads, Yusuf al-Thaqafi, the father of Hajjaj. Finally Zayd was killed and they hung his nude body on a tree for four years. Then they burnt his body and allowed his ashes to be thrown into the rivers of Iraq.

The Umayyad empire now began to shake as the people became frustrated. The banner that they raised was "al-Rida min Aal Muhammad." This meant that leadership should go back to Aal Muhammad. The people who raised this slogan began to write letters to Imam as-Sadiq (as).

Abu Muslim al-Khorasani and Abu Salama al-Khallal were the first ones to write the Imam a letter. Imam as-Sadiq (as) turned towards the people who brought him the letter. They said, "Imam! Imam! There is a movement to remove the Umayyads and they want Aal Muhammad to come into power. Imam! This is your opportunity!" Imam took the letter and burnt it. The man said to him, "Imam? What's wrong? The Bani Hashim are going to return [to power]." Imam said, "I am telling you it will not happen. Those people who are raising the banner are my cousins. I know who they are. They are using our name to win all of your support. I promise you they will not let you touch their government."

The people were astonished and the first to oppose Imam as-Sadiq (as) were his own cousins, Abdullah b. Hassan II b. Imam Hassan, and his two sons Muhammad and Ibrahim. They said to Imam as-Sadiq (as), "What do you mean? This is our opportunity. We are going to remove the Umayyads and come to power." Imam as-Sadiq (as) said, "I promise you that we will not get any power. This Saffah and Mansur al-Dawaniqi are the ones who will rule."

Later the Umayyads were replaced by the Banu Abbas. The Abbasids were the descendants of Abbas, the uncle of the Prophet (pbuh). Therefore they were the cousins of Imam as-Sadiq (as). Nobody caused trouble for Imam Muhammad al-Baqir (as) up to Imam Hassan al-Askari (as) like the Banu Abbas, despite being cousins. Imam Muhammad al-Baqir (as), Imam as-Sadiq (as), Imam al-Kadhim, Imam ar-Ridha, Imam al-Jawad (as), Imam Ali al-Hadi (as) and Imam Hassan al-Askari (as) were all killed by their cousins.

Thus Imam as-Sadiq (as) said to the descendants of Imam Hassan, "I swear to you, you will not taste any power. These people are making the excuse that they want Aal Muhammad to rule over the Muslims, but it is not us; they are referring to themselves." And it so happened that as soon as the Umayyads were defeated, the people said, "Give the leadership to Imam as-Sadiq (as)," and the Banu Abbas said, "Are you joking? We are the representatives of Aal Muhammad, not them. We are the sons of Abbas, they are the sons of Abu Talib; we have an equal right to this authority."

The Banu Abbas were so treacherous that the Umayyads seemed mild in comparison to their treachery. When al-Mansur al-Dawaniqi came to power, the only difference between him and the Umayyads was that the Umayyads spent more money on the Muslims and were extravagant upon themselves. Al-Mansur al-Dawaniqi was known to be the stingiest caliph throughout the 1400 years of Islamic history. The only time he would give money to the poor was if they recited a piece of poetry that no one had ever heard. But even then, the money he would give would be equivalent to the weight of the paper the poetry was written on. He would tell the people, "O people, I am your caliph, not Ja'far as-Sadiq. Leave him and come to me and I will give you money."

When the people would come to his courtroom, he would say, "I will give you money if you recite poetry for me, but only if that poetry has never been heard before, will I give you payment. If it has been heard before, you will not get anything; and if it has never been heard before, I will give you money equal to the weight of the paper you have written it on." He would then hide two people behind the curtain. They were specialists in Arabic grammar. They could memorize poetry very fast. So even if a person recited a poem, those two would memorize it as it was being read, and then come out and repeat it as if they had heard it before and it was nothing new.

One day al-Asmai came to al-Mansur al-Dawaniqi and said, "O caliph, I have come because I want a donation." Al-Mansur al-Dawaniqi said, "Very good. Recite some poetry and if we have never heard it, we will give you the money equivalent to the weight of the paper that the poem was written on." Al-Asmai said, "Are you ready?" Al-Mansur al-Dawaniqi said, "Yes." He looked at the other two of his men and said, "Are you two ready?" They said, "Yes." Al-Mansur al-Dawaniqi said, "Yes, go ahead, go ahead." Al-Asmai began to recite poetry with the most difficult words in the Arabic language, and he twisted them. Al-Mansur al-Dawaniqi was looking at him thinking, "I have never ever heard a person say anything like this. What's going on?" So he looked at the two of his men behind the curtain and the two of them were also baffled. So al-Mansur al-Dawaniqi said, "You have done well. Give me the paper you have written it on."

He said, "I did not write it on a piece of paper. I wrote it on that big black rock over there." That day al-Mansur al-Dawaniqi never slept because he almost lost his entire wealth that night. The rock weighed a ton.

Al-Mansur was also a ruthless killer, imprisoning and killing many of the descendants of Imam Hassan who rebelled against him. Thus Imam as-Sadiq (as) saw al-Mansur al-Dawaniqi establish his position and that it was wiser to refrain from openly rebelling against him. Instead he focused on teaching the School of Ahlulbayt to the people. In the beginning al-Mansur al-Dawaniqi was not happy with Imam as-Sadiq (as)'s teaching.

Al-Mansur al-Dawaniqi was sitting in his royal box at hajj one day. The Barmaki family were on one side, and ar-Rabi'i was on the other. Al-Mansur al-Dawaniqi was preventing pilgrims from reaching the Hajr ul-Aswad. He saw someone walk towards the Hajr ul-Aswad. The Hajr ul-Aswad has a love for the Ahlulbayt that when they walk towards it, it opens for them. Thus al-Mansur al-Dawaniqi turned around to the person next to him and said, "Who is that who is walking there?" The person next to him said, "He is the god of the people of Iraq." "What do you mean?" "They call him Ja'far b. Muhammad; they say he is as-Sadiq and they say that he is a man of piety." "That's interesting. I have never met this man before." The narrations say that all of a sudden a person came to al-Mansur al-Dawaniqi and said to him, "We have a case of law that we do not know how to answer." Al-Mansur al-Dawaniqi said, "What is it?" "We have found a dead body. We want to know what the blood money is for this body and how much is to be paid to the inheritors because we do not know who the inheritors are." "Well, I do not know how to answer this question. You guys are the people of knowledge. Tell me." "We do not know." "Then who would know?" "Ja'far b. Muhammad would know." "Then call him."

So Imam Ja'far as-Sadiq (as) came. Al-Mansur al-Dawaniqi said, "I hear that you are a man of knowledge." "I am not of the ignorant." "We have found a dead body and the head has been severed. What is the blood money?" "A hundred dinars." "How did you answer that so quickly?" "Because the Quran says that there are five stages in the life of the human being. There is the stage of sulala, then nutfa; and the stage of the mudhga, and the stage of idham; and the stage of death…" Imam mentioned the five stages and said, "Because there are five stages, that means twenty dinars for each stage, and until death it comes to a hundred dinars." "How about the inheritance?" "If there are no inheritors, you pay the money as sadaqa."

Mansur looked at the people around him and said, "Would you have been able to answer like Ja'far as-Sadiq?" They said, "No." He said, "This man's knowledge must be something else."

Al-Mansur al-Dawaniqi noticed that Imam Ja'far as-Sadiq (as) had a stick. This stick had travelled down from the Prophet (pbuh) to Imam

Ali (as) who then gave it to Imam al-Hassan (as), who gave it to Imam Hussein (as) and it finally reached Imam Ja'far as-Sadiq (as). Al-Mansur al-Dawaniqi said, "I want that stick." Imam Ja'far as-Sadiq (as) said, "Here, take it." "You gave it to me very easily." "If these are the things you care for in life, then have them."

"I will allow you to teach because you're a man of knowledge, but you cannot teach near me. Go to Kufa and teach over there." That was the biggest mistake al-Mansur al-Dawaniqi made because when he allowed Imam Ja'far as-Sadiq (as) to move to Kufa, he reignited the school of Amir al-Mu'mineen in Masjid al-Kufa. Nobody had taught like that since the days of Amir al-Mu'mineen.

While Imam Ja'far as-Sadiq (as) was in Kufa, there were nine hundred circles of classes that were being conducted there, and each teacher would say, "I heard from Ja'far b. Muhammad..."

The first thing Imam Ja'far as-Sadiq (as) did as a teacher before he taught was to practice what he preached. You can teach, but if you do not practice what you preach, no one will listen to you. On a Monday, Imam Ja'far as-Sadiq (as) would say, "Love for others what you would love for yourselves." On a Tuesday he would say, "Oppose the oppressor and support the oppressed." On Wednesday he would say, "We, the Ahlulbayt, do not take back that which we have given."

On Thursday when he entered the mosque and there was a man in the mosque. Mualla b. Khunais narrates, "I saw a man in the mosque and he had a thousand gold coins next to him. When he finished his salat, he looked around, and there were no more gold coins. He got angry and shouted, 'Where are my gold coins?' There was no one in the mosque and Imam Ja'far as-Sadiq (as) had just walked in. When Imam walked in, that man looked at the Imam and said, 'You are the one who took my gold coins.'" Imam Ja'far as-Sadiq (as) looked at him and said, "I promise you, my brother, it was not me. It must have been someone else." He said, "No, it is you. The coins were here. You are the only one in this mosque." Imam Ja'far as-Sadiq (as) said, "Brother, I'm telling you, it was not me. But if you need those gold coins urgently, I will arrange for them to be given to you." [The day before Imam Ja'far as-Sadiq (as) had said, 'We, the Ahlulbayt, do not take back that which we have given away.'] Imam Ja'far as-Sadiq (as) turned to someone and said, "Can you get me a thousand gold coins?" The person said, "Yes." He brought a thousand gold coins and gave it to that person. The man said, "Thank you. Now leave me. You people steal from Muslims." As he walked out of the mosque, he saw his bag with a thousand gold coins at the door of the mosque. He came running back to the Imam, and as he was running back he asked someone, "Who is that man?" They said, "Ja'far b. Muhammad." He said, "Which Ja'far b. Muhammad? Ja'far b. Muhammad as-Sadiq?" There were two Ja'far b. Muhammads at the time. They said, "Yes." He came to Imam Ja'far as-Sadiq (as) and said, "I beg you, forgive me. I did not know it was you, and I was wrong to accuse you; I have found my bag at the door of the mosque. Here are your thousand gold coins." Imam said, "We, the Ahlulbayt, do not take back that which we gave away."

Thus the first aspect of his teaching was that he practiced that which he preached. Today we have teachers who tell the community to remain united whereas they are the cause of disunity. They tell other people not to abuse other Muslims whereas they are the cause of abuse.

Students who Studied under Imam as-Sadiq (as)

Most of the narrators who related hadith reports from Imam Sadiq (a) were not residents of Medina; rather, they were from different regions such as Kufa, Mecca, Sana, Wasit, Qum, Isfahan, Basrah, Mashhad, Halab, Rayy, Damascus, Yemen, Daylam, Taef, Kabul and Andalus, with the majority from Iraq, especially the city of Kufa. These people who lived in different parts of the Muslim world during the 34 years of Imam Sadiq's (a) tenure sometimes were able to go to Medina and hear the hadiths from the Imam (a). These sessions took place mostly during the hajj season, because people who went for pilgrimage would make a short stopover in Medina and during this time sometimes were able to meet the Imam (a) and listen to his statements. The number of narrators who related hadith reports on the authority of Imam Sadiq (a) is 3,224.

The most famous, and the first of the students of Imam Ja'far as-Sadiq (as), was Nu'man b. Thabit, who was most famously called Abu Hanifa. 31% of the Muslim world follows Abu Hanifa in fiqh. If you go to India or Pakistan and you ask them, "Who is your teacher in fiqh?" They say their master is Abu Hanifa. If you ask them, "Do you know who Abu Hanifa's teacher was?" Many of them will say, "We don't know." Abu Hanifa used to say, "If it wasn't for my two years with Ja'far as-Sadiq, I would have been finished." He studied under Imam Ja'far as-Sadiq (as) for two years. Numerous books have been written about Abu Hanifa, yet many of them do not even mention Imam Ja'far as-Sadiq (as). Abu Hanifa did not just study law under Imam Ja'far as-Sadiq (as), he even studied political science under him. Because of Imam Ja'far as-Sadiq (as)'s teachings, Abu Hanifa gave ten thousand dinars to Zayd, the uncle of the Imam, when Zayd spoke out against the Umayyads. When al-Mansur al-Dawaniqi was caliph, Abu Hanifa would not lead the salat for al-Mansur al-Dawaniqi because of his respect for Imam Ja'far as-Sadiq (as). They put Abu Hanifa in prison because of his love for Imam Ja'far as-Sadiq (as). If you go to the Hanafis (followers of Abu Hanifa) today and ask, "Do you know who taught Abu Hanifa?" Many of them will not know.

25% of the Muslim world follows the second student of Imam Ja'far as-Sadiq (as), who is known as Malik b. Anas. If you go to Morocco, Algeria or Tunisia and ask them, "Which man do you follow in fiqh?" They will say, "We follow Malik b. Anas." Ask them, "Do you know who Malik's teacher was?" Many of them do not know that Malik's teacher was Imam Ja'far as-Sadiq (as). Malik b. Anas used to say, "No eye has seen and no ear has heard a man with knowledge like Ja'far as-Sadiq." He used to say, "It is as if I see Imam Ja'far as-Sadiq (as) in front of me now." He would also say, "He was always in one of three states - either he was fasting or he was in salat or he was teaching or reading the Quran. I swear by Allah that Ja'far b. Muhammad never discussed religion except that he was in a state of taharah." Imam Ja'far as-Sadiq (as) would never give a lecture unless he had done wudu' before the lecture. He would say, "How can I give a lecture about the Prophet while I have not done the wudu' of the Prophet?" Malik was from the people of Medina.

Jabir b. Hayyan was the third student of Imam Ja'far as-Sadiq (as). He was the master of chemistry. If you Google his name, or type it in Wikipedia, you will find that he was the man who translated Pythagoras, Plato, Aristotle and Socrates in the Islamic world; the man who wrote on crystallization, distillation and evaporation in the Islamic world; the man who wrote 110 volumes on chemistry in the Islamic world; 400 of his treatises are in Paris. This man taught the world about chemistry. When you read his biography, it is written that "Jabir b. Hayyan [was] the master of chemistry." Ask the world, "Do you know who the teacher of Jabir was?"

When Jabir b. Hayyan would talk about chemistry, he would say, "My master Ja'far as-Sadiq taught me about calcium…and he taught me about evaporation…and distillation…and crystallization…and everything within chemistry I learnt from my master Ja'far as-Sadiq." In Paris, when they teach about Jabir b. Hayyan, there is not one reference to Ja'far as-Sadiq, and that is our fault. We have not sponsored people to write about the master of Jabir.

Ja'far al-Barmaki was one of the leading men of the Islamic empire. When his daughter Hassana became ill, they asked who the best person was to consult regarding her illness. The people said to him, "Ja'far as-Sadiq has a great student called Jabir b. Hayyan al-Tartusi as-Sufi Abu Musa." They brought Jabir to the Barmaki family's house. As soon as he looked at Hassana, he said, "I know what her problem is." "What is it?" "She has a lack of calcium. And my master Ja'far as-Sadiq taught me that this will produce weak bones, so there needs to be an increase in her calcium so that she is stronger."

As a result of this incident, Jabir married the daughter of the Barmaki family. They gave him the Jama' al-Umawi. Today it is a famous tourist spot known as the Umayyad palace in Syria. After the Umayyads, it was taken over by the Abbasids and was later given to Jabir as a gift. Every lesson that Jabir would begin, he would say, "My master Ja'far as-Sadiq taught me…"

Imam Ja'far as-Sadiq (as)'s fourth student was a man by the name of Hisham b. Hakam. There are two Hishams in history and they are known as the "Hishamayn," and they are the great disciples of Imam Ja'far as-Sadiq (as). One of them was Hisham b. Hakam. This Hisham learnt how to debate atheists through Imam Ja'far as-Sadiq (as). Hisham said, "Whenever an atheist would debate me, I would go and ask Imam Ja'far as-Sadiq (as). He would give me an answer and I would go and tell the atheist and then he would become a Muslim."

He narrates that one day an atheist came to him and said, "Hisham, do you believe in God?" Hisham said, "Yes." "Can your God do anything?" "Yes." "If your God exists, can He fit the whole universe into an egg without the egg getting bigger or the universe getting smaller?" Hisham went to Imam Ja'far as-Sadiq (as). Imam looked at him and said, "Hisham, what's the matter?" Hisham said, "Imam, I've got a question and I cannot answer it." Imam Ja'far as-Sadiq (as) said, "You look like you have travelled; go and rest and come back to me tomorrow.".

He came back the next day. Imam Ja'far as-Sadiq (as) said, "Now tell me your question." Hisham said, "An atheist asked me, 'If God exists, can He fit the whole universe into an egg without the egg getting bigger or the universe getting smaller?" Imam said, "Do me a favor and go up to the top of our house and have a look at everything and come back." Hisham went to the terrace; he looked around and came back. Then Imam asked him, "Hisham, how many senses do you have as a human?" Hisham said, "Five." "Name them." "I can see, and I can touch, and I can taste, and I can smell, and I can hear." "What is the smallest source for your senses, Hisham?" "The smallest sources for sensory perception are my eyes." "What do you see with your eyes? What did you see when you were on top of the house?" "I saw trees and humans and buildings." "If Allah can fit all of those into your eyes, then why can He not fit the universe into an egg?"

If you go to New York and you see all those skyscrapers, have you ever wondered how Allah fits the image of a whole building into an eye?

On another day Hisham came to the Imam and said, "There is an atheist who wants to see you." Imam said, "Let him come to me." The atheist arrived and Imam Ja'far as-Sadiq (as) said, "Ask your question." He said, "Ja'far?" "Yes." "Show me God." "Simple. Look at the sun." He looked at the sun and then he turned his eyes. Imam said, "What is wrong?" He said, "The rays of the light of the sun are blinding me." "If you cannot bear to see the created, how do you expect to see the Creator?"

While the Banu Abbas were trying to stabilize their power, Imam Ja'far as-Sadiq (as) was controlling the situation from another perspective.

Another atheist came to Imam and said, "I can be like your God!" Imam said, "What do you mean?" He said, "You say your God creates?" "Yes." "I can create as well." "How?" "Give me some mud and some compost, and give me the right environment and the right temperature, I will let worms be created." "Go ahead, do it."

So the person went and got the mud and got the compost and within no time the worms were moving. Imam Ja'far as-Sadiq (as) said, "So what do you think now?" He said, "I am God." Imam said, "You are God?" He said, "Yes." "And these are your creatures?" "Yes, these are my creatures." "Very well, so these worms are of your creation?" "Yes, they are of my creation." "Let me ask you three questions about them because you know them so well." "Go ahead." "What is the gender of your creation?" "I do not know." "Okay, do not worry. What is the weight of each of your worms?" "I do not know." "Okay. Your worms are going one way; you as their god, order them to go another." "I cannot." Imam said, "I have never seen a god who does not know the weight of his creation and does not know the gender of his creation and cannot order his creation to go in the opposite direction." The person came towards Islam immediately saying, "I believe in your God, and I am not God."

Another student of Imam Ja'far as-Sadiq (as) was Sufyan al-Souri. Our Sufi brothers say that there were eight great Sufis; one of them was Sufyan. If you study Sufism, there are two things you will notice about this movement. Firstly, you always find the Sufis going back to the Imams of the Ahlulbayt, and secondly, many Sufis love Sufyan al-Souri. They say he was very spiritual. But ask them, "Do you know who his teacher was?" Many of them will say, "We do not know."

Sufyan studied under Imam Ja'far as-Sadiq (as). Sufyan used to say, "Do you know where I got my spirituality from? I got my spirituality from Ja'far b. Muhammad."

He narrates, "Wallah! I remember one day I was in his house, and he came and sat near me and he began to cry. I said to him, 'O Imam, why are you crying?' He said, 'Something happened to me yesterday that I have not recovered from.' I said, 'What is it?' He said, 'I had guests in my house and I asked one of the maids to bring the food. She brought the food along with her baby and the hot soup dropped on the baby and the baby passed away.' I said, 'Imam, why are you crying?' He said, 'I cannot believe that I as a master in my house brought such fear into one of my workers that my worker had to rush because of me. What type of master am I that I made my workers fear me? I am saddened by the fact that I made my worker rush and because of that her child passed away.' Wallah! I could not believe the humility of this man with so much knowledge, yet he could not sleep because of how much he was crying over this incident."

Thus, these students from the famous schools of Islam, all of them had studied under Imam Ja'far as-Sadiq (as).

Yet Imam Ja'far as-Sadiq (as) was not just a teacher in the classroom. He was a teacher outside of his classroom as well, even in his manners and his discipline. Imam Ja'far as-Sadiq (as) would speak out against al-Mansur al-Dawaniqi when he would see what he was doing to the Islamic State. One day Imam Ja'far as-Sadiq (as) was next to al-Mansur al-Dawaniqi and Imam saw a fly irritating him. Al-Mansur tried to move it away again and again, and then he asked Imam Ja'far as-Sadiq (as), "Ja'far b. Muhammad, why did God create flies?" Imam said, "Allah created flies so that they can humiliate the oppressors." Imam could have stayed quiet but he chose not to because he knew this man was an oppressor, and where there is oppression, there is also a need to stand up against oppression.

Some of the Imam's own cousins were giving him trouble towards the end of his life. Even his own Shi'a would come up to him and would say, "O Ja'far b. Muhammad, you can see these Abbasids are oppressing the people. Why don't you speak out? We are with you. We will fight them." He said, "You really want me to fight them? I do not have enough loyal Shi'as to fight these people." The person said, "Imam, I am here for you, and they are your Shi'a." Imam said, "Are you willing to do anything for me?" He said, "Yes, Imam. I am ready to do anything for you." Imam said, "You see that oven? Open it and go and sit inside it." (indicating unconditional submission) He said, "Imam? Come on." Harun al-Makki was walking by and Imam Ja'far as-Sadiq (as) looked at Harun and said, "Harun?" Harun said, "Yes, my master?" Imam said, "Do you see the clay oven?" He said, "Yes." Imam said, "Go and sit inside it." Harun said, "Okay," and went towards the oven, opened it and sat inside. Imam looked at the questioner who was stunned. He was thinking that Harun was getting burnt inside the oven. Then Imam said, "Harun, come out of the oven." Harun came out and walked away. Imam said to the man, "Did you see what happened?" He said, "Tell me." Imam said, "Harun al-Makki did not know that there was no fire in that oven. He went and opened it and he went inside because Ja'far b. Muhammad asked him to do so. You come and tell me, 'Let's fight al-Mansur al-Dawaniqi.' I asked you to do one thing and you run away? If I had more loyal people like Harun al-Makki, I would fight, but I do not have people like him."

In other words, Imam Ja'far as-Sadiq (as) could have revolted but it would not have led to success without loyal followers. He decided that the best option for him was to spread knowledge in that period. War would not have brought positive results whereas training students led to the revival of faith in their families and communities.

Words of Wisdom for His Shi'a Before He Passed Away

In the last moments of the life of Imam Ja'far as-Sadiq (as), there are some interesting things that occur which are lessons for all of us.

Imam Ja'far as-Sadiq (as) told his wife, "I want you to give seventy dinars to my cousin Hassan." She said, "Imam, your cousin, who tried to stab you because you did not fight Banu Abbas?" Imam said, "Yes, give him seventy dinars." She said, "How can you give money to someone who tried to stab you?" Imam said, "Oh my wife, do you want me to be of those to whom Allah looks down upon on the Day of Judgement because I never observed silat al-rahm?"

It is said that paradise can be smelled from two thousand years away but a person who had been disobedient to his parents and has broken relations with his family will never be able to smell paradise.

Imam's last words before he died is a message for all of us. He looked at his family and he said, "Tell my Shi'a that those who neglect their prayers will not receive our shifa'at (intercession) on the Day of Judgement."

He used the word "neglect" rather than "abandon," meaning those who take their prayers lightly, i.e., if the time to pray is at 1:00, they pray it at 6:00. The true 'Ja'fari' follower of Imam as-Sadiq (as) is one who never neglects his salat but rather ensures that his salat is disciplined and well looked after.

Just before he passed away, he said, "I promise those of my followers that if they perform my ziyarah in Medina, I will ask Allah to forgive their sins on the Day of Judgment and I will make sure that they never die in a state of poverty."

Time and again Imam would say, "Please, O my followers, be truthful and trustworthy and do not go against your promises because when you do that, people will say, 'That is the true Ja'fari follower of Ja'far as-Sadiq,' and if you do things which embarrass us, then people will say, 'Look at Ja'far as-Sadiq, he did not know how to bring up his followers.'"

It is vital for us that when we call ourselves "Ja'fari" and we honor the true message of Imam as-Sadiq (as).

Lecture 9

Imam Musa b. Ja'far al-Kadhim (as)

Imam Musa b. Ja'far (as) was born on the 7th of Safar in the 128th year after Hijra and died on the 25th of Rajab in the 183rd year after Hijra. He was a man from whose life many a lesson may be learnt and many an outstanding principle may be derived; he is a man revered for his patience, humility, piety, justice and stand against oppression. Imam Musa b. Ja'far (as), unfortunately, has not received systematic study. There are many who know of his existence but few know about his impact, both spiritually in terms of the legacy he left behind for the religion of Islam, and also in terms of his own character, from which there are many, many lessons that can be learnt which can then be applied in our everyday lives.

It is unbelievable to see the number of people who go to visit his shrine in Baghdad without knowing absolutely anything about his life. There are many who will travel to his shrine, stand there, pay their salutations and regards, but without the same emotion they show at other places of pilgrimage. The reason is due to their lack of knowledge regarding the life of Imam Musa b. Ja'far (as). Had a person studied the life of Imam Musa b. Ja'far (as) in depth then he would show much greater respect towards him and more emotion than the little that is shown by those who have not.

Therefore, let us examine this man, who was tortured more than any other of the Imams of Aal Muhammad (pbuh), and see what kind of impact his life has on our lives today.

His Birth and His Parents

The Imam was born on the 7th of Safar, and that is why the wiladah (birth) of Imam Musa b. Ja'far (as) is hardly celebrated in our communities because Safar is normally a time of grief. It is a time where the family of the Prophet (pbuh) was taken to the land of Syria in chains. That is why, for that forty-day period, or in some cases a sixty-eight day period, you find that many of our mosques will not necessarily honor his birth. He was born on the 7th of Safar in an area known as al-Abwa, between Mecca and Medina.

Mufadhil b. Umar narrates that "Imam Ja'far as-Sadiq (as) had a home that was a place where he would visit on his journey, for example, towards hajj or on his journey from Mecca back to Medina. This place was in an area called al-Abwa." He says, "I used to remember seeing Imam Ja'far as-Sadiq (as) in the middle of the hottest day plowing the earth and working. I would say to him, 'Imam, you are a man of knowledge and one for whom others would work on your behalf, why are you working like this? Why don't you let us do the work for you?' Imam replied by saying, 'And what is the shame in me earning a lawful living?'"

Just like everybody else, there were prophets who worked. Prophet Idris was a tailor; Prophet Musa was a shepherd; Prophet Dawud used to work with iron; Prophet Isa was a carpenter; the Holy Prophet himself worked for Lady Khadija.

One day in al-Abwa, Imam Ja'far as-Sadiq (as) was sitting with Abu Basir. Abu Basir narrates, "We had our breakfast; Imam Ja'far as-Sadiq (as) used to have a grand breakfast, from which he would make you eat and he would give you a wide variety of foods to choose from. All of a sudden somebody came up to him and said, 'Your wife Hamida is now going through labor and she wants you to be by her side.' Imam Ja'far as-Sadiq (as) left them and he went to Hamida. He came back later and said, 'I have glad tidings that Allah has given me the best gift and that is a son whose face resembles the face of Nabi Musa (as) and therefore I have decided to name him Musa.'"

He is the only Imam of the Imams of the Ahlulbayt who is named after a Prophet of God besides the Holy Prophet (pbuh). Thus Imam Musa b. Ja'far (as)'s father was Ja'far b. Muhammad (as); his mother's name was Hamida and she was from North Africa. One may ask, "Why would

Imam Ja'far as-Sadiq (as) marry a woman from Africa? Does not Imam Ja'far as-Sadiq (as) have enough women to choose from in Medina? Also, Imam Ja'far as-Sadiq (as) is a sayyed and is from the line of Amir al-Mu'mineen (as); aren't sayyeds only meant to marry sayyedas?"

If Imam Ja'far as-Sadiq (as) believed that sayyeds must only marry sayyedas or that Arabs must not marry non-Arabs, why did Imam marry a lady from North Africa? He could have easily said, "I am the son of Muhammad al-Baqir, who is the son of Zayn ul-Abideen, who is the son of Ali b. Hussein, who is the son of Hussein, who is the son of Ali, I have to marry only from that lineage." On the contrary, Imam Ja'far as-Sadiq (as) married someone from North Africa. He was highlighting to us that in Islam there is no such thing as marrying someone from your own caste. In Islam you can marry someone who is from your religion but from a different cultural background; someone whose race may be different from your own race. Thus the Imam was trying to show us that we should never reach a stage in our communities where we have even an inch of racism in our culture.

Imam Ja'far as-Sadiq (as) used to praise Hamida very highly. He used to say, "Allah is pleased with Hamida and she is pleased with whatever Allah has given her." He would also say to the ladies of Medina, "Whenever you have a question to ask, do not ask me. Ask my wife Hamida because my wife answers in exactly the same way I answer." One can only imagine at what level Hamida must have been. This is how a husband and wife's relationship should move forward together. In our communities today, either the husband is too religious and the wife is not; or the wife is too religious and the husband is not. Unfortunately, this causes a bit of friction at home. Sometimes the balance does not mean that both have to be religious, but that both of them are trying to become more and more religious. Unfortunately today, we have a situation where one is too religious while the other is not interested in the religion at all and of course this causes friction within the home. When Imam Ja'far as-Sadiq (as) married Hamida, he could have easily said, "I am the Imam. I am knowledgeable. You just act as my wife." On the contrary, his relationship was as if he was telling her, "Both of us will become religious together; both of us will gain knowledge of each other; both of us will interact with each other with our understanding of Islam." Therefore, when you have a mother who is as knowledgeable as she was, and a father who is knowledgeable, then naturally the young Imam will be extremely knowledgeable as well.

His Childhood

Imam Musa b. Ja'far (as), at the age of five, was teaching Abu Hanifa lessons about Islam. If you go to Pakistan and India and you ask the people, "What is your jurisprudence?" and they reply to you, "We are Hanafi," say to them, "Did you know that not only did Imam Ja'far as-Sadiq (as) teach Abu Hanifa, but that if Imam Ja'far as-Sadiq (as) would be busy, Imam Musa b. Ja'far (as), at the age of five, used to answer on his behalf?"

Abu Hanifa came one day to the house of Imam Ja'far as-Sadiq (as). He knocked at the door and Imam Musa b. Ja'far (as) emerged. When he emerged, Abu Hanifa said to him, "Is your father here?" mam said, "Yes, but he is a bit busy." Abu Hanifa said, "Then I will wait." Imam said, "Is there anything I can help you with?" "No, no, I think your father can answer it for me." "No, no. Ask me." "Okay, young man. When we commit a sin, is it Allah who makes us sin? Is it Allah and us? Or is it us alone who commit a sin?" "O Abu Hanifa, if it is Allah who makes us commit a sin, then it would not be fair that He would put us in hell when He made us commit the sin; if it is us and Allah then once again it is not fair that we would be punished when He was part of the crime; therefore it is us who have been given the choice of free will. We can either stay away from sin or we can continue sinning." Abu Hanifa was in his old age when Imam Musa b. Ja'far (as), at the age of five, answered his question.

On another occasion Abu Hanifa came to Imam Ja'far as-Sadiq (as) one day and said to him, "Ja'far b. Muhammad, I saw your son Musa al-Kadhim praying today, but I do not think he knows how to pray properly." Imam Ja'far as-Sadiq (as) looked at him and said, "What do you mean?" "When someone walked past him in salat, he did not stick his hand out."

If you walk past our brothers in Islam in salat, do not be surprised if their hand comes out like that. This is because they say that you should not walk past someone in salat.

Imam Ja'far as-Sadiq (as) said, "O Abu Hanifa, why don't you go and teach him?" Abu Hanifa said, "Very well." He came to Imam Musa b. Ja'far (as) who was five years old at the time. He said to Imam, "Young man, I need to teach you about salat." Imam said, "Go ahead." "When someone walks past you in your salat, you must put your hand out and block them. I just saw someone walk past you now and you did not block them." "O Abu Hanifa, Allah says that He is closer to me than my jugular vein; while I was praying, I was so focused on my Lord that I did not see any human being walk past me."

Thus, at that young age, Imam Musa b. Ja'far (as), being the student of his father and his African mother Hamida, was able to achieve this prowess; and that is why many people were in awe of the young Imam Musa b. Ja'far (as). Many people used to love him because they saw a young man who had all the pleasures of the world in front of him but went towards Allah (swt). The Holy Prophet (pbuh) used to say, "Allah loves to see nothing more than a youth who turns away from all of these forbidden acts and turns towards Allah (swt)."

People used to say, "When we would pass that small house, we would know that the young Imam Musa b. Ja'far (as) would be in the house as we could hear him reciting his prayers in the most beautiful voice; and you could see the tears coming down from his eyes and you could hear him say, "Ya Mohsin, qad ata kal Musi - O Doer of Good and O You who is All-Good, the sinner has come to you."

Imam Musa b. Ja'far (as) lived during the reign of many caliphs. He saw the reigns of as-Saffah, al-Mansur, al-Hadi, al-Mehdi and Harun ar-Rashid. All of them lived in huge palaces some of which are present in Baghdad even today. The names of some of the palaces are Dar ur-Raqeeq, Qasr ul-Ghul, Qasr ush-Shakiriyyah. While the caliphs lived there, Imam Musa b. Ja'far (as) lived in a small house. Today we ask, "Which palace adorns Baghdad 1,200 years later?" Now it is the grand palace of Imam Musa b. Ja'far (as) that stands in Baghdad.

The Beginning of His Imamate

Imam Musa b. Ja'far (as) was twenty years old when his father died. When Imam Ja'far as-Sadiq (as) died, al-Mansur al-Dawaniqi tried to play a trick on him in order to end the Imamate, which Imam Ja'far as-Sadiq (as) had already foreseen and defeated. When Imam Ja'far as-Sadiq (as) died, al-Mansur al-Dawaniqi wrote to his governor in Medina, "I have heard the news that Ja'far b. Muhammad has died; find out whom he has said will be the leader after him in his wasiya and behead the person." Al-Mansur al-Dawaniqi believed that these Imams had to be killed off to safeguard his rule.

The governor in Medina was called Sulayman. He got the will of Imam Ja'far as-Sadiq (as) and read it to see whose name he had written in it. He went through the list of all his wishes in the will and finally came to the part where it was written, "...and my successors are five: al-Mansur al-Dawaniqi; Sulayman (the governor of Medina, and the one who was reading the wasiya); Abdullah; Hamida; and Musa b. Ja'far." Now Sulayman was wondering what to do, as al-Mansur al-Dawaniqi's orders were to behead whoever's name was on the list. So he wrote back to al-Mansur al-Dawaniqi, who was anxiously waiting for the message to arrive from Sulayman. When it finally came, he said, "Give it to me quickly. Quickly." As al-Mansur read the names, he realized he could not execute anyone on the list because he would also have had to get someone to kill him as well.

Thus Imam Musa b. Ja'far (as) was safe and began his Imamate at the age of twenty. When he began his Imamate, the first thing people noticed in his Imamate was that he was a man who was able to restrain his anger however much disrespect one showed him. His title was "al-Kadhim." There is a verse of the Quran (3:34) which says, "Wal Kadhimin al-ghaiz..." "Kadhim" means the one who is able to restrain his anger in a moment of difficulty.

When he received the Imamate at the age of twenty, there were people who used to insult him and curse him and never in his life did he ever reply back to them. That is why each one of us should be a Kadhim, especially when we have an Imam who was such. How many of us have an anger problem in our lives? Then ask yourself, "Why am I not like my Imam Musa b. Ja'far (as)?"

One day as Imam Musa b. Ja'far (as) was walking, this man came up to him and said, "Curse be on your father and on you!" The companions of Imam Musa b. Ja'far (as) wanted to approach the man, but the Imam said, "Wait, wait, wait...leave him." A couple of days later Imam Musa b. Ja'far (as) said, "How do you think we should approach this man?" It is vital that, when we hear these stories of the Ahlulbayt, we must implement their attributes in our life. They said, "Imam, we should punish him... attack him...confiscate his... " He said, "No. Leave this man to me." A few days later, the Imam inquired about the man and he was told that he was in his garden. Imam walked towards the garden of this man. As he entered the garden, the man saw him and said, "What are you doing here? You son of..." Imam looked at him and said, "What is the problem?" He said, "You have already damaged my garden with your footsteps." Imam said, "How much have you spent on this garden?" He said, "One hundred dinars." "How much do you expect to make from it?" "Two hundred dinars." "Here, take this."

When the man counted it, it was exactly three hundred dinars. The man looked at Imam Musa b. Ja'far (as) and said, "But look at the way I cursed you. I cursed Ja'far as-Sadiq and I cursed you." Imam said, "We, the Ahlulbayt, have been taught to instill akhlaq not only in the lives of mankind but in our lives as well. I could have easily replied to you, but I want you to understand that humanity will never survive if each of us attack each other like that." Thus people would call him "al-Kadhim."

One person said, "Wallah, I saw him one day in his house when someone dropped water all over his cloak, and the person looked at him and said, "Bismillah al-Rahman al-Rahim… wa'l-Kadhimin al-ghaiz…" Imam said, "I have restrained my anger…" "Wal afeena an in-nas…" "I have forgiven you…" "Wallah yuhibb al-muhsineen." "I have freed you for the sake of Allah (swt)!"

This attribute of Imam Musa b. Ja'far (as) was at the beginning of his life, and he would later need this same trait when he was in prison for more than fifteen years. It was due to this attribute that people would respect him and learn from him. If your akhlaq is good, people will listen to your knowledge, but if your knowledge is good and you do not have akhlaq, then no one will listen to you. Imam Musa b. Ja'far (as) first touched the people through his morals so that they could know that he was sincere in giving this knowledge.

One day Imam Musa b. Ja'far (as) was walking; he went past a house where music was being played. He saw a lady sweeping outside that same home. He said to her, "May I ask you a question?" She said, "Go ahead." "Is the owner of the house a free man or a slave?" "Of course, he is a free man." "Yes, of course he is, because if he was a slave he would know which master was watching him." She heard him and thought, "I had never thought about it like this; if truly I am an 'abd' (slave of Allah), then how much am I not respecting my master by playing music at home?"

The narrations state that she went back in the house and her husband asked her what happened. She said, "Oh, I was just talking to someone outside." "What did he say?" "I do not know. He looked like a very humble man and he just asked me a question." "What was the question?" "He said, 'Is the owner of the house a free man or a slave?' So I said to him, 'He is a free man.'" "What did he say then?" "I heard him say, 'Yes, definitely he is a free man because if he was a slave then he would know that the master was watching him.'" "Can you describe him to me?" "Yes. He had this kind of complexion, beard, height." "That is Musa b. Ja'far!" He ran out of the house without even wearing his slippers. He looked for Imam Musa b. Ja'far (as) until he found him. He said, "O Imam, forgive me. Wallah, I have never thought of music in the way you described it. In the past I heard people say that music was haram but it never made sense to me. But the way you described it, it made sense. How can I play music in a house when I claim to be a servant of Allah (swt)." "Do not worry. If you regret it and performed tawba, Allah will forgive you."

That person is held in very high esteem by the Sufis today; they call him Bishr al-Hafi. Al-Hafi in Arabic means "the one who walks barefoot." They call him that because he ran out of his house to Imam Musa b. Ja'far (as) barefoot. Look at the lesson Imam Musa b. Ja'far (as) taught. He did not tell him straight to his face, "Music is haram; you are going to be punished if you listen to music." No. He subtly implied, how can you say in salat that you are an "abd" of Allah, yet in your house you are listening to the people who oppose Allah (swt)? An interesting article, published in Islamic Culture, is Hamid Algar's 1990 analysis of the Imam in Sufi tradition.

The Political Situation During His Imamate

That aspect of Imam being "Kadhim" was needed in his life because the amount of oppression committed against the Shi'a at the time was severe. There has never been a period in Islamic history when the Shi'a of Aal Muhammad have been oppressed in such a way as they were during the time of the Imamate of Imam Musa b. Ja'far (as). Under the reign of the caliphs of his time, the Shi'a could not practice their faith openly; they had to adopt "taqiyya." This is when you have to conceal your belief because you are in a life or death situation. Many of the great companions of Imam Musa b. Ja'far (as) had to resort to taqiyya. Ibrahim al-Jofi, Ahmed al-Halabi and Ahmed al-Bazanti were a few, amongst others, who had to conceal their faith.

Those caliphs were terrorizing anyone who was a follower of Aal Muhammad. Imam ar-Ridha had a hadith that said, "If it was not for the event of Karbala, the worst tragedy to have affected our Ahlulbayt was the tragedy of Fakh." Dabbal b. Ali al-Khuza'i even has poetry about their graves in Fakh. What happened in Fakh?

After al-Mansur al-Dawaniqi died, his son Hadi became the caliph. Hadi had a governor in Medina who used to oppress the Shi'a so much that he made a sign-up sheet in his palace where, if you were a Shi'i or an Alid (a descendant of Imam 'Ali or Lady Fatima) living in Medina, you had to sign in every morning and evening. This was so that he knew what you were doing and record all of your movements. It was mandatory for every Shi'i, whether man, woman or child, to come in the morning and evening and sign in in the palace. Imam Musa b. Ja'far (as) had two cousins: Hussein b. Ali al-Khair and Hassan al-Aftas. This governor of Hadi caught Hassan al-Aftas and whipped him two hundred times in public for being a follower of Ahlulbayt. And on top of that, he spread rumors about him that, "because we caught him drinking, we have to punish him and we need to parade his body on a donkey." Hussein b. Ali al-Khair went to this governor and said, "Listen, I know my cousin was not drinking; moreover, the punishment for drinking alcohol in Islam is eighty lashes. Why have you punished him with two hundred lashes? Also, in Islam you do not parade a body on a donkey." The governor said, "Who are you to speak to me like that? You and your Shi'a are not even allowed to practice your faith under my rule! Get out!"

Hussein b. Ali al-Khair decided to tell all the Shi'a to rise and not sit and watch. The narration states that Hassan al-Aftas removed the governor and went on top of the governor's palace. He said, "Hayya alas salat; Hayya alal Falah; Hayya ala khairal amal! All of you rise!" The family of the Aal Muhammad (pbuh) rose under the leadership of Hussein and Hussein's sister, Zaynab. History repeated itself a hundred years after Karbala. Two hundred and thirty-two members of Aal Muhammad (pbuh) rose up against these people. Hussein told Zaynab, "My sister Zaynab, when the blood reaches your ankles, then cast this paper, which lists the names of our followers, in the blood because we do not want our followers to get caught if we die."

When Hussein got killed, the governor took all the children of Aal Muhammad (pbuh) who survived to Baghdad to meet the caliph, al-Hadi.

All these children were sitting in front of al-Hadi. Imagine all the children of the Ahlulbayt and grandchildren of Lady Fatima (as), all of them were standing in front of al-Hadi. He looked at them and said, "Who are they?" He was told, "They are the grandchildren of Fatima Zahra." He said, "Oh, they are the ones related to Musa b. Ja'far?" "Yes." "Very well, bring me a sword." "What are you going to do?" "I want you to make them all stand next to each other. Let's see how many heads I can cut at the same time."

Today we have followers of the Ahlulbayt who say, "It is hard for me to be religious." In reality, they do not know an inch about those who came before them.

Al-Hadi got his sword and he beheaded them one by one. Imam ar-Ridha said, "Were it not for the incident of Karbala, the worst incident to affect us was the incident of Fakh."

Al-Hadi told everyone there, "I swear this whole uprising is because of Musa b. Ja'far!" Abu Yusuf al-Qazi was there and he said, "No, I can swear on my children that Musa b. Ja'far did not tell anyone to rise." Al-Hadi said, "I will find Musa b. Ja'far and I will kill him!" The narration states that Yaqtin (the father of Ali b. Yaqtin, a great companion of the Imam) said to Imam Musa b. Ja'far (as), "Imam, be careful; this al-Hadi wants to find you and kill you." Imam said, "Let me just recite salat." After salat he recited the dua Jawshan as-Sagheer and after finishing he said, "Now do not worry. You will hear the news of his death shortly." No sooner had Imam said this and they got the news of his death.

After al-Hadi died, al-Mahdi assumed the caliphate. After him, the worst caliph, in terms of his cruel treatment towards an Imam of the Ahlulbayt, was Harun ar-Rashid. If Harun found out that anyone was part of the Shi'a, they were immediately beheaded.

Nobody could teach or attend Shi'a gatherings. The only way they could do it was, for example, if a Shi'i sold butter, then while selling butter, he would educate a fellow Shi'i about the teachings of the Ahlulbayt. As soon as the guard of Harun ar-Rashid would walk past them, he would change the conversation and say, "Okay, three kilograms of butter? Here you go."

Another companion of Imam Musa b. Ja'far (as) was Ali b. Yaqtin, who was the minister for Harun ar-Rashid. First when Ali b. Yaqtin came towards the Ahlulbayt, he wrote a letter to Imam Musa b. Ja'far (as) and said, "Imam, how do us, the followers of Ahlulbayt, do our wudu'?" Imam wrote back to him saying, "We perform our wudu' by washing our face, and then washing our hands, and then wiping our head, and then washing our feet." Ali b. Yaqtin said, "When I read the letter, I was shocked to see that he said 'washing our feet.' We do not wash our feet. We wipe our feet. But Imam Musa b. Ja'far (as) would not make a mistake, so what do I do? Do I wash or do I wipe?"

Someone was jealous of Ali b. Yaqtin and told Harun ar-Rashid, "I think that Ali b. Yaqtin is a lover of Musa al-Kadhim." Harun ar-Rashid said, "Why?" He said, "Because I've seen him talk about him and he talks about him in a pleasant way." Harun ar-Rashid said, "Ali b. Yaqtin would never leave my way. This is not true." That person said, "No, it is. I promise you it is." Harun ar-Rashid said, "Very well, tomorrow I will find out." The person said, "How?" Harun ar-Rashid said, "We will go and spy on Ali b. Yaqtin in wudu'." (There is a moment in your life where you unconditionally submit to your Imam or you pick and choose what of Islam you like and what you don't like. Ali b. Yaqtin was reading a letter where Imam Musa b. Ja'far (as) said to him, "Wash," whereas Ali knew you have to wipe; but if your Imam says, "Wash," then you have to wash.)

Harun ar-Rashid was watching him through the window. Ali was doing his wudu'; he washed his face, then his hands, wiped his head, and then it was the moment of truth where he was thinking, "Do I listen to my Imam or do I do what I think is right?" As he approached the masah of his feet, he chose to listen to his Imam, and he began washing his feet. Harun ar-Rashid immediately said to the man, "I told you he hasn't joined Musa al-Kadhim; look, he washes his feet like we wash our feet." On many occasions the Imam would direct his companions thus.

Harun ar-Rashid had put the Imam in prison for two reasons: Harun ar-Rashid looked at Imam Musa b. Ja'far (as) one day and said, "Why do you sons of Ali b. Abi Talib think you are better than us, the sons of Abbas?" They were cousins. Imam was from the line of Abu Talib whereas Harun ar-Rashid was from the line of Abbas. Abu Talib and Abbas were brothers; but sometimes cousins can hate each other.

Imam Musa b. Ja'far (as) said, "Harun, we come from Abu Talib; you come from Abbas; the Prophet's father Abdullah is from the same father and mother as Abu Talib whereas Abbas's mother is different." Harun ar-Rashid said, "But Abu Talib died and Abbas remained alive and the heritage of the Prophet remains with Abbas not Abu Talib." Imam said, "Yes, but the heritage of the Prophet remains in his child not in his uncle and we are the sons of Fatima; O Harun ar-Rashid, if the Prophet came to propose for your daughter would you give your daughter to him?" Harun ar-Rashid said, "Yes, it would be my honor." Imam said, "But I could not give him my child because he is the father of our mother; he would never come to us for marriage. Therefore our line is a straight connection and yours is an indirect connection."

Harun ar-Rashid was not happy at hearing this at all. It made him envious, and he needed a rumor to be spread about Imam Musa b. Ja'far (as). He used Imam's brother Isma'il to spread this rumor. Isma'il was the brother of Imam Musa b. Ja'far (as) from a different mother, and he died before Imam Ja'far as-Sadiq (as). Some of the Shi'as believed that because he was the eldest son, that meant he should be the Imam after Imam Ja'far as-Sadiq (as); and even if he was dead, his son should become the Imam, whereas in the School of Ahlulbayt, it is not the eldest son who becomes the Imam, but rather whomever Allah chooses becomes the Imam.

Isma'il had a son called Muhammad. Yahya Barmaki told Ali, "We will pay you a certain amount of money if you come to Baghdad and spread rumors about Musa b. Ja'far." The narrations say that before Muhammad b. Isma'il left Medina, Imam Musa b. Ja'far (as) asked his nephew, "Where are you going?" He said, "I am going to Baghdad." "I have debts which I need to pay." "Ali, I will pay your debts. You do not need to go to Baghdad." "No, I want to go. Give me a piece of advice, O uncle." "Do not be the cause of the bloodshed of me and my family; Muhammad, here is three hundred dinars." One of Imam's companions asked him, "Imam, why did you give him three hundred dinars? You know what this man is going to do." Imam said, "The Prophet used to say, 'Look after your relatives; if your relatives do evil to you later, that is Allah's concern not yours.'"

Muhammad travelled all the way to Harun ar-Rashid. On reaching his palace, he saw Yahya Barmaki sitting next to Harun. "What is it Muhammad?," Harun said. Ali said, "You know this Musa b. Ja'far? He is sitting in Medina and collecting weapons and he is raising an army to kill you." He did this all for money. Harun ar-Rashid said, "O people, did you hear this?" They said, "Yes." He said, "Now do you allow me to put him in my prison?" The people said, "Yes." Muhammad b. Isma'il said, "Now can I have my reward?" Harun ar-Rashid gave him the pouch. When he went to open the pouch, he saw that there was two hundred dinars in the pouch whereas Imam had given him three hundred. When he saw the two hundred dinars, he could not believe it and he choked and died at that moment. He let down his uncle, and from then on Harun ar-Rashid took over Imam Musa b. Ja'far (as)'s life.

Imam's Life in Prison

Imam Musa b. Ja'far (as) was moved from prison to prison; he spent more than fifteen years in prison. The first prison was in Basra; then they took him to Qantara prison; then they took him to the prison of Fadl b. Rabi'i. When Imam Musa b. Ja'far (as) first entered the prison, his first words were, "Ya Allah! All my life I have asked you to give me the honor of worshipping you in a place alone. I now thank you that you have given me this honor."

When the Imam was transferred to Fadl b. Rabi'i's prison, Fadl said to Ahmad al-Qazwini, "Ahmed, come with me to my prison," so he came. Fadl said to him, "What do you see in the prison?" He said, "I see a white robe." Fadl said, "No, no, no. Look closer." He said, "I see a white robe." "No, that's Musa b. Ja'far in sujood; the whole time in prison he is steady in his sujood."

Harun ar-Rashid sent the most beautiful girl in all of Arabia to Imam Musa b. Ja'far (as)'s prison cell. When she entered the prison cell, she said to Imam, "O man, whatever you want from me, I will give it you," and he did not reply. She asked a second time and he did not reply, and the third time she said, "Please, whatever you want, I will give it you. The caliph has sent me." She narrates, "He turned around to me and said, 'O lady, why would I want what you offer when Allah has offered more?'" By the time the guards entered the prison, they saw Imam Musa b. Ja'far (as) in sujood and the lady behind him in sujood.

Harun ar-Rashid used to send people into the prison who did not speak Arabic to try and torture the Imam, but eventually even they would come out as Muslims. Harun ar-Rashid would ask them, "What's wrong with you? You people were meant to kill Musa b. Ja'far!" They said, "The man started speaking to us in our language and we became Muslims from his words." Fadl b. Rabi'i used to say, "How can I torture a man who fasts in the daytime and prays in the night?"

Then they transferred the Imam to the prison of Fadl b. Yahya, and towards the end they took him to the prison of as-Sindhi. Although the other prisons were tight spaces; as-Sindhi's prison was a pit so narrow that one had to remain standing inside it. On top of the hole they would place a rock so that one wouldn't know the difference between day or night. Imam Musa b. Ja'far (as) used to say to the guards, "I do not know the difference between the day and night. When you want to pray your salat, I beg you to come and tell me so I can attempt to pray my salat."

There is a narration that states that one day, they once removed the rock from the top of the hole and Imam Musa b. Ja'far (as) tried to look outside for some daylight. All of a sudden a man came and smacked him and began to kick the face of Imam Musa b. Ja'far (as) with his legs. There are so many of us today who go to the grave of Imam Musa b. Ja'far (as) and do not cry by his grave because we do not know anything about his life. No Imam of Ahlulbayt was tortured like Imam Musa b. Ja'far (as). Of course there are no days like Aba Abdullah, but there are no years like Imam Musa al-Kadhim (as).

We cannot even imagine how they must have tortured Imam Musa b. Ja'far (as) in prison. Normally an Imam has a great threshold for pain and troubles, but Imam al-Kadhim's last dua in prison throws some light on his state. He said, "Ya Allah! All my years I asked You to allow me to worship You alone and I thank You for that honor, but Ya Allah, I beg you now to release me from the prison of Harun."

Ali b. Su'ade narrates, "I got through to the prison of Imam Musa b. Ja'far (as) and asked him, 'O Imam, when are you coming out? Your Shi'a are waiting!'" Imam said, "O Ali, I will be out on Friday morning on the bridge of Baghdad." Ali narrates, "I went and told all our Shi'a that Imam Musa b. Ja'far (as) is going to be released so let's all gather on the bridge of Baghdad on Friday. On Friday, we went to the bridge of Baghdad and we heard a man saying, 'There is a janaza here!' When we went there we saw a body lying on the ground on the bridge of Baghdad. We came towards the body and we were wondering whose body this was. When we went closer, we saw that it was Imam Musa b. Ja'far (as)'s body that was on the bridge. There was a Christian doctor with me and I said to him, 'Come and look at this body'; when he came and looked at the body, he said, 'Does this man have any family?' I said, 'Why?' He said, 'Because they should ask for blood money.' I said, 'Why?' He said, "Because the poison has surrounded his whole body."

Sheikh Ahmed al-Waeli is one of the greatest reciters in Islamic history and he narrates his experience: One day in Baghdad I came home and I saw my wife and daughter crying. I asked why they were crying and my wife told me that while my daughter was playing with a glass, it broke and a piece went in her eye and her entire eye was cut open. I rushed and got a doctor who examined my daughter and said that she would never be able to see with that eye again. I immediately said, "I am going to Imam Musa b. Ja'far's grave in Baghdad!" I went there and stood by the grave and said, "O Imam, I have said you are Bab ul-Hawa'ij! Show me now. My daughter's eye is cut and she cannot see." I returned home and my wife was smiling. I said to her, "What is it?" She said, "Look at your daughter." I looked at my daughter and her eye was back in the same state again. That was the day I realized the meaning of Bab ul-Hawa'ij. When the Christian doctor saw the girl again, he said, "I cannot believe that the eye is back to normal like this!"

Lecture 10

Imam Ali b. Musa ar-Ridha (as)

Imam Ali b. Musa ar-Ridha (as) was born on 11th of Dhil Qad'ah in the 148th year after Hijra. He died, according to varying reports, on the 23rd Dhil Qad'ah in the 203rd year after Hijra. He is a man from whose life extraordinary lessons may be learnt and many principles may be derived, especially principles concerning politics and society within which we live our everyday lives. Unfortunately, his life has been understudied. There is not enough value that has been given to the status of Imam Ali b. Musa (as), in the idea that there may be many who admire him but do not necessarily have enough knowledge about his biography. And indeed you find that the period within which he was living in was one of the most turbulent times for any of the Imams of Aal Muhammad. The Abbasid Empire had established itself and therefore he had to find his position within the empire. Until today, unfortunately, many people ask the question, "How could Imam Ali b. Musa take a position under a tyrannical leader?" Through the examination of his biography we will address this question and appreciate his legacy.

His Parents

Imam Ali b. Musa (as) was one of thirty-seven children. Imam Musa b. Ja'far (as) had nineteen daughters and eighteen sons, which is even more extraordinary when you read that Imam Musa b. Ja'far (as) spent a lengthy part of his life in prison. That is why today you will find the legacy of Imam Musa b. Ja'far (as) is so great that most of the Sadat (Sayyeds) are Musawi. There are many Musawis in Lebanon, Iran and Pakistan; and they are so numerous because of the fact that Imam Musa b. Ja'far (as) had many children. Therefore, Imam Ali b. Musa (as) was one of the thirty-seven children of Imam Musa b. Ja'far (as). Of course, the thirty-seven children came from the various wives of Imam Musa b. Ja'far (as), and Imam Ali b. Musa (as) was born from the wife who was from North Africa. Therefore, she was the second of the wives of the Imams of Ahlulbayt from North Africa. According to certain reports her name was Arwa; other narrations mention her as being called Najma; and yet other narrations also mention her as Tuktum. Possibly, some of these names could be her actual names and some may be her titles.

Imam Ali b. Musa ar-Ridha (as)'s mother was of North African decent and Imam Musa b. Ja'far (as)'s mother was North African as well. Some people ask, "Why would the Imams of Ahlulbayt marry women from North Africa? Why did they not stick to the women of their own city of Medina?"

As mentioned earlier, the first reason is that Islam wanted to break all racial boundaries. Islam wanted to come as a religion where everybody is welcome, not just a certain race. A religion that only caters to a certain race is a racist religion; and do not be surprised if that type of religion exists today where it is very difficult for you to convert to that religion. Islam, from day one, focused on the fact that everybody is equal and all of us came from Adam, and Adam came from Allah (swt). Therefore, the first reason was to remove racism.

On a second level, the Imams wanted to exemplify to those areas that had been colonized and conquered by Islam, such as Africa, that you should not see yourself as second-class citizens just because we have conquered you. You are as much a part of our religion as we are. When the Imam married a lady from North Africa, the Imam was exemplifying the fact that if I am an Arab and the caliphs have conquered Africa, then the Africans who have come into Islam are as much a part of our religion as we are. The Muslims today try and tell people who have only recently converted to Islam that, "You are latecomers while we are veterans who have precedence over you," whereas when the seventh Imam married the eighth Imam's mother, he was implying that she is as much part of this religion as I am.

The third reason is that sometimes the traits and attributes of a different culture may be different from ours; an Arab culture may be known for its generosity but the African culture may be known for its humility. If people from these two cultures marry each other, then those beautiful attributes can come together.

Therefore, Imam Ali b. Musa (as)'s mother was from North Africa, and his parents decided to name him Ali. Someone asked, "From the twelve Imams, why are four of them called Ali?" The reason was because, from the time of the Umayyads until Banu Abbas, they kept on trying to erase the name Ali, but the Ahlulbayt kept on bringing it back: Imam Ali b. Abi Talib (as), Imam Ali Zayn ul-Abideen (as), Imam Ali ar-Ridha (as), and Imam Ali al-Hadi (as). The reason Aal Muhammad were stressing the name Ali was because every generation of an Islamic Empire always tried to execute people who were named Ali.

For example, Mu'awiya once looked at Abdullah b. Abbas and said, "I heard you have good news?" Ibn Abbas said, "Yes." "I hear you have a newborn baby." "Yes." "What have you decided to name him?" "Ali." "And what is the title you are giving him?" "I'm going to give him the title, Abul Hassan." "So you are giving both of these names to the child, Ali and Abul Hassan?" "Yes." "Ibn Abbas, pick one of them and not two if you want to survive in my community. I am not allowing both the names."

Similarly, Hajjaj b. Yusuf al-Thaqafi, once asked his men on Eid ul-Adha what the people slaughter on that day and he was told, "Sheep." He said, "Very well, then we will slaughter anyone called Ali, Hassan and Hussein."

So when the Ahlulbayt named Imam Ali b. Musa ar-Ridha (as) with the name Ali, the motive was that they did not want this name ever to be erased, because the hatred towards Imam Ali b. Abi Talib (as) moved from one generation to another.

From a young age Imam Ali b. Musa ar-Ridha (as) faced very difficult circumstances. Imagine a child born into this world who asks, "Where is my father?" and he is told, "He is in prison in Basra." Five years later, again that child asks, "Where is my father?" and he is told, "He is in prison in Baghdad."

Thus, in the beginning of his life, Imam Ali b. Musa ar-Ridha (as) faced the most difficult trial in that he could hardly see Imam Musa b. Ja'far (as).

They were moving Imam Musa b. Ja'far (as) from one prison to another and therefore there was an added responsibility on the shoulders of Imam Ali b. Musa ar-Ridha (as) because, firstly, the followers of Ahlulbayt could not reveal their true identity, and those that could, could not go to the Imam of their time, so they would all approach Imam Ali b. Musa ar-Ridha (as).

The First Part of His Life

Imam Ali b. Musa (as)'s life is divided into two sections: the first thirty-five years of his life when his father was alive but was in prison and the next twenty years of his life when he became the Imam. In those first thirty-five years when Imam Musa b. Ja'far (as) was in prison, Imam Ali b. Musa ar-Ridha (as) knew that there was no way he could speak out against the Banu Abbas because many of his Shi'a were in taqiyya (concealing their true faith), so he decided that it was better for him to sit in the mosque of the Prophet in Medina and give lessons to the Muslims on how to build a Muslim community. Most people only know about Imam Ali b. Musa ar-Ridha (as)'s life in Mashhad or Toos, but Imam Ali b. Musa (as) spent the first thirty-five years of his life in the Prophet (pbuh)'s mosque in Medina. The Ahlulbayt used to love the land of Medina; that was their home.

Imam knew that the Muslims at the time had forgotten the concept of "a community." During the rule of the Banu Abbas and the Umayyads, there were different schools and segments of Islam and Muslims and there wasn't a united community. He wanted to build a community where people would begin to realize their role within the community that they lived in. There were four key lessons that he taught about how to build a successful Muslim community.

The first lecture he gave was a lecture about cleanliness. He said, "Keep yourselves clean for it is the manners of the Prophets of Allah." A community can never survive if there is no cleanliness. For example, ask a person who is smoking outside a mosque and throws his cigarette butt on the ground and walks away, "Would you do the same thing in your home? Do you smoke your cigarettes and throw them in your front yard? Or do you make sure that you actually look after your yard?" For some people it is a very natural reaction to use something and then throw it on the ground. There are so many unmaintained Muslim mosques in the world today where one may see a banana peel lying on the ground, rice on the floor and smelly carpets whereas Imam Ali b. Musa ar-Ridha (as) used to insist on the community being clean as his grandfather, the Prophet (pbuh), had a famous saying, "Cleanliness is part of faith." Therefore, do not call yourself a believer if you have no concept of cleanliness. It is very surprising to see that in modern day Muslim communities there is so much trash lying around their institutions and homes. When you ask them about this, they casually disregard it by saying, "There are cleaners who will come and pick it up." The question to ask them is, "Are you not a cleaner of Allah's earth? Do you have no respect of Allah's environment over your own mosque?"

But is cleanliness only about that? Cleanliness also targets our own personal hygiene. How many of us have been for ziyarah and seen the state of our public lavatories? When one sees the conditions of those restrooms, one cannot help but ask, "Are we all followers of Imam Ali b. Musa ar-Ridha (as)?" How many times has it happened that when you come to the mosque and sit next to a person and it seems that he has not had a bath in years? That same person may go to a wedding and cover himself with perfume. Is it normal to come to the house of Allah smelling so awful? Some people are of the opinion that it is part of being modest to come smelling like that to the mosque. On the contrary, religiosity comes when you are in a state of cleanliness. Thus Imam Ali b. Musa (as)'s first lecture was on cleanliness.

Another lecture of the Imam was about dishonesty in a community. He said, "A Muslim who is dishonest with another Muslim is not one of us." Sometimes we find in our communities that there is a person who recites the salawat loudly and enthusiastically, but in his personal life he has been extremely dishonest with many Muslims. He has lied to people, stolen people's money, and he backbites about the people in his community, whereas Imam says that a community cannot be built if people are dishonest with one another.

In his third lecture about the community, the Imam said, "The worst of you is one whose existence is of no use to the community." These are the type of people who will attend the gathering at the mosque, hear the sermon and then leave and complain. Every time you ask them to help, they say they are busy but they will be the first to complain about the community and will do nothing to help solve the issues.

His fourth lecture was regarding how to employ people and treat those employees in your community. He taught the people through his own actions on how to do so. Once Imam passed a particular field with his companions. He looked in the field and asked, "Who is that over there?" His companion said, "That is a worker who just started to work today." Imam said, "How much are we paying him?" The companion said, "At the end of the day we will see what he's done and then we will pay him." The companion narrates, "I saw Ali b. Musa ar-Ridha's face become red. He looked at me and said, 'What did you say?' I said, 'Imam, we will fix his wage at the end of the day.' Imam said, 'How many times have I told you that before someone works in the community, fix their wage; do not leave it until after they have finished for they may be expecting a certain amount and you may give them less than that amount.'" Then the Imam said, "A sign of a follower of Aal Muhammad is that he always gives a bit more than he agreed upon."

Thus, in those early years, Imam Ali b. Musa ar-Ridha (as) spent a lot of time talking about the uplifting of his community.

The Political Conditions During the Second Part of His Life

Then when Imam Musa b. Ja'far (as) passed away, Imam Ali b. Musa ar-Ridha (as) was thirty-five years old, and that is when he had to now come into public life. Imam Ali b. Musa ar-Ridha (as) became the Imam in the most difficult of times. The Banu Abbas were masters in the art of public relations. On the surface they looked like the best leaders in Islamic history as the people could not see what was happening in their private lives. Even today, when you look at many Muslim countries, and you go to visit them in the Gulf, you will see the grandest mosques, and the grandest libraries and buildings. If a non-Muslim were to see it, they would say, "Oh my God! This Muslim Empire is magnificent! Look how modern it is!" But they wouldn't know about the corruption that exists deep within that state. They do not know about the people who are tortured and persecuted.

Thus, Imam Ali b. Musa ar-Ridha (as) became the Imam in such a time when the Banu Abbas had begun one of the best acts of public relations ever done in Islamic history. They created an institution called Bayt ul-Hikma (House of Wisdom). Many non-Muslims praise Harun ar-Rashid and al-Ma'mun today because of this institution, but they are unaware about how Imam Musa b. Ja'far (as) was tortured in prison. They see this grand institution that survived four hundred years. In that institution they would translate many works of the Persians and Greeks into Arabic, such as literature, astronomy, philosophy, mathematics and algebra.

The Bayt ul-Hikma was a big magnificent house which was a big translation library. If you walked passed it, you would be like, "May Allah bless Harun ar-Rashid!" Why? Because you are looking at people like Khwarizmi in there; you are looking at algebra and the best of mathematics and astronomy. Thus the people from the outside were marveling at the Banu Abbas, but they could not see what the Banu Abbas were doing from the inside.

Imam Ali b. Musa ar-Ridha (as) could see the inside as well as the outside. On the inside, it was a different story. For example, Harun ar-Rashid one day came to his friend Humayd b. Qahtaba and said, "Humayd, I want to ask you a question. What are you willing to sacrifice for me?" Humayd said, "I will sacrifice my life for you." "No, no. What else are you willing to sacrifice for me?" "I will sacrifice my wealth for you." "No, no. What else?" "I will sacrifice even my religion." "Very well. You see that prison there?" "Go in there with the jail warden, take a sword, open each door; whoever you find inside each door, behead them."

The Banu Abbas were publicly magnificent but behind closed doors the killing of the sons of Imam Ali b. Abi Talib (as) used to take place. Humayd entered the first door and came across twenty of the grandsons of Imam Ali (as) hung from ropes; he beheaded all of them. He opened the next door and again came across twenty of them, and the next door also had twenty of them. Humayd beheaded them all and then came out and said, "Now what do you want me to do?" Harun ar-Rashid said, "Put a name tag next to each of their heads and we will put it in a treasure chest and send it out." That was the norm inside the palace of the Banu Abbas.

On another occasion, Harun ar-Rashid had a clash with Yahya b. Abdullah b. Hassan. A war took place between them and then they signed a treaty in which they agreed that none would fight the other. Harun ar-Rashid was one day sitting with the chief judge of Baghdad. The chief judge said to Harun ar-Rashid, "You look sad." Harun ar-Rashid said, "Yes." "Why?" "I signed a peace treaty with Yahya b. Abdullah who is from the grandsons of Hassan b. Ali, but now I am more powerful than him and I wish I had not signed that treaty so I could kill him." The chief judge bent down towards his socks and took out a knife and said, "Where is the contract?" Harun ar-Rashid said, "Here it is." Yahya tore it up and said, "The contract is no more; go do what you have to do." Thus the judges were under their control, the palaces were under their control and so were the prisons.

As soon as Imam Ali b. Musa ar-Ridha (as) announced his Imamate, some of his own Shi'a began to say, "That is not our Imam!" When Imam Musa b. Ja'far (as) passed away, there were sixty-seven witnesses who had heard the Imam say, "Ali b. Musa ar-Ridha is my successor."

Imam Musa b. Ja'far (as) had people who used to collect khums for him. Amongst those people who used to collect khums was Ziyad b. Marwan and Ali b. Abi Hamza. These people collected a lot of khums, and sometimes when you collect a lot of khums, you start forgetting Allah and you start thinking about yourself. So Ziyad b. Marwan collected seventy thousand dinars or gold coins and Ali b. Hamza had collected thirty thousand gold coins. When Imam Ali b. Musa ar-Ridha (as) announced his Imamate, he was already facing opposition from the Banu Abbas who had swayed the public into believing in them; and now he had to deal with companions like Ziyad and Ali. Yunus b. Abdur Rahman, who was one of the great companions of the Imam, came up to both of them and said, "Now Ali b. Musa is the Imam, so the khums has to be given to him." They said, "No." Yunus said, "What are you saying? This khums does not belong to you. It belongs to the Imam." They said, "Listen, Yunus, we are all khums collectors; how much do you want us to give you so that you may remain silent?" Yunus said, "What are you talking about?" They said, "Look at the amount of money we have collected from khums. Do you really think we care about the Imam anymore? We are more concerned that the money remains in our hands." Yunus said, "I will never go with a group of people like you."

They formed a Muslim sect called "al-Waqifiyya." "Waqf" means "to stop." So they are the ones who have stopped at Imam Musa b. Ja'far (as). They said, "Imam Musa b. Ja'far was our Imam; now he is gone into occultation and he is the Imam Mahdi."

This episode gives us a glimpse of how difficult the circumstances were becoming for Imam Ali b. Musa ar-Ridha (as). Thus, during his Imamate, the Banu Abbas had maintained a good public image; a group of his own

Shi'a were not willing to follow him and when Harun ar-Rashid died, his sons fought an intense civil war against each other.

Before Harun ar-Rashid passed away, he declared, "Al-Amin, my son from my wife Zubaida, will be my successor; al-Ma'mun can be governor of Khorasan in Iran."

When Harun ar-Rashid died, Imam Ali b. Musa ar-Ridha (as) was present and so was al-Amin and al-Ma'mun. Al-Amin was supposed to give the leadership after him to his brother al-Ma'mun, but he refused, saying, "I am not going to give the caliphate to him; he was born to a slave girl whereas I am from an Arab mother." So he decided to give the caliphate to his son al-Musa. When al-Ma'mun heard this, he launched a vicious attack against al-Amin under the command of Tahir b. Hussein; they entered Baghdad and ransacked it. He caught al-Amin and beheaded him. Al-Ma'mun now returned back to Khorasan and needed to cement his position of power. He knew that the way he had secured his position was not good for his reputation, so in order to make up for that, he announced, "I have come to lead you, O people, but I am more sincere than my brother al-Amin, and I am going to make Ali b. Musa ar-Ridha my successor."

Al-Ma'mun's choice of al-Ridha as his heir-apparent has been of interest to many scholars writing in western languages. F. Gabrieli, Hamdi D. Sourdel, M. Watt, M. Zahniser, H. Kennedy, M. Rekaya and J.A.Nawas have all suggested explanations for al-Ma'mun's decision. So too has W. Madelung, who has also translated two important documents about the event.The same is the case with P. Crone and M. Hinds who have translated another document concerning it.Some primary sources previously overlooked, such as Abu Ja'far ibn Habib's Asma' al-Mughtalin minal-Ashraf and al-Rafi'i's al-Tadwin fi Akhbar Qazwin treatise must be analysed in relation to this event.

Imam Ali b. Musa ar-Ridha (as) was living in Medina at the time. Al-Ma'mun ordered Imam Ali b. Musa ar-Ridha (as) to leave Medina and become his successor otherwise he, along with his family, would all be killed. Imam Ali b. Musa ar-Ridha (as) left Medina, performed Umra and then proceeded to Basra. On his way to Basra, he stopped at Qum and performed the first ten nights of majalis for Imam Hussein (as) in Qum. Then from Qum he reached Khorasan where al-Ma'mun was sitting on his throne. He saw Imam Ali b. Musa ar-Ridha (as) and said, "Welcome my heir and my successor!"

Imam Ali b. Musa ar-Ridha (as) said, "I do not want to be your successor; I am not interested and it will not come to me anyway." "No, you are my successor and I want to look after you." "I do not want it." "Why?" "If Allah has chosen you to be the leader, then it is not for you to give your share to someone else, but if you have chosen it yourself, and it does not belong to you, then you have no right to give it to others." "Listen to me very clearly. Your grandfather Ali b. Abi Talib took part in a Shura of six; and Umar said to all six of them, 'If you do not participate, we will behead you.' Is my message loud and clear or no?" "Allah has ordered us not to kill ourselves; very well, I will take up your position as your so-called'heir.'" Al-Ma'mun was delighted. He put his stamp and the name of Imam Ali b. Musa ar-Ridha (as) on the coins of the country. The letters and the poets all had to praise Imam Ali b. Musa ar-Ridha (as).

His life in Khorasan as the Successor of al-Ma'mun

Some of Imam's own Shi'a came up to him and asked him, "How dare you claim to be the son of Hussein b. Ali and you take a position under Ma'mun?" This was the arrogance of some of his Shi'a who claimed to be the followers of the Imam, but the Imam's vision was wider than theirs. Imam replied, "May I ask you a question? Who is greater, a Muslim or a Mushrik?" He said, "A Muslim, of course." "Who is greater, a Prophet or a Wasi?" "A Prophet, of course." "What if I tell you of a Prophet who took a position under a Mushrik? What would you say?" "Who?" "Nabi Yusuf; the Quran says in Sura 12:55 (Joseph) said: "Set me over the storehouses of the land: I will indeed guard them, as one that knows (their importance)."' Did not Yusuf, a Prophet of God take a position under a Mushrik leader of his country?" "Yes." "Yusuf voluntarily took a position, while I have been forced by al-Ma'mun to take this position."

That is why they called him Imam ar-Ridha. Some people say that they called him Imam ar-Ridha because those that liked him and those that did not like him were pleased with his allegiance. This is not true. On the contrary, those who did not like him hated him; they were not pleased with his allegiance to al-Ma'mun. The reason why he was called ar-Ridha is because he was pleased with whatever trial Allah put him in – "Al-Radhi bi'l-Qadar wa'l-Qadha - He accepts whatever Allah has ordained."

Many people do not realize how difficult it must have been for Imam Ali b. Musa ar-Ridha (as) to leave Medina and go and live alone with no family around him. Why do we say in the ziyarah, "Assalamu alaika, ya Ghareeb al-Ghuraba - Salam upon you, O Stranger of Strangers?" In those days, was there anyone from Aal Muhammad living in Toos (Mashhad)? He had to leave Imam al-Jawad (as), when he was so young, to go and live alone in Mashhad just to protect the School of the Ahlulbayt. But Imam Ali b. Musa ar-Ridha (as) did not allow al-Ma'mun to get away with his mischief.

One day al-Ma'mun said to him, "Now that you are going to be my successor, you have to lead the Salat ul-Eid." Imam said, "I will lead Salat ul-Eid the way I am going to lead it." "Yes, that's fine." "You have no problem with that?" "No, no problem." On Eid morning, all the people including the entire staff of Ma'mun's palace were waiting for the Imam. The people of Ma'mun's palace were all wearing golden robes and were adorned with their best jewels. They were all waiting for Salat ul-Eid to begin and were thinking, "Where is Ali b. Musa?" All of a sudden Imam Ali b. Musa ar-Ridha (as) started coming towards them. He was barefooted just like the Prophet (pbuh) used to be when he would go to pray Salat ul-Eid. As he was walking barefoot, he kept saying loudly, "Allahu Akbar! Allahu Akbar! Allahu Akbar!," just like the Prophet. Narrations state that al-Ma'mun could not hear himself think because by that time the whole of Khorasan was shouting, "Allahu Akbar! Allahu Akbar!"

During that time, some people came to Imam Ali b. Musa ar-Ridha (as) and said, "O Ali b. Musa, can you give us a piece of advice?" The piece of advice that the Imam gave them was called "The Golden Chain." Imam said, "O people! Do you want a piece of advice?" They said, "Yes." He said, "I heard from my father Musa b. Ja'far, who heard from his father Ja'far b. Muhammad, who heard from his father Zayn ul-Abideen, who heard from his father Hussein b. Ali, who heard from his brother Hassan b. Ali, who heard from his father Ali b. Abi Talib, who heard from the Prophet, who heard from Jibra'il who heard from Allah (swt) that, 'La ilaha illallah is my fortress; whoever enters my fortress will be secure from my punishment.'""Is that it?" "No. I am one of the conditions of la ilaha illallah."

On various occasions, al-Ma'mun tried to force the Imam into the arena of complex debates with various groups and creeds. He used to conduct scientific and intellectual sessions to which he invited giant thinkers, leading scientists, the atheists of the century, and debaters whose scientific might was feared and before the stubbornness of whose complex arguments the evidence was muted and due to the fierceness of whose doubt the proof was weakened. In all such debates, the Imam would come out victorious over his opponents due to the tremendous power of knowledge he possessed without forcing himself into the sophistry of arguments to which some might have resorted in order to demolish the structure of his opponent's argument and weaken his ability to provide evidence. Rather, he depended in his debate upon honest arguments in order to prove right to be right, his miraculous ability of conviction, and his calm stylistic method. These debates have been discussed by academicians such as David Thomas, Binyamin Ibrahimov, David Wasserstein, Steven Wasserstrom, M.A. Buyukkara fascinating Phd from Edinburgh in 1997, Michael Cooperson as well as Madelung's seminal 1981 work published by the American University of Beirut. These debates do certainly reflect an early Shii theology, crystallized in a period of great theological discussions within the empire.

Al-Nawfali tried to warn the Imam against attempting to deal with the debates of such people when the Imam asked him why al-Ma'mun had invited him to debate them, for al-Ma'mun had asked the Catholic archbishop, the High Rabbi, leading Sabians, the Hindu high priest, followers of Zoroaster, Nestus the Roman medical scientist, and a group of orators, to enter into a scientific debate with Imam . He sent Yasir the servant to the Imam to tell him about the time when the debate would start, requesting him to attend. When Yasir went out and al-Nawfali was alone with the Imam, the Imam turned to him and asked him in the form of a dialogue, "O Nawfali! You are an Iraqi, and the heart of an Iraqi is not severe; so, what can you gain from causing your cousin to require us to meet with disbelievers and rhetoricians?" Al-Nawfali answered, "May my life be sacrificed for yours! He wants to put you to test, and he loves to know how much knowledge you possess. He has, indeed, built his assumption on a shaky foundation, and doomed, by God, what he has built." He asked, "And what has he built?" He answered, "Scholars of theology and innovators are opposite of the scholars. A scholar does not deny the undeniable, whereas rhetoricians and polytheists are people who deny and try to prove what is not true. If you argue with them and tell them that God is One, they would say, `Prove His Oneness,' and if you say that Muhammad is the Messenger of God, they would say, `Confirm his Message,' then they would press their lies on a person while he tries to disprove their lies, and they would continue to prove that he is mistaken till he abandons his argument; so, beware of them, may my life be sacrificed for you." He smiled and asked, "O Nawfali! Do you fear that they will disprove my argument?" He answered, "No, by God! I have never worried about you, and I hope God will enable you to have the upper hand over them." The Imam asked again, "O Nawfali! Would you like to know when al-Ma'mun will feel regretful?" He answered, "Yes." He said, "When he hears me argue with the people of the Torah quoting their own Torah, with the people of the Gospel (Bible) quoting their own Gospel, with the people of the Psalms quoting their own Psalms, with Zoroastrians arguing in their Persian language, with the Romans in their own Latin, and with rhetoricians using their very rhetoric. So, if I closed all the avenues of argument in the face of each arguing party and disproved his claim, making him renounce his statement from its onset and referring to my own statement, then al-Ma'mun would know that he would not achieve what he aspires. It is then that he will feel regretful; We are God's, and Unto Him is our return." Thus does the Imam show that he was taking lightly and was not concerned about such persons whom al-Ma'mun wished to gather together against him trying to embarrass him with their falsification and arguments which he hoped might close for the Imam all the avenues of argument.

When the session starts and the Imam is invited to join it, the discussion starts and the Imam starts his debate with the Catholics, making the Bible his reference to prove his own defense of the Unity of God and disprove the Godhead of Christ by those who regarded him as a god besides God. Then he follows with a magnificent discussion proving that the Bible in circulation today is not the same which God had revealed to Christ (A.S.) and that it is authored by some of the disciples of Jesus (A.S.) who are the authors of the four gospels, depending in his argument on the fact that the details presented by each one of them stand in flagrant contradiction with those of the other. The Catholic archbishop slipped into an obvious self-contradiction; for he on one hand sanctified the authors of the four gospels and held them above lying while, on the other hand, he admitted to the Imam that they did tell lies about Christ. Then the Imam goes to debate the High Rabbi, scholar of the Jews, to prove the prophethood of Prophet Muhammad from the previously revealed divine testaments, after which he follows with a very logical debate. Having argued with him that one of the requirements of a Prophet was to perform something all other creation are unable to perform, he asked him about the reason why they, the Jews, refrained from believing into the miracles of all prophets other than Moses son of Imran, and the High Rabbi answered him saying, "We cannot admit the prophethood of any who professes prophethood except after bringing us knowledge similar to that brought by Moses." Imam said to him, "Then how come you admitted the prophethood of other prophets who preceded Moses who did not split the sea, nor cleave the stones so that twelve springs would gush forth from it, nor took their hands out shining white as Moses did, nor did they turn a cane into a snake?!" It was then that the High Rabbi overcame his stubbornness, submitted to the argument, and admitted that any supernatural act beyond human capacity was indeed a proof of prophethood. The Imam asked him then about the reason why they did not believe in the prophethood of Jesus despite the fact that he brought forth miracles beyond human capacity such as bringing the dead back to life, healing those who were born blind and the lepers, and about the reason why they did not believe in the prophethood of Muhammad despite his bringing an extra-ordinary miracle, that is, the Holy Qur'an while he was neither a scholar nor a writer. The High Rabbi had no answer at all. Then came the turn of the Zoroastrian high priest whom the Imam debated depending on the priest's belief in the prophethood of Zoroaster. The Zoroastrian tells the Imam that Zoroaster brought them what no other man had ever brought them before. "We did not see him," he continues, "but the stories of our ancestors told us that he legalized for us what no other person before made legal; so, we followed him." The Imam asked, "You believed in the stories which came to you about him, so you followed him, didn't you?" "Yes," he answered. The Imam said, "This is the case with all other nations. Stories came to them about what the prophets had accomplished, what Moses , Jesus, and Muhammad had all brought them, so why did you not believe in any of these prophets, having believed in Zoroaster through the stories that came to you about him saying that he brought forth what others did not?"

After sometime al-Ma'mun approached the Imam again and said, "All the doctors of other faiths have written a book on medicine. O Ali b. Musa, what knowledge do you have about medicine?" The story of this dissertation is that al-Ma'mun had a very inquisitive mind eager for knowledge, fond of obtaining more of it. During one of his scientific debates, a group of physicians and philosophers in Nishapur, including Yohanna

(John) ibn Masawayh the physician, Jibraeel (Gabriel) ibn Bakhtishoo' the physician, Salih ibn Salhama the Indian philosopher, in addition to others, had gathered. Discussion turned to medicine and how in it the bodies are improved. Al-Ma'mun and his attendants were involved in a very lengthy discussion of the subject, and how God created the human body and the contradictory things in it, the four elements, the harms and benefits of various types of food, while the Imam kept silent and did not take part in any of that. Al-Ma'mun, therefore, said to him, "What do you have to say, O father of al-Hassan, in today's subject of our discussion?" Abul-Hassan (A.S.) said, "I have of this the knowledge of what I have personally tested and came to know about its accuracy by experience and by the passage of time in addition to what I was told by my ancestors of what nobody can afford to be ignorant of nor excused for leaving out. I shall compile that with an equal share of what everyone need know." Al-Ma'mun then rushed to Balkh and Abul-Hassan did not accompany him; therefore, al-Ma'mun sent him from there a letter asking him to fulfill his promise and make that compilation, so the Imam wrote to him saying: "In the Name of Allah, Most Gracious, Most Merciful; My reliance is upon Allah I have received the letter of the commander of the faithful regarding what he ordered me about acquainting him with what is needed of matters I have tested and heard about foods and drinks, medicines, venesection, blood letting, bathing, poisons, what should be avoided, and other things which manage the health of the body, and I explained what is needed to be done regarding one's own body, and God is the One Who gives success." After that he initiates the dissertation. A good number of scholars attempted to write commentaries on the dissertation including Tarjamat al-Dhahabiyya by mawla Faydallah 'Usarah al-Tasatturi who was an authority on medicine and astrology during the regime of Fath-Ali Khan. This book was written under the cover of secrecy in about 107 A.H. A handwritten copy of the manuscript dated 1133 A.H. is available at Mishkat Library of the Tehran University. Thus al-Ma'mun said, "I do not want it written in ink; I want it written in gold." And so they wrote it in gold.

Al-Ma'mun was now seeing the popularity of Imam Ali b. Musa ar-Ridha (as) on the rise; he knew then that he had made a big mistake allowing Imam Ali b. Musa ar-Ridha (as) to become his successor. So now Ma'mun wanted to get rid of him according to Shaykh al-Saduq.

Abu Salt narrates that he went to Imam Ali b. Musa ar-Ridha (as) one day and he said, "I saw the Imam, and he was sad and looked tired. I said to him, 'Imam, you are looking sad and tired.' Imam said, 'Abu Salt, I miss Medina. I miss my family in Medina, and this man oppresses me and tortures me and tries to humiliate me, but I am ar-Ridha, I am pleased with what Allah has given me.'"

Al-Ma'mun told his companion one day, "Lengthen your fingernails." So his companion lengthened his fingernails for a couple of weeks; when they got long enough, al-Ma'mun told him, "Now stick them in the pomegranate juice." The juice was full of poison. He said, "Now take your fingernails out and put them in a different glass. I will drink from one glass and Ali b. Musa will drink too."

As soon as Imam Ali b. Musa ar-Ridha (as) drank the juice, he felt the pain go directly into his body because they had put a lot of poison in his juice. The narrations say that the Imam went home and said to his people, "Look after my burial ceremony and shroud me; you will see someone who will come and bury me. Remove all the carpets from my house and remove the mattress; let me lie on the ground." His companions wondered why they should remove the carpets, the Imam said, "Just for a few moments I want to feel what Aba Abdullah felt when he lay on the ground on the tenth of Muharram."

Lecture 11

Imam Muhammad b. Ali al-Jawad (as)

Imam Muhammad b. Ali al-Jawad (as) was born in the 195th year after Hijra and died in the year 220 after Hijra, at the age of twenty-five. He is revered as being the embodiment of knowledge, wisdom, humility and patience, and he is indeed a leader whose life has to be examined in great depth. There are many practical lessons to be learnt from him and many theological principles to be derived from his leadership.

Imam Muhammad b. Ali al-Jawad (as) lived in a period in which there was a greater understanding of the principles of the Imamate. He is a role model for youth and elders alike. The fact that he died at the age of twenty-five means that he would be an ideal exemplar not only for adults but even for people who are still in their twenties.

Unfortunately, many in their twenties are not able to discuss the life of Imam al-Jawad (as). There are many who have not scrutinized his life in depth, whereas when you actually examine his life, you find some of the most profound discussions on Islamic law, theology and ethics were explored in his lifetime. Therefore, there is a need for us to dissect his life in depth and try and apply as many of these principles in our discussions today.

His Parents

The Imam was born in the 195th year after Hijra. That would mean that his father, Imam Ali b. Musa ar-Ridha (as), was forty-six years of age when Imam al-Jawad (as) was born. Up until that time many people were coming up to Imam ar-Ridha (as) and saying to him, "Imam, every Imam before you had a son, and all of them had their son at a young age, whereas you are in your forties and you still do not have a son."

Many people questioned the Imamate of Imam ar-Ridha (as) due to the activities of a group called the "Waqifiyya" who had believe that Imamate ended with Imam Musa b. Ja'far (as). Normally, when an Imam became the Imam of his age, his successor was already living and ready to succeed them. For example, Imam Ali (as) had Imam al-Hassan (as) and Imam al-Hussein (as); and from Imam al-Hussein (as) there was Ali b. Hussein (as), then Muhammad b. Ali (as) and then Ja'far b. Muhammad (as); then Musa b. Ja'far (as) and then Ali b. Musa ar-Ridha (as); but now people doubt Imam Ali b. Musa ar-Ridha (as) since he was forty-five years of age and still did not have a son. So now they were beginning to wonder, is this the lineage we are meant to follow? Now even if Ali b. Musa ar-Ridha (as) had a son, then this son was going to be very young by the time the Imam had passed away.

Therefore, a number of companions of the Imam began to ask, "Imam, have you obtained a son yet?" The Imam would reply back by saying, "No, we have no son yet." And the questions would keep coming, "Imam, do you have a son yet?...No we do not have a son yet...Imam, do you have a son yet?...No, we do not have a son yet…" Imagine if your wife has not yet given birth to a son and people intrude into your life by constantly asking you, "Do you have a son?...Do you have a son?..."

Each time Imam Ali ar-Ridha (as) would reply by saying, "Allah (swt) determines when my son will come into my life." Eventually, when Imam Ali ar-Ridha (as) was forty-five or forty-six years of age, hadith collections tell us that Imam al-Jawad (as) was born. The narrations state that Imam Ali ar-Ridha (as) had married, like the rest of the Imams, a lady from Africa. Some of the books mention her name as "Khaizaran"; others mention her name as "Sabeeqa." This lady was seen as one of the most pious ladies in the School of Ahlulbayt. Finally, Lady Sabeeqa gave birth to a son.

The Greatest Honor for the Shi'a of Aal Muhammad

When people would come to Imam Ali ar-Ridha (as) and say, "Tell us about your son," he would say, "I have a son who will inherit from the line of Prophet Dawud (as); and this son of mine is the son whose birth is the greatest honor for the Shi'a of Aal Muhammad (pbuh)."

Why would Imam Ali ar-Ridha (as) say that the birth of Imam al-Jawad (as) was the greatest honor to be given to any of the followers of Aal Muhammad? Isn't Ali b. Abi Talib (as) the greatest honor? Isn't Imam al-Hassan (as) the greatest honor? Isn't Imam al-Hussein (as) the greatest honor, or for that matter the rest of the Imams? So why does Imam Ali ar-Ridha (as) say that Imam al-Jawad (as)'s birth is the greatest honor for all the Shi'a? Many scholars have come forward and wondered what Imam Ali ar-Ridha (as) meant when he said that this birth is the greatest of the "barakah," or honors, to be given to the Shi'a of Aal Muhammad.

One group of scholars came up with some reasons as to why Imam Ali ar-Ridha (as) must have said this. They said one of the reasons was because Imam al-Jawad (as) was born at a time when the followers of Ahlulbayt were not really as oppressed as they had been before. They explained further by saying that Imam al-Jawad (as) was born in the 195th year after Hijra. Al-Ma'mun, at that time, was not acting in an oppressive manner towards the followers of the Ahlulbayt. He was more concerned with capturing Yemen and Mecca, and he was more concerned with conquering Baghdad and the caliphate. Hence al-Ma'mun had his brother, al-Amin, killed by a man named Tahir b. Hussein.

Then scholars say that al-Ma'mun returned Fadak back to Aal Muhammad. Fadak, when it left Lady Fatima Zahra (as), was passed from one caliph to another. Umar b. Abdul Aziz gave it back to the Ahlulbayt; then al-Mansur al-Dawaniqi and Harun ar-Rashid took Fadak back for themselves. When al-Ma'mun came to power, he looked at Fadak and asked, "Where are the sons of Fatima Zahra?" They replied to him, "These are the sons." He said, "What are the arguments they put forward for the land of Fadak?" They said, "The land of Fadak was given by the Prophet (pbuh) to Lady Fatima in her lifetime and therefore it does not come under the laws of inheritance." Inheritance is that which you receive after you die. Al-Ma'mun asked, "Did Fatima provide any witnesses?" The reply was, "Yes." "Who?" "Ali b. Abi Talib." "So why wasn't he accepted?"

"Because the caliph of the time said that Ali was her husband." "Did she provide any other witnesses?" "Yes." "Who?" "Hassan and Hussein." "Why weren't they accepted?" "Because Hassan and Hussein were too young." "Did they provide any other witnesses?" "Yes." "Who?" "Umm Ayman." "Why wasn't she accepted?" "She was a non-Arab, and in those days the witnessing of a non-Arab would not be accepted." Al-Ma'mun finally said, "None of this makes sense to me. Fadak goes back to the sons of Fatima Zahra."

Thus the scholars say this could also be one of the reasons that Imam Ali ar-Ridha (as) had said that Imam al-Jawad (as) was the greatest honor for the Shi'a of Aal Muhammad (pbuh).

Another reason they give is that al-Ma'mun began the praise of Ali b. Abi Talib (as) and started telling people the truth about the character of Mu'awiya b. Abu Sufyan. He would say to the people, "There is none in equality to Ali b. Abi Talib, and there is no one worse in the history of Islam like Mu'awiya b. Abu Sufyan."

Someone may ask, why was al-Ma'mun saying this? Did he believe this? No. Al-Ma'mun wanted power, and the best way to get power in those days was by giving every case of injustice against the Ahlulbayt back to them. So the first opinion of the scholars is that when Imam Ali ar-Ridha (as) says that the greatest honor given to the followers of Aal Muhammad is the birth of Imam al-Jawad (as), it is because in the time of Imam al-Jawad (as) the followers of Ahlulbayt were being treated very well.

But we reject this. Why? Just because al-Ma'mun was giving all of this back does not mean that he was treating them well. Al-Ma'mun still had prisons where the Shi'as would be killed. They would be executed behind closed doors. Yes, publicly these announcements occurred but this was only to win favor, as privately al-Ma'mun was still killing Shi'as. He knew he had poisoned Imam Ali ar-Ridha (as), so he tried to cover it up.

So the question is, then why would Imam Ali ar-Ridha (as) say the greatest birth, which was an honor to the followers of Aal Muhammad, was the birth of Imam al-Jawad (as)? O Imam Ali ar-Ridha! Ali b. Abi Talib wasn't the greatest birth? Imam al-Hassan? Imam al-Hussein? What do you mean Imam al-Jawad (as) is the greatest honor?

Imam Ali ar-Ridha (as) was indirectly saying that up until the point of Imam al-Jawad (as) many people were still not certain that Imamate was a special position. They had seen Ali b. Abi Talib (as) become an Imam at thirty-three. So they said, "His knowledge was not special; up until thirty-three one can learn the Quran and hadith." Then they saw Imam al-Kadhim (as) become an Imam at twenty. They said, "Twenty is not special; someone who is clever and has a good memory can easily learn hadith." They saw Imam Ali ar-Ridha (as) become an Imam at thirty-five. They said again that thirty-five was not special; anyone could become knowledgeable at thirty-five. When Imam Ali ar-Ridha (as) said that the greatest honor for our Shi'a was the birth of Imam al-Jawad (as), it is because Imam al-Jawad (as), at the age of eight, highlighted how Aal Muhammad's knowledge was absolutely higher than everybody else around them. Before that time nobody had ever heard of an eight year old Imam.

Ask yourselves sincerely, if you were a follower of Aal Muhammad in those days and Imam Ali ar-Ridha (as) had said to you, "When I pass away my young son al-Jawad is going to be my successor," would you accept an eight year old as your Imam? Some will say, "Of course! I would listen to anything my Imam says!" But in reality there would be many of us who would look and think, "Hold on, this young boy is going to teach me about Islam?"

There is a narration that someone came to Imam Ali ar-Ridha (as) and said, "O Imam, when you did not have children at the age of forty-five, we kept on saying, 'Where's your son? Where's your son?' Now that you have a son can you tell us who is going to be an Imam after you?"

Imam Ali ar-Ridha (as) used to give a distinction to Imam al-Jawad (as). From the age of two he used to call him "Aba Ja'far." So Imam Ali ar-Ridha (as) looked at his companion and said, "The Imam after me is this one, Aba Ja'far."

The companion looked at him and he said, "Imam? He is three years old. How long is it going to be until he is an Imam? At three, what type of knowledge will he have?" Imam Ali ar-Ridha (as) looked at him and said, "Jesus spoke from the cradle and no one doubted that, so why should you doubt him? This one is chosen by Allah (swt)."

When the Muslims read in the Quran that Jesus was talking from the cradle, did you hear any Muslim say, "How could Jesus answer questions like this?" No. But the funny thing about the Muslim world sometimes is that we may have many principles from the Quran but we never apply them again.

Thus Imam al-Jawad (as) became an Imam at the age of eight. So when Imam Ali ar-Ridha (as) said those words, he was implying that the complete foundation of Imamate was now cemented. What does this mean?

When someone asks us, what are the attributes of Imamate? We say there are three main attributes of Imamate:

1. Designation from God

2. Ismah, or infallibility

3. Knowledge which is higher than all the knowledge around them

Until Imam al-Jawad (as) people would say, "Imam al-Kadhim and Imam as-Sadiq, were old and the knowledge they had, they probably memorized from books; that is how they had that knowledge." But when it came to Imam al-Jawad (as), this was the first time they were saying to themselves, "How is an eight year old answering like that?"

His First Encounter with His Shi'a

The first group to question his authenticity was his own Shi'a. They saw Imam Ali ar-Ridha (as) die and then they were discussing among themselves, asking each other, "So who is the Imam?" Oh, the eight year old." "The eight year old is the Imam? Ali b. Abi Talib was thirty-three; Musa b. Ja'far was twenty; Ali b. Musa was thirty-five, and now this eight year old has become an Imam? Let's go and ask him some questions."

When they got there, Abdullah, the son of Imam al-Kadhim was there. Abdullah, who was also of course the brother of Imam Ali ar-Ridha (as), said, "Oh people! I am the Imam now from Aal Muhammad." The people said, "What do you mean?" He said, "I was the one chosen." So the Shi'a came up to him and said, "Well then, let us ask you a couple of questions, let's see if you can answer them." He said, "Go ahead." "What do you say about a man who says to his wife, 'I have divorced you according to the number of stars there are in the sky?'" He looked at them and said, "Yes...the divorce is valid as per the three stars...the three stars of Gemini." Then they asked him the next question, "What do you say about a man who has a physical relationship with an animal?" He said, "The man's hands should be cut and he should be whipped a hundred times."

They said, "Excuse me? You're not the Imam. Your first answer, nobody even understands what you are talking about; and your second answer, we have the books of fiqh from Imam as-Sadiq, and the manuscripts do not say the same thing."

Imam al-Jawad (as) was also present at the time. They addressed him and said, "Young man, you claim to be the Imam of the followers of Aal Muhammad. You are the eight year old?" He said, "Yes." They said, "So what's the answer to our first and second question?" He said, "As per the one who says, 'I divorce my wife according to the number of stars there are on the sky,' the answer is in chapter 2, verse 229, which says, 'After divorcing her twice, either keep her or release her,' only the third divorce [is irrevocable]." (Meaning, a man who makes such a statement has only divorced her once if the proper requisites are present). They said, "Yes, this is what the Quran says. And how about our second question?" The Imam said, "The punishment is the discretionary punishment of the judge of the Islamic state; and the animal must have a mark on it which is clear, and the animal must be banished from the land so that the animal does not come back to bring more embarrassment for the person who performed this act." They said, "Very well, we accept you as our Imam."

His First Encounter with al-Ma'mun

Al-Ma'mun now had a problem. Imam Ali ar-Ridha (as) had died and people were saying that al-Ma'mun was the one who caused the killing of Imam Ali ar-Ridha (as). Al-Ma'mun was now trying to cover up his act. He had his first meeting with Imam al-Jawad (as), which made him recognize that this child was not a child; he had something special about him.

Al-Ma'mun was riding with his horses and there were children sitting in the street. When al-Ma'mun came, all the children ran away except Imam al-Jawad (as). Al-Ma'mun looked at this child and did not know who he was. He said, "Young man, why do not you move? Can't you see me and my soldiers are riding in this street?"

Imam al-Jawad (as) looked at him and he said, "There are two reasons I am not moving; the first reason is that the roads are wide enough for your horses to go on the other side and the second reason is that I have not done anything wrong to you for me to run away from you. So I will stay here, and the road is wide." Al-Ma'mun said, "Okay...what is your name?" Imam al-Jawad (as) said, "My name is Muhammad." Al-Ma'mun said, "Okay."

Al-Ma'mun was going hunting and he had a hawk in his hand. Al-Ma'mun used to love his hawk. So after hunting, when he returned, he saw Muhammad there. He said, "Young man! You seem like a young man full of wisdom." Imam al-Jawad (as) said, "Yes, sure. Ask." "I want to ask you why God created hawks. Oh, but instead of telling me this, I want you to first tell me something else." "Yes, what is it?" Al-Ma'mun clenched his fist and put it towards the Imam and said, "Tell me, what do I have in my fist right now?" Imam said to him, "God created hawks for the kings, and these hawks fly in the sky; and when they come back down between the heavens and the earth, there are fish that come out from the sea, and go back in; and come out and return once again; the hawk catches the fish as it comes out of the sea; and the hawk takes a fish to a caliph, the caliph puts the fish in his fist and then asks the sons of Aal Muhammad, 'What is in my fist?'" "Give me your name again?" "Muhammad." "Son of who?" "Son of Ali." "Ali, son of who?" "Son of Musa, son of Ja'far, son of Muhammad, son of Ali, son of Hussein, brother of Hassan, son of Ali, son of Muhammad, chosen by Allah (swt)." Al-Ma'mun said to him, "You need to marry my daughter." "Sorry?" "You have to marry my daughter. I have a daughter called Umm al-Fadl. I do not want anyone to marry her; you two do not have to get married now. Marry her in ten years, marry her in fifteen, but I want you to be accepted for my daughter from this moment."

His Encounter with the Scholars of Baghdad

Why did al-Ma'mun want him to be accepted as a husband for his daughter then? It is an interesting issue. Firstly, he wanted to keep an eye on this young man because he knew that if this young man was left loose, al-Ma'mun's rule would be threatened by him. Secondly, he wanted a son from this young man one day so he could combine the Abbasid line with the Alid.

Now al-Ma'mun gathered all his judges and said to them, "I want to make an announcement; my announcement is that my daughter Ummul Fadl is to be engaged to Muhammad b. Ali al-Jawad." Yahya b. Aktham was there. He was the chief judge of the entire area. He said to al-Ma'mun,

"Muhammad al-Jawad, the kid?" Al-Ma'mun said, "The what?" Yahya said, "The kid." Al-Ma'mun said, "Do not say that to him. I am telling you he comes from a school of knowledge chosen by God." "What do you mean? A kid is a kid. An eight year old is an eight year old. You are going to give Ummul Fadl to him? Be patient, wait for one of the grand scholars." "So why don't you test him?" "What do you mean?" "Well, you are saying he is a child, so why don't you get every alim in Baghdad to debate him?"

Before Imam al-Jawad (as), the prerequisites of the Imamate were hotly debated. When Imam al-Jawad (as) appeared it became apparent that the Imams were definitely chosen by Allah. Was the Imamate of Imam al-Jawad (as) difficult to accept for loyal Shi'a? No. We believed in him; but others (like the Zaydi Qasim al-Rassi previously mentioned) doubted that he was the rightful Imam.

Thus Yahya said, "Okay, I am inviting nine hundred of the ulema of Baghdad, put the eight year old in front of us all." These nine hundred ulema of Baghdad were masters of fiqh. They had discussed and studied Islamic law thoroughly for many years. Thus Imam al-Jawad (as) came and the stage was set. Yahya b. Aktham said, "Muhammad b. Ali! That is your name, isn't it?" "Yes." "I have a question to ask you." "What is it?" "What is the kaffarah (atonement) for a person who goes hunting while wearing the ihram?"

There are some of us who are in our forties and fifties and cannot answer this question, and there are some of us who do not even know the meaning of kaffarah. And to study the laws related to worship and pilgrimage takes years, doesn't it? You cannot, at the age of eight, know about kaffarah, ihram and hunting altogether.

So Yahya b. Aktham asks the question, "What is the atonement of a pilgrim who has gone hunting?" and he takes one glance at the audience as if to say, "Now get ready for this embarrassment! O people! Let's see if the kid can answer this!" Imam al-Jawad (as) said to him. "Your question is not clear." "Why? You cannot answer it?" "No. Is the pilgrim a free man or is he a slave? Is it in the period of hajj or in the period of umra? Is it in the daytime or in the night? Does he have knowledge of the act or no knowledge? Is he ignorant or not ignorant? Is it in Mecca or outside of Mecca? Is it a wild animal or is it not a wild animal? If it is a wild animal, is it a bird or another type of wild animal?"

The Imam put forward sixteen different points about this one issue. Yahya b. Aktham was stunned. He thought the young man said the question was not clear because he didn't know the answer, but the young man continued and said, "If he is a free man, then he must do this…if he is a slave, then he must do this…if he is in the period of hajj, then this…If not, then this…If it was in the day time, then this…if night, then this..." He gave the answer and described all the atonements one had to give in every situation.

Now Imam al-Jawad (as) turned around and said to Yahya, "Let me ask you a question." Yahya was thinking to himself, "I asked this question and I got sixteen different issues. Now I do not know what he's going to ask me." Everyone in the crowd was saying, "Yahya, come on! You're the one who said the child does not know!" Thus Imam said, "A man gets up in the morning and looks at something and it is haram for him; then as the day continues, it becomes halal for him; then as the day continues, it becomes haram for him; then in the afternoon, it is again halal for him; then in the evening, it becomes haram for him; then at the end of the day, it becomes halal for him. What is the thing he looked at?"

Do you know eight year olds who know things like this? It is very rare, isn't it? Yahya b. Aktham said, "I might as well admit that I do not have a clue." Imam said, "The person looked at someone else's slave girl. When he looked at her in the beginning, it was haram. So he purchased her, and she became halal; he freed her and she became haram; he married her and then she became halal; he then said to her, 'You are to me like the back of my mother' (this act is called "dhihar," which was very common among Arabs), so she became haram; he paid the kaffarah and then she became halal; he then divorced her, and she became haram. At the end of the day he revoked the divorce and she became halal for him again."

At that moment, al-Ma'mun looked at Yahya and said, "I told you. This is the person for my daughter." This was the beginning of Imam al-Jawad (as)'s Imamate. Can you imagine how much pressure this young man was under? We do not appreciate Imam al-Jawad (as) the way he deserves to be appreciated. His seventeen year long Imamate began with this sudden influx of knowledge.

Pearls of Wisdom During His Imamate

His Imamate lasted seventeen years and this is how it began. From the beginning he was forced to marry Ummul Fadl. It wasn't his choice. While being married to her, he travelled back and forth from Baghdad to Medina.

Do you know why he was called al-Jawad? Al-Ma'mun used to give him a salary of a million dinars a year. The whole of the million dinars he would use to help the poor of the Muslim community. "Jawad" means "the one who is generous." And so the Imam was named al-Jawad because he would distribute a million dinars a year amongst the poor.

When he would leave Baghdad and get away from al-Ma'mun, he would go to Medina. He would sit in the mosque of the Prophet and give lectures about the religion. Some of the most beautiful narrations in Islam are from Imam al-Jawad (as). All of these hadiths were narrated while he was fourteen, fifteen, sixteen and seventeen. He was a teenager and would narrate the most beautiful hadiths. Some of which are as follows.

Imam al-Jawad (as) has a famous lecture on the hadith, "Do not be a friend of Allah in public but an enemy of Allah in private." One may ask, "What does this mean?" It has two meanings: The first meaning is that in the community (the public) we all love to act religious. Why? The Mawlana is watching me…my dad's reputation is on the line...my future wife may be in this community…so I have to think a hundred times about the way I behave. Thus I slow down my salat in front of people, and also during fasts, I will come to the mosque and give out some food…And I'm smiling with everyone. But as soon as I get home, in private, when the community does not watch, and my parents do not watch, and the people who care do not watch, that is when I can act in disobedience to Allah. The very base of hypocrisy is this. "Do not be a friend of Allah in public and an enemy of Allah in private."

The second hadith of Imam al-Jawad (as) is when he asked the question, "Do you know what tawba (repentance) means? Tawba has four stages.

1. You regret the act you have performed in the past.

Sometimes you speak to people who are older and ask them, "Remember when you were young and irreligious? Do you regret it?" Often times you hear them say, "No. I was young. It happened. Everyone who is young goes through that." Sometimes you hear people saying, "Oh they were the good ol' days, so carefree..." Imam Zayn ul-Abideen (as) says, "Do not look at the act but look at Whom you were disobeying." Amir ul-Mu'mineen (as) says, "The biggest sin is the one you think is the small one." Imam as-Sadiq (as) says, "Half of repentance is regret."

2- You must say, "Astaghfirullaha Rabbi wa atubu ilaih."

3- You must never perform that act ever again.

4- You must ensure the completion of all obligatory acts.

The third hadith of Imam al-Jawad (as) in Medina was whilst he was giving a talk. He said, "Sincerity is the best worship." Sometimes, when we do a good deed in the community, there is no sincerity. We do it to simply show off. "Put my name on the top, or in the front; make sure everybody knows it is me." But Imam said, "Sincerity is the best worship." So when your niyyah (intention) is a pure niyyah, when you are doing it purely for the sake of Allah, then that sincerity can move any rocks in front of you.

The fourth hadith of Imam al-Jawad (as) says: "The one who hears about oppression and the one who aids oppression and the one who smiles when they hear about oppression, all of them are partners of the oppressor."

I hear about oppression in my community, and I listen to the people speaking about it, and I am pleased when I hear about it. Imam al-Jawad (as) says, "You are just as much of an oppressor as the one who is oppressing." Sometimes in our community, when we sit down and hear about someone who's oppressing a fellow community member, instead of saying to them, "Stop, that's my brother in the community. Do not talk about him like that. Do not be rude. If you have a problem with him, then talk to him face to face. Do not backbite him," but no; with us, we enjoy hearing about it. Imam al-Jawad (as) says, "One who hears and allows it to be reported and is pleased with it, he is an oppressor himself."

His Encounter with People of Other Schools of Thought

Imam al-Jawad (as), at that young age, would give lectures promoting these hadith. People would come from far and wide to ask him questions; but the akhlaq of Imam al-Jawad (as) was such that even the non-Shi'a would love to sit with him. Today the Sunni and Shi'a cannot sit together without having an argument or dispute. Instead of the Sunni and Shi'i sitting at one table of brotherhood, you find that disputes occur in which they end up hating each other. Where has that heart and spirit of the Prophet gone?

People from other schools of faith would come to see him. One day a person came to him and said, "You are Muhammad b. Ali al-Jawad?" He said, "Yes, it is me." "You're the one about whom they say, "His knowledge is so great at such a young age that everybody from around the world asks him questions and he's able to answer?" "I will try to answer." "I have a problem with your history." "What's the issue?" "You say Ali b. Abi Talib should have been the successor of the Prophet whereas I say that the first and the second caliph are the rightful successors."

Today we cannot talk like that with each other, can we? But this person knew that Imam al-Jawad (as) was the very embodiment of humility. So he continued and said, "O Muhammad b. Ali! I have heard so many hadith which praise Abu Bakr and Umar, so how can you tell me they are not the rightful successors of the Prophet?" "Oh my dear brother in Islam, ask me. Let's discuss it. You can agree or at the end you can say, 'I disagree.' What are the narrations that you have heard? Ask me." This was the spirit of the Imams of Aal Muhammad. They do not arrogantly deny everything. The Quran says, "Hold onto the rope of Allah, do not disunite." The man continued, "O Muhammad b. Ali, there is a hadith which says, 'Allah told Jibra'il, 'I am pleased with Abu Bakr. Is Abu Bakr pleased with me?'

Imam al-Jawad (as) looked at him and said, "Before I begin answering, know one thing. The Prophet said that after he passes away there will be many who will lie about him and the worst of him is the one who lies purposely, for hell is his abode; and that whenever we get any hadith, should not we put it alongside the Quran? Will that be our principle?" "Yes." "Very well then. You say this first hadith where Allah says, 'I am pleased with Abu Bakr. Is Abu Bakr pleased with me?' My dear brother, Allah says in the Quran, 'I am closer to you than your jugular vein,' so why would

Allah need to ask Jibra'il to ask Abu Bakr if he is pleased with Him, when Allah is closer to Abu Bakr than his jugular vein?" "Thank you, O Imam. May I ask you another question?" "Please. Feel free to ask." "O Imam, I have read a hadith that says, 'The position of Abu Bakr and Umar in this world is like Jibra'il and Mikaeel in the heavens.' "That is not accepted." "Why?" "Jibra'il and Mikaeel are angels of God who have never, ever disobeyed God once [in the thousands of years they have lived] whereas would you admit that…, [and this is something that] Abu Bakr and Umar themselves admit, before they became Muslims…they were polytheists and lived most of their lives as polytheists?" "Yes." "So how can someone who was a disbeliever for most of his life be put in comparison with someone who is an archangel who has never disobeyed?"

"Your answer makes sense. Now question number three: O Imam, I have a hadith in front of me which says that, 'Abu Bakr and Umar are the masters of the elders of Paradise,' just like Hassan and Hussein are the masters of the youth.""O man, in Paradise, there are only youth; there are no elders."

"O Imam, I have another hadith which states that, 'The Prophet (pbuh) said that, 'If there was a prophet after me, it would be the second caliph Umar.' "O man, in the Quran, Allah (swt) has a verse where He says, 'We made a covenant with all the prophets, and with you, and with Prophet Nuh.' This means Allah made a covenant with the prophets before the physical creation of mankind, He had already decided on His prophets. It would be absurd to believe that God would consider sending as a prophet someone who committed polytheism and lived most of his life as a polytheist. [Thus the hadith 'If there was a prophet after me, it would be Umar,' contradicts this verse in the Quran, as Umar was not like those who took part in this covenant]."

"You are right, O Imam. May I ask you about another hadith?" Imam al-Jawad (as) was only thirteen or fourteen years of age at the time. "Please go ahead and ask me." "I have read a hadith that says, 'Abu Bakr and Umar are the lights of Jannah.' "This hadith is rejected." "Why?" "Allah has one hundred and twenty-four thousand prophets in Jannah. I would think they would provide the lights for Jannah." "You are right."

"O Imam, may I ask you about another hadith?" "Go ahead." "O Imam, I have read a hadith where the Prophet (pbuh) said, 'Tranquility came down on the tongue of Umar b. Khattab.' "Do you believe Abu

Bakr is greater than Umar?" "Yes." "Abu Bakr himself was heard saying, 'Please help me because I know sometimes Satan affects my tongue,' so how could Umar have tranquility on his tongue while Abu Bakr is greater?"

"Imam, I have another question." "Go ahead." "Imam, I have a hadith that the Prophet (pbuh) said, 'I sometimes feel that if the revelation does not come to me, it has gone to the family of Khattab [instead].' At this moment the Imam looked at him and said to him, "This would mean that the Prophet (pbuh) sometimes doubted his own prophethood and this is impossible. Since God selects angels and men as Messengers (Quran, Chapter 4, Verse 77), it would be absurd for Him to send revelation to one who committed shirk in place of the one whom He had selected [for prophethood]."

Imam al-Jawad politely, but plainly demonstrated the incompatibility of such hadith with the Quran and the fundamentals of Islamic theology.

Many Attempts Made on His Life

Most hadith indicate that Imam al-Jawad (as) was around sixteen years of age when he married Ummul Fadl. Some say fifteen, but most say sixteen. So they were engaged until they were married at the Tigris river. Al-Ma'mun organized the ceremony. Do you think this Ummul Fadl was a barakah (blessing) in his life?

This was a torment in his life. The only reason al-Ma'mun made her marry Imam al-Jawad (as) was because he wanted a son from them. She kept on trying to have a son, but do you think Allah would give a son to someone like her?

One day she went to her father and said, "O my father! However much we try to have children, we are not having them; and this man has gone off to marry someone else, and she is giving him children. But with me there are no children."

Al-Ma'mun had been drinking that night when he heard this. He picked up a sword. Ummul Fadl herself narrates, "My father picked up a sword, and he went to the house of Imam al-Jawad, and entered the house. Imam al-Jawad was sitting with his wife and children; he came and struck Imam al-Jawad with a sword. I was sure Imam al-Jawad died. I took my father back home, as he was really drunk.

My father woke up the next day and said, 'What did I do with the sword yesterday?'" Ummul Fadl said, "You struck Imam al-Jawad." Al-Ma'mun said, "I struck him, and did he die?" She said, "Yes." He said, "Quickly, let us go and arrange for his body to be removed."

The narrations state that as they went to the house they saw Imam al-Jawad (as) sitting down very normally. Al-Ma'mun asked, "How come you are alive? I struck you." Imam al-Jawad (as) took something out and said, "This is the hirz of my grandmother, Fatima Zahra. This hirz was passed to me in the line of Imamate until it reached me. This hirz protects you from everyone except Malik ul-Mawt. I had worn it last night when you tried to attack me, and Allah protected me because of the hirz of my grandmother, Fatima."

Thus they tried and tried, until al-Mu'tasim took over from al-Ma'mun. When al-Ma'mun died, al-Mu'tasim came in to power. Al-Mu'tasim did not attack Imam al-Jawad (as) for the first year; but then it was Imam al-Jawad (as)'s knowledge that killed him. The Prophet (pbuh) used to say, "The disease of the scholars is envy." How many times do you find scholars who are envious of each other? There are many scholars who dislike others.

Al-Mu'tasim once had a difficult case and this was the case that killed Imam al-Jawad (as). A thief came to al-Mu'tasim, and putting forward his two hands towards al-Mu'tasim, said, "Purify me!" Al-Mu'tasim said, "What do you mean?" He said, "I am a thief and I want you to purify me!"

Al-Mu'tasim was looking at him, wondering, "What does 'purify' mean? What is he talking about? Purify me? What shall I do to him?" So the people around him told al-Mu'tasim, "He means cut his hands, as the Quran states it as a punishment for stealing. That way he will be purified." Al-Mu'tasim said, "Where do we cut from?" They said, "The hand." He said, "What's the hand?"

He asked an interesting question. He wanted to know, does the hand refer to the entire hand up till the elbow, or just till the wrist, or half the hand, or the fingers? He said, "Bring me all the ulema. I want to ask all of them." So the ulema came. Al-Mu'tasim said, "The one who convinces me the most, he is the one who will decide the judgment."

Thus all the ulema came and al-Mu'tasim asked all of them. He pointed to one and said, "You. Tell me, how do I solve this?" He said,

"You have to cut from the elbow." "What do you mean from the elbow?" "The Quran says, 'O you who believe! When you get ready for prayers, wash your faces and your hands, until the elbow..." The hands include the elbow. Get a sword and chop his elbow off." Al-Mu'tasim said, "This does not make any sense to me, move." He looked at the second person and said, "Tell me, you. What does it mean?" He said, "You have to cut the hand only." "Why?" "Because that same verse then later says, '…rub your head and your feet...' and to rub, you need to make sure that you are using your hands; so the verse refers to the hand and that is where you must cut from." Al-Mu'tasim said, "I'm still not sure. Where is the young man?" "Who?" "Muhammad b. Ali. Where is he? He is the one who answers all the questions. He makes sense to me."

They called Imam al-Jawad (as). He knew this was the sign of his end. Isn't it a shame that the grandson of the Prophet thinks that his answering the questions will be the cause of his death. They brought Imam al-Jawad (as), and he said, "Please, I do not want to answer; the others are there, ask them." Al-Mu'tasim said, "No, you answer." Imam al-Jawad (as) said, "You have to cut the fingers only; when a thief steals, there are nineteen conditions. If all the conditions are fulfilled, then you have to cut the fingers only." "Why?" "Chapter 72 in the Quran, verse 18." "What is it?" "And that, the places for sajdah (prostration) are for God" "What do you mean by this?" "Aren't there seven places for sujood (prostration)?" "Yes." "What are they?" "The seven places for sujood are your palms, forehead, feet and knees." "Therefore, for sujood to be done, you need your palm. So you only cut the fingers because, if this thief repents later, and if you cut his hand or his elbow, he will never be able to do sujood again. Whereas sujood is for Allah, and if the thief repents, then at least if you are going to cut his fingers he can still do sujood properly." Al-Mu'tasim said, "What a beautiful answer! Only someone from your family can answer like that!"

The ulema sitting alongside al-Mu'tasim felt that "this is now enough. This Muhammad al-Jawad makes a fool of us. Every time we answer, his answer is closer to the Prophet! His answer is closer to the Quran!"

Two scholars, one was b. Duad, and the other, some narrations say, was Abu Dawud…they both came to al-Mu'tasim and said, "Mu'tasim, are you not reflecting upon yourself?"Al-Mu'tasim said, "What do you mean?" They said, "Do you want to stay in power?" These were the ulema of Islam. But sometimes the biggest troublemakers in Islam are those people who call themselves ulema.

They said, "You are letting this young man answer questions instead of us? We are your servants, and we are your scholars; whatever law you want, we will make; but this young man will not make those laws; and if the people hear that this man is answering questions like this, from the day he was eight and now he is twenty-five, are you going to allow this? And your relative Ummul Fadl is not getting any children from this young man, whereas his other wife has given him Ali al-Hadi, and has given him others. Isn't it about time you got rid of him?"

Al-Mu'tasim said, "You know what? You make sense; maybe it is about time I got rid of this young man. Maybe this young man is not good for our community." What did he mean "not good?" This man was serving Islam! So he turned around to Ummul Fadl and said, "Get me the poison that will hurt him the most."

Imam al-Jawad (as), at twenty-five years of age, was buried next to his grandfather in Kadhimayn. The next time you visit his grave, do not just stand there, but reflect on what this young man went through.

They used the worst poison and as it began to circulate in the body of Imam al-Jawad (as), he knew that these were his final moments. At the age of twenty-five, the world ended up killing this youth from Aal Muhammad, who had served the religion of Islam with his knowledge all his life.

Lecture 12

Imam Ali b. Muhammad al-Hadi (as)

Imam Ali b. Muhammad al-Hadi (as) was born in the year 214 after Hijra and died in the year 254 after Hijra at the age of forty. This is a man from whose life many a lesson may be learnt and many a principle may be derived. He is indeed a man who is recognized for his extraordinary knowledge, bravery, passion and sacrifice. When we examine Imam Ali b. Muhammad al-Hadi, there are many lessons to be learnt about the political environment which faced the Imams of Ahlulbayt preceding the advent of the Mahdi (ajfs) from Aal Muhammad (pbuh).

When we dissect his biography, we begin to realize the meaning of the word house arrest and why there was so much political pressure on the last few of the twelve Imams of the Ahlulbayt. Unfortunately, Imam Ali al-Hadi (as)'s life has not been studied in depth. His life has a historical base but a contemporary significance, in that it was only a few years ago that we witnessed the bombings of his shrine and the shrine of his son, Imam al-Askari (as). One would think that many people would have gone on to study his life and biography, after witnessing the bombing of those shrines in Samarra.

Unfortunately, that bombing did not have any effect on people except for their emotions. There were many who were emotionally affected by Samarra but not intellectually. If you were to ask many people, when they heard that Samarra was bombed, did it effect them emotionally? They would say yes, but did it affect them enough to go and read a book on Imam Ali al-Hadi and Imam al-Askari? Not really. There are many until today who do not know much about Imam Ali al-Hadi (as) and Imam al-Askari (as) whereas what we do not realize is that the beginning of the political pressure on the Imams, because of the recognition that Imam al-Mahdi (ajfs) was coming, began with Imam al-Hadi (as). In the lifetime of the Imams, it is well known that our Sunni brethren would narrate that the Prophet (pbuh) said, "There will be twelve caliphs after me and all of them are from Qureish." This hadith indicates that the Abbasid caliphs, due to their relationship to Sunni hadith scholars, were expecting the Mahdi (ajfs) to appear.

So, when we study the life of Imam al-Hadi (as), we are now approaching that final part of the history of the Imamate where there is going to be major surveillance on the houses of the Imams of the Ahlulbayt. Let us dissect his life and see what we can learn from it.

His Parents

Imam al-Hadi (as) was born in the year 214 after Hijra. His mother was called "Sumana al-Maghribiyya." "Maghrib" today refers to Morocco. In other words, his mother again was a lady from North Africa. One cannot help but notice that there isn't any movement of going back to ladies from Medina, or ladies from Mecca, on the part of the Imams. Many of the ladies now are of North African decent. Once again the reasoning behind this is to remove any racism from Islam; never should a Muslim community not allow their sons to get married to a lady who is from the followers of the Ahlulbayt just because of her race. That is why when you read about Imam Ali al-Hadi (as) or Imam al-Jawad (as) you will notice that they say that their skin was a bit darker than normal Arab skin. Naturally, if they are marrying women from North Africa, then their sons aren't going to have the lighter Arab complexion. They would have been a bit darker in complexion. Notice therefore that this Sumana from al-Maghrib, the narrations say, was one of the most pious women of Arabia. This lady was a devout woman, a lady of the Quran and Sunna of the Prophet (pbuh). Imam al-Jawad (as) was married to Ummul Fadl, the daughter of al-Ma'mun. Ummul Fadl did not give him any children; he married Sumana and she gave him Imam Ali al-Hadi (as).

The Initial Period of His Imamate

The beginning of Imam al-Hadi (as)'s life was even more difficult that Imam al-Jawad (as). Why? Imam al-Jawad (as) was eight years old when they tested him on his Imamate. If Imam Ali al-Hadi (as) was born in the year 214 and Imam al-Jawad (as) died in the year 220, how old was Imam Ali al-Hadi (as) when he was announcing his Imamate? Six. That is why, when we come to Imam al-Zaman (ajfs), we will notice that he was five. Some people ask, "How come a five year old?" Well, we just spoke about a six year old, and before that an eight year old. Notice that now there begins a trend where you have Imams at a very young age. Imagine, when Imam al-Jawad (as) passed away, Imam al-Hadi (as) was six.

The caliph, al-Mu'tasim, now makes an announcement. He called his companion, Umar b. Faraj, and said to him, "Umar, you know al-Jawad was eight when he became an Imam? Do you remember?" He said, "Yes." Al-Mu'tasim said, "Do you believe his knowledge was truly from God? Or do you think maybe he had a private tuition when he was young which affected his knowledge?" Sometimes Allah can show you the light but you still do not believe. Umar said, "It does not matter. It might not be from God; it might be from a private tutor." Al-Mu'tasim said, "Very well. Now that al-Jawad is dead, his son Ali al-Hadi is six. Maybe if we get to Ali al-Hadi at this age, he will not have the knowledge al-Jawad had."

You see how the mind works? Six? eight? five? These are all from the lines of Ahlulbayt. These are all people who inherit knowledge, one from another.

So now they brought a private tutor by the name of Ubaydullah al-Junaydi. He was a master of law, a master of Quran, a master of hadith, a master of ethics and a master of Arabic grammar. He had mastered absolutely everything. He came to al-Mu'tasim, and al-Mu'tasim said to him, "Listen, you know that six year old there?" Ubaydullah al-Junaydi said, "Which six year old?" Al-Mu'tasim said, "The one, there." "O Ali? Son of Muhammad?" "Yes. We want you to be his tutor from now."

Umar b. Faraj then interrupted and asked Ubaydullah al-Junaydi, "Do you know why we want you to be his tutor?" Ubaydullah asked, "Why?" Umar said, "We want you to get to his mind before another person gets to his mind." Ubaydullah said, "What do you want me to instill in his mind?"

Umar said, "Instill in his mind the hatred towards the religion of Islam." Ubaydullah al-Junaydi said, "But I too am from the scholars of Islam." Umar said, "Okay, then instill this idea of hatred towards the family of the Prophet. Let him believe in something else." Ubaydullah al-Junaydi said, "Leave this to me. I am a man of age; this is a six year old. His father was eight, maybe he had a private tutor." Ubaydullah al-Junaydi went in.

The next day someone saw him and asked him, "Ubaydullah, how is your servant from Bani Hashim doing?" Ubaydullah al-Junaydi said, "Which servant?" He said, "The six year old. How is he doing?" Ubaydullah al-Junaydi said, "Do not call him a servant. He is one of the scholars of Aal Muhammad." "What do you mean?" "When I entered the house, I said to the kid, 'Child, recite for me a surah from the Quran,' so the child said to me, 'You name the surah, I will continue reciting.' So I picked the longest surah in the Quran and this child began reciting everything by heart; and his voice was equivalent to the voice of Prophet Dawud (as). I have never heard a voice like this, that when the Quran says, 'Dawud's voice was amazing,' I guarantee you his voice was like Dawud's. But shall I tell you something more extraordinary, which tells me that they have got knowledge from God and not from a private tutor?" "What is it?" "Every verse of the Quran I ask him about, he tells me when it was revealed, where it was revealed, and about who it was revealed. Can you tell me how a six year old can know all this already? Do not leave me with this child because it is not me disciplining him, he's disciplining me." When al-Mu'tasim heard this, he thought, "Yes, I know they have knowledge but surely there could be someone who could question them."

Do you know whom al-Mu'tasim called again? Sometimes we do not learn from our mistakes, do we? He called Yahya b. Aktham again. Yahya b. Aktham had already gone through the most embarrassing day of his life with Imam al-Jawad (as). Now he came back again. Al-Mu'tasim said to him, "Yahya, I want you to ask this young man some questions." "You mean the child who is the son of the one that al-Ma'mun asked me to pose questions to?" "Yes." "Do we have to go through this again?" "Yes, Yahya. Ask him." "You know these people; their knowledge is different. These people aren't chosen by man. There is someone else who chooses them and that is Allah (swt)." "Do not talk like that to me. Ask him. I did not see what al-Ma'mun saw. For all I know it is not real." Sometimes people can tell you something, but you choose not to listen. Yahya b. Aktham looked at al-Mu'tasim and said, "So we will ask Ali al-Hadi?" Al-Mu'tasim said, "Yes, ask Ali al-Hadi." Yahya approached Imam Ali al-Hadi and said, "Ali, I have some questions to ask you." Imam al-Hadi (as) said, "About what?" "I have some questions about Prophet Adam, about Prophet Sulayman, about Prophet Yusuf and about Ali b. Abi Talib and about the Quran."

How old was Imam al-Hadi (as)? Very young. Six or Seven. Do not let anyone ever make you doubt your Imams; your Imam's knowledge was miles ahead of anyone who surrounded them. Have pride when when you attend the wiladah or shahada of Imam Ali al-Hadi (as). Do not let anyone tell you, "This is a small shahada." Do not let the mosques be empty; these are the beacons of knowledge from the Ahlulbayt. Come and honor their knowledge.

Yahya looked at Imam al-Hadi (as) and said, "The first question I want to ask you about is Prophet Adam. What was the tree that he ate from?" "It was originally known as the 'Tree of Envy.'" "Yes, you are right. Al-Mu'tasim, are you happy now?" Al-Mu'tasim said, "No, ask him another question. That was too easy."

Yahya said, "Prophet Sulayman said, 'Who can bring me Queen Sheba's throne?' and the Queen of Sheba's throne was in one part of the world, Prophet Sulayman said, 'I want it in front of me now.' So one of the jinns said, 'I can bring it,' and then Asif b. Barkhiyya said, 'I will bring it without the blinking of the eye,' and the throne came straight away. O Ali al-Hadi, could not Prophet Sulayman have done it himself? Why did he need to ask?" "Oh no, he could do it himself, but he wanted to make clear to the people who is the successor after he dies." Al-Mu'tasim said, "Ask again." Yahya asked, "Aren't we meant to do sujood (prostration) only to Allah?" Imam al-Hadi (as) said, "Why?" Yahya said, "How come Yaqub does sujood to Yusuf in the Quran?" Imam al-Hadi (as) said, "We have two types of prostrations in Islam: we have a prostration to Allah and a prostration which is obedience to Allah." Yahya said, "What do you mean?" Imam al-Hadi (as) said, "When Allah asked the angels to prostrate to Adam, can we prostrate to a human? No. But it was not the prostration of worship, it was the prostration of obedience. Likewise, when Yaqub did prostration to Yusuf, it wasn't the prostration of worship, it was the prostration of obedience." Yahya said, "Thank you. Let me ask you another question. When people fought Ali b. Abi Talib at Jamal, he let them escape after the battle but he never let those at Siffin escape. Why?"

Now imagine this scenario. Here is a young boy of about six or seven and he is talking about something that has happened almost 200 years before him. He said, "Imam Ali let the people of Jamal escape because once the war had finished those people were not intent on instigating a further fight; they surrendered and the verse in the Quran says, 'Bring peace between the people,' whereas those at Siffin wanted to continue fighting, and however many times they were given a chance, they would pick up a weapon again and come back and fight. By the time Jamal finished, those at Jamal were still believers, whereas those in Siffin had become infidels." Yahya said, "Okay, I also have a question about surah 31, verse 27." Al-Mu'tasim looked at Yahya and said, "If he answers this question that will be enough for me; I will let the him go."

So Yahya said, "Surah 31, verse 27, says, 'If all the trees were pens, and the seven seas were all ink, they would not be able to exhaust the words of Allah.' Name me the seas and name me the words." Al-Mu'tasim looked again and he said, "If he can answer this, I will let him go."

Imam al-Hadi (as), only seven or eight years old, looked at al-Mu'tasim and then he looked at Yahya b. Aktham and said, "The seven seas are; the sea in Yemen, and the sea of Tabariyya, and the sea of Kibreet, and the sea of Bahran, and the sea of Barhout, and the sea of Lisan, and the sea of Saylan." Yahya said, "Okay, and what are the words of Allah?" Imam al-Hadi (as) said, "The words of Allah are us Aal Muhammad, that if you got all the trees and they were pens, and you got the seven seas and they were ink, all of them, if they came together, would not be able to exhaust the virtues of Muhammad and Aal Muhammad." Yahya said, "You have answered my question now. I will let you go."

After this incident, al-Mu'tasim said to Imam al-Hadi (as), "Very well, you can teach in Medina."

Some of His Teachings in Medina

After al-Mu'tasim died, al-Wathiq became the caliph. During that period they allowed Imam Ali al-Hadi (as) to teach and there wasn't much oppression against the Imam. He would give lessons in the Prophet (pbuh)'s mosque in Medina. The first of the lessons would be on the Saheefa of Ali b. Abi Talib (as). "What is that?," one may ask.

Ali b. Abi Talib (as) would sit under the Prophet, and while the Prophet would give lessons, Ali b. Abi Talib (as) would write the lessons down. Ali b. Abi Talib (as) kept these lessons or lecture notes. He then gave them to Imam Hassan (as), from him to Imam Hussein (as), from him to Imam Zayn ul-Abideen (as) until they reached Imam Ali al-Hadi (as). This saheefa is with Imam al-Zaman (as) right now. Imam Ali al-Hadi (as) would sit in the mosque of the Prophet (pbuh) with the Saheefa of Imam Ali (as) and would say, for example, "Ali b. Abi Talib heard the Prophet say, 'Faith is in the heart, and it is supported by your deeds and they are unified by your tongue.'"

Faith is where? In the heart, but the heart is not enough. Sometimes you hear Muslims who say, "I do not pray and fast but I have a good heart. What will happen to me on the Day of Judgement?" Allah will take your heart and put it in Jannah and the rest he'll put in Jahannum. What's the point of having a good heart with no actions?

So the heart is the locus of faith but it should be supported with action. What is the point of saying, "I love Hussein! I love Hussein!," but my actions are the opposite of Hussein? The Quran says, "Verily those who believe and do good deeds…" In the Muslim world today we have so many who believe, but there are no good deeds.

After Imam Zayn ul-Abideen (as), no Imams of the Aal Muhammad have left us as many duas as Imam Ali al-Hadi (as). People would say, "He is the second Zayn ul-Abideen (as)." According to one investigation, there is a minimum of forty-three duas of Imam Ali al-Hadi (as). Imam Zayn ul-Abideen (as) had fifty-one. Most of Imam Ali al-Hadi (as)'s duas focus on "the whispering of Satan." Many times the troubles that you see in the community or at home is due to the whispers of Satan, isn't it? Imam Ali al-Hadi (as) would sit with his students in the mosque in Medina and he would say to them, "Listen to the following dua..."

After teaching them duas, he taught them a ziyarah called Ziyarah al-Jamia'a, which after Ziyarat Ashura is arguably the most powerful ziyarah in the religion of Islam. Many scholars say, "If you want to understand the true position of the Imams, read Ziyarat al-Jamia'a." He talks about the role of the Imam, the position of the Imam and the meaning of the Imams of Aal Muhammad in this ziyarah.

His Move from Medina to Samarra

During the reign of al-Mu'tasim, and then al-Wathiq, Imam Ali al-Hadi (as) had a relatively peaceful time. But then after they died he had to face one of the worst caliphs in Islamic history. His name was al-Mutawakkil; he was the one who tried to destroy Imam Hussein (as)'s grave in Karbala forty-seven times. In other words, virtually every month in his reign as caliph al-Mutawakkil would try and cause the destruction of the grave of Aba Abdullah (as). If it were not for Allah (swt) that grave would not be there today.

Narrations state that when al-Mutawakkil became the caliph he was in Samarra; Imam Ali al-Hadi (as) was in Medina. Al-Mutawakkil knew that the Mahdi (ajfs) would be coming very soon, and he would be from the line of Fatima (as), and that Imam Ali al-Hadi (as) was also from the line of Fatima (as). He also knew that al-Ma'mun and al-Wathiq did not create a lot of problems for Imam Ali al-Hadi (as). So he thought to himself, "If I give him an easy ride, then this person will end up taking the masses."

No caliph put an Imam under house arrest like al-Mutawakkil. He told his advisor Yahya b. Harthama, "Yahya, I want you to go to Medina with three hundred of your soldiers." Yahya said, "Why?" He said, "Ali b. Muhammad al-Hadi lives in Medina. I do not want him to stay there; tell him we are in Samarra, and so he has to come and live in Samarra."

Do you know why the Abbasids were living in Samarra? They were worried about the Turks, who were now more powerful than the Abbasids. Samarra is in northern Iraq (towards Tikrit). So they made their capital Samarra.

Yahya b. Harthama says, "At the time I did not really believe Ali al-Hadi was an Imam who was worth following. On our way to Medina, I had a soldier who was from the Khawarij (who hated Imam Ali (as)) and I had a soldier from the Shi'a of Ali al-Hadi. (Sometimes you may be a believer but you are working for the government.) On our way to Medina, these two had a debate.

The Kharijite looked at the Shi'a and said, 'Ali b. Abi Talib has some hadith which do not make any sense. How do you follow this man?' The Shi'a said, 'Which hadith?' The Kharijite said, 'You have a hadith in which Ali b. Abi Talib says, 'Every part of the earth will be a grave for a human being one day.' How can every part of the earth one day be a grave for a human being?' The Shi'a said, 'If Ali b. Abi Talib says this, then Ali b. Abi Talib must be right.'

Anyway, so they debated on this issue while they were on the part of the journey to Medina. We got to Medina and found where the house of Ali al-Hadi was and we were ready to give him the orders to pack up. As soon as we got to the house of Ali al-Hadi, we saw people who were knitting, and people who were stitching, people who were making saddles and people who were making large coats. I looked at this man and I said to myself, 'This is the man they call their Imam?' This man does not have any common sense whatsoever.

(Why? Because it was summer; Iraq in the summer is one of the hottest places on earth. He thought, Ali al-Hadi is asking his people to knit in the summer?) So I said, 'Ali, you have to leave.' Ali said, 'Where?' I said, 'Al-Mutawakkil wants you in Samarra.' Ali said, 'Why?" I said, 'Al-Mutawakkil says you have to be under house arrest in Samarra. You are not allowed to live your life or practice your teachings freely in Medina.'

Ali al-Hadi looked at me and said, 'You see our people knitting and stitching? Do you mind? They are going to finish tomorrow and then we can leave on the third day.' I said, 'Okay, on the third day we will leave.' I thought to myself, I do not know why people are knitting. I do not know why people are stitching. It is hot. What do you need knitwear for? We left on the third day and we were taking the desert route back towards Samarra and we reached the place where the Kharijite debated the Shi'a. When we reached that place, Ali al-Hadi said, 'Keep this knitwear with you, and also the armor, and keep it next to you.' I asked him, 'Why?' and he said, 'Just keep it.' All of a sudden we saw from faraway a blizzard coming, the like of which we had never seen before. When this blizzard came, Ali al-Hadi said, 'Quickly, wear what I gave you!'

Some of us wore it, some of us did not; the blizzard came and a few moments later it left. We got up. I had three hundred soldiers in the beginning of the journey, eighty of them had now died. Ali al-Hadi looked at me and said, 'Ali b. Abi Talib was right when he said, 'Every part of the earth will one day be a grave for a human being.' I looked at him and I thought, 'How did he know what we discussed on the way here? Where did he have the knowledge that we were here and we discussed this issue?' That is when I believed in the Imamate of Imam Ali al-Hadi (as). I took him and we went to Samarra."

His House Arrest and Frequent Harassment by the Caliph

When Imam Ali al-Hadi (as) reached Samarra, he went inside his house and sat down. This was the beginning of his house arrest. Al-Mutawakkil did not even come to meet him. They put the Imam in a small house in Samarra. The narrations state that al-Mutawakkil said, "Let the man stay in that house; he will not leave that house without us watching his every move." A couple of days later al-Mutawakkil fell ill. He had eaten something which had been poisoned. Al-Mutawakkil's mother came to the house of Imam Ali al-Hadi (as) and said to him, "O Ali b. Muhammad, I am sorry about the way my son has treated you. Do you mind coming to his house? He is on his deathbed. I beg of you, look after him, say something, and tell us what we should do."

An Imam of Aal Muhammad could have easily turned around and said, 'No. Your son is a man who has hurt me!" But Aal Muhammad have hearts that are the hearts of generosity. Imam Ali al-Hadi (as) said to her, "O mother of al-Mutawakkil, let him eat a part of lamb and let him also have some rose water, and inshallah he will be cured."

She went back and sat next to her son (who tried to destroy the grave of Imam Ali al-Hadi (as)'s grandfather forty-seven times). She gave him some lamb and some rose water to drink. Al-Mutawakkil had made a vow that, "If I survive this, I will give 'mal kathir'" (a great amount of wealth). He managed to survive. His mother secretly came back to Imam Ali al-Hadi (as) and said to him, "I thank you very much. My son has survived. Here is ten thousand dinars in a bag."

Someone saw her come into Imam Ali al-Hadi (as)'s house. That person was called Abul Hassan al-Bathai. When he saw her, he went to al-Mutawakkil and said, "Al-Mutawakkil, I think Ali al-Hadi is trying to instigate people against you." Al-Mutawakkil said, "How?" He said, "I saw your mother go to his house; and she gave him a bag." Al-Mutawakkil said, "Very well, this Ali al-Hadi is of no good to us. At midnight send Saeed to his house; I do not care if his family is awake or asleep, wake him up and find out what he has in his house."

Saeed narrates, "I went to the house of Imam Ali al-Hadi in the middle of the night; all of a sudden I heard a voice saying, 'Saeed, wait. I will give you a candle.' (It was Imam Ali al-Hadi (as) telling him this.) Imam Ali al-Hadi (as) got up and said, "Saeed, what is it?" He said, "Ali, we need to search your house because we think you are getting money to fight us. What is this ten thousand dinars?" "It is a bag from al-Mutawakkil's mother; when al-Mutawakkil was dying, I told her what al-Mutawakkil should eat." "What is this?" "It's a mattress." "What is that?" "It's a jug." "What's that?" "A prayer mat." "You have nothing else in this house?" "I swear we have nothing else in this house; this is all we live on." "Very well. I still do not accept this. Come with me outside the house. We are going to walk to the king's palace."

Imam Ali al-Hadi (as) had to walk in the middle of the night to the palace. When Imam Ali al-Hadi (as) reached there, al-Mutawakkil looked at him and said, "What is going on?" Imam Ali al-Hadi (as) said, "Why don't you ask your friend?" Al-Mutawakkil looked at Saeed and said, "Saeed, what does he have in his house?" Saeed said, "He has a bag with ten thousand dinars." Al-Mutawakkil looked at Imam and said, "What is the ten thousand for?" Imam said, "Your mother gave it to me." Al-Mutawakkil said, "Why did my mother give you ten thousand dinars?" Imam said, "Because when you were poisoned and dying, I told your mother what you should eat and that is why you are alive now." Al-Mutawakkil said, "Forgive me. Let the man go back to the house."

They would do this to the Imam every week. They would enter his house in the middle of the night and pull him out. Why? To try and hurt him. They would barge into his house in the middle of the night. "Get out!" "What happened?" "The king wants to see you. Now!"

One time when they took Imam to the palace, al-Mutawakkil was drinking and he said to Imam Ali al-Hadi (as), "Why don't you have a drink as well?" Imam Ali al-Hadi (as) looked at him and said, "I do not want any of this." Al-Mutawakkil said, "Ali b. Muhammad, recite some poetry for me." Imam said, "We are not people of poetry." Al-Mutawakkil said, "Recite." Imam said, "All I remember is poetry from my father Amir al-Mu'mineen..." And Imam recited those lines where he told him, "There will be a day...where are the crowns? Where are the declarations? Where is the glory? At the end all you'll be is a human being underground with worms eating you from the inside out."

When al-Mutawakkil made the vow, he said, "When I become well, I will give 'mal kathir,'" but when he became well, he said, "I wonder. I said 'mal kathir.' Kathir means a lot; how much should I give?" So they went to one of the guards of al-Mutawakkil and asked, "How much is kathir?" He said, "One thousand dinars." Then they went to the ulema and asked, "How much is kathir?" They said, "One hundred thousand dinars." Al-Mutawakkil said, "No, no, no. None of you are right. Get me Ali al-Hadi; I want to see what he thinks."

They pulled Imam Ali al-Hadi (as) out of his house in the middle of the night. They refused to wait until morning. They always went to his house in the night, deliberately. Al-Mutawakkil said to him, "I made a vow." Imam Ali al-Hadi (as) said, "What was it?" Al-Mutawakkil said, "I made a vow that if I became well, I would give mal kathir; but now I do not know what a lot is. What is kathir?" Imam said, "You should give eighty-three dinars." Al-Mutawakkil said, "Sorry?" Imam Ali al-Hadi (as) said, "Eighty-three dinars." "Only eighty-three? "Yes." "Why?" "Because of the verse in the Quran." "Which verse?" Imam Ali al-Hadi (as) said, "Bismillah al-Rahman al-Rahim...Allah has given you victory in 'mawatin katheera.' You want the word 'kathir' in the Quran? This is the verse where the word 'kathir' is used." Al-Mutawakkil said, "What does the verse mean?" Imam said, "Allah gave the Prophet eighty-three victories in his life. Therefore you should pay eighty-three dinars on this issue." Al-Mutawakkil looked at him and said, "Only you people have knowledge like this," and he let him go.

On another occasion, he called him again in the middle of the night while Imam Ali al-Hadi (as) was asleep. They entered the house and ransacked it, saying, "Everyone wake up! Wake up! Where is Ali al-Hadi?" Then Imam al-Hadi would get up. "What is it?" "Come to the castle of al-Mutawakkil!" So he went to al-Mutawakkil's castle and there was a Christian man standing there. Al-Mutawakkil said, "Ali b. Muhammad, this Christian man committed zina (adultery) with a Muslim woman. I have asked that alim, Yahya b. Aktham. You know Yahya b. Aktham?" "Yes, I know him." "I asked Yahya b. Aktham to punish him, and we are about to punish him but this Christian man read his shahada. Yahya says that the Christian man should be forgiven because when you read your shahada all your sins [that you committed before becoming Muslim] are forgiven; and this alim here says he should be whipped. What's your opinion?" Imam said, "The person has to be whipped until he dies." Al-Mutawakkil asked, "Why?" Imam said, "The verse in the Quran says, '...when they see Our punishment that is when they say, 'We believe in Allah.' It is easy for a person, who commits zina, to say 'I have become a Muslim' when you are about to give him the punishment.'" Thus the punishment was meted out to him.

Week after week Imam Ali al-Hadi (as) would go through this. That is why his Shi'a found it difficult to reach him. In the beginning, his Shi'a would just have to step out of their homes and could meet him outside his house, but not anymore. People like Yunus Naqash and Isa were his companions.

Yunus Naqash narrates, "I came to Imam Ali al-Hadi secretly one day. I said, 'Imam, save my life!'" Imam said, "Yunus, what is it?" "One of the Abbasids has told me to engrave something on a gem stone. Imam, while I was engraving the gemstone, it fell and broke into half." "Yunus, do not worry; tomorrow you will receive good news." "Imam, what do you mean? I have broken the gem of this Abbasid caliph's daughter. You think he's going to forgive me? He'll kill me." "Do not worry, tomorrow you'll wake up and will receive good news."

Yunus left and narrates, "Imam Ali al-Hadi told me this, but surely, surely, these Abbasids are going to kill me. The next day the Abbasid caliph called me. He said, 'Where is the gem stone?' Now I knew I was going to die. I looked at the caliph and said, 'What do you mean?' He said, 'Can you do me a favor?' I said, "What is it?' He said, 'My two daughters have had an argument about the gemstone. Can you split it in half?'"

Yunus came back to the Imam and said, "O Imam, 'He said that his daughters were in an argument and he wanted it cut in half,' and I looked at him and I said, 'I will think about it.' He did not know in my heart I virtually had a heart attack and died. Now I'm designing it in my own way."

There was another companion by the name of Isa. He said, "We used to never get access to Imam Ali al-Hadi. One day I saw the Prophet in my dreams. The Prophet gave me thirty dates. When I woke up, I thought to myself, 'thirty dates?' It must mean that I am going to live for thirty years. I was walking and I saw Imam Ali al-Hadi (as) sitting on the ground. He was giving out dates and he gave me thirty dates. I looked at him and I said, "O Imam al-Hadi, why do not you give me more dates?" He looked at me and said, "If my grandfather the Prophet would have given you anymore, I would have given you more as well."

One day al-Mutawakkil was in trouble. A case was brought to him for which he made Imam Ali al-Hadi (as) wake up in the middle of the night to answer. A lady was brought to al-Mutawakkil. He asked, "Who is this lady?" They said, "Zaynab." "Zaynab who?" "Daughter of Ali b. Abi Talib." "Sorry?" "Zaynab, daughter of Ali." "Which Ali?" "Ali b. Abi Talib." "What do you mean Ali b. Abi Talib? Ali b. Abi Talib died two hundred years ago and Zaynab died after him." He said to the lady, "Oh Lady, explain yourself." She looked at him and said, "Yes, I am Zaynab, daughter of Ali, and sister of Hussein." Al-Mutawakkil said, "Listen, I drink a lot, but today I have not drunk anything; I am in my senses today, and I am looking at you today and I know I am not drunk. How are you Zaynab, daughter of Ali?" "Because every night in my dream the Prophet touches me so I get my youth back." Al-Mutawakkil said, "This is confusing. Go wake up Ali al-Hadi."

Imam Ali al-Hadi (as) was woken up from his sleep and brought to the palace. Al-Mutawakkil looked at him and said, "Ali, we have an issue." "What is it?" "This lady says that she is Zaynab, daughter of Ali." Imam Ali al-Hadi (as) said, "Which Ali?" The lady said, "Ali b. Abi Talib." Imam Ali al-Hadi (as) said, "You mean my great-grandfather? Who are you?" "I am Zaynab." "Which Zaynab?" "Zaynab, daughter of Ali, and sister of Hussein." "You mean Hussein, my great-grandfather, and Zaynab, my aunt, the one who was in Karbala?" "Yes, that's me." "How did you get your youth back?" "Oh, every night I see your grandfather the Prophet. He touches me on my shoulder and I get my youth back." Imam said, "Very well." Al-Mutawakkil said to the Imam, "How are we going to resolve this?" Imam Ali al-Hadi (as) said, "Simple. Al-Mutawakkil, you still have your lions in the cage?" Al-Mutawakkil said, "Yes, my lions are there. They are sitting and they are happy." Imam Ali al-Hadi (as) said, "If she is truly Zaynab, daughter of Ali, let her enter the cage of lions; none of the lions will come near her." She said, "Well, if you are Ali, and you are truly the grandson of Muhammad, then you go into the cage of lions." She turned it around on him. Imam Ali al-Hadi (as) said, "Very well, al-Mutawakkil. Allow me to enter the cage of your lions."

He opened the cage of lions, Imam Ali al-Hadi (as) went and sat in there. The hadith narrated in our books and in the books of our Sunni brothers in Islam says, "When Imam al-Hadi sat in the cage, every lion came and sat next to Imam Ali al-Hadi (as)." He turned around and said to her, "Now, are you Zaynab?" She turned around and said, "No, no. I promise I am not Zaynab," and she walked away. So in this way Imam Ali al-Hadi (as) was harassed constantly.

The Beginning of His Correspondence with His Shi'a

Since the Shi'as did not get access to their Imam so easily, the first system of letter writing began with Imam Ali al-Hadi (as). There is a book available in the Tabligh library called The Biography of Imam Ali al-Hadi (as). In it there is an entire chapter about all the "masa'il fiqhiyya" (Islamic jurisprudential queries and legal issues) which were written as letters to Imam Ali al-Hadi (as) and Imam Ali al-Hadi (as)'s answers to them.

Today people ask, "How do these ulema today answer questions? Where do they get their knowledge from?" A lot of their knowledge comes from Imam Ali al-Hadi (as)'s letters. Since he was under house arrest and the Shi'a could not get access to him, many of them would write fiqh letters to Imam Ali al-Hadi (as). Imam al-Askari (as) preserved those fiqh letters and they continued with all the ulema of Aal Muhammad (pbuh). Those fiqh letters remain with us until today. The great companions of Imam Ali al-Hadi (as) would make sure those letters would reach him.

People like Shah Abdul Azeem al-Hassani, Ali b. Mahziyar, Ahmad b. Muhammad b. Isa, Ayyub b. Nuh and Hassan b. Rashad were great companions of Imam al-Jawad (as) and Imam Ali al-Hadi (as) and would make sure the letters would reach Imam Ali al-Hadi (as). Until today, if you study to become a mujtahid, you need to study the letters of Imam Ali al-Hadi (as) and his answers to those questions.

Many of our fiqh masa'il come from Imam Muhammad al-Baqir (as), Imam Ja'far as-Sadiq (as) and Imam Ali al-Hadi (as). For example, they wrote him a letter saying, "O Imam, how do we wash the corpse of a believer in the presence of the Murje'ah? Do we wash it in the way of the Murje'ah or can we do it the way you have taught us?" Murje'ah are a sect of Islam who used to say, "What is important is not your actions, it is your heart that is important." These people would not use the palm branch in the ceremonial washing of the dead. Imam said, "Do it in our way but try to secretly use the palm branch without them seeing."

Another letter said, "O Imam, I am a Shi'a who lives far away from you; I live in an area where I know it is forbidden for me to wear a belt which is made from the leather or fur of an animal that is haram to eat. Or from an area where it is haram because of the slaughter. O Imam, but the problem is all the animals here are slaughtered in the haram way. O Imam, is there any animal which we are allowed to use the fur of in this situation?" Imam replied, "The fur of the beaver is an animal you are allowed to use in the situation you are living in." Another letter said, "O Imam, if someone walks past me in salat in my area, is my salat invalid, or does my salat remain?" Imam said, "Your salat does not become invalid by someone walking past you."

Another letter said, "O Imam, my wife is breastfeeding in the month of Ramadan; does she have to fast?" Imam replied, "Your wife is not obliged to fast in the holy month of Ramadan if she is breastfeeding."

Thousands of letters were written to Imam Ali al-Hadi (as) which are preserved until today. Al-Mutawakkil was killed by his son al-Muntasir. Why? Al-Muntasir saw al-Mutawakkil hurt Imam Ali al-Hadi (as) and so he got upset and killed his father. What did al-Muntasir see his father do?

Al-Mutawakkil began a comedy stage show where he would get an effeminate man to play Ali b. Abi Talib (as). The man would put a cushion under his dress and he would make himself look bald and he would say, "I am Ali b. Abi Talib." Al-Muntasir despised the way his father behaved. He went to Imam Ali al-Hadi (as) and said, "What is the ruling on someone who curses Fatima Zahra (as) and Ali b. Abi Talib (as)?" Imam Ali al-Hadi (as) said, "That person is to be killed." He said, "What happens if that is someone's father?" Imam said, "That will be the end of his son's life; his son will die shortly afterwards because he has broken ties with his father." Al-Muntasir said, "While I am alive my father will not do this." Thus he went and killed his own father, al-Mutawakkil, and six months later al-Muntasir himself died.

One caliph after another died until al-Mu'tazz came into power. When al-Mu'tazz found out that Imam Ali al-Hadi (as) had that much of a following, al-Mu'tazz decided, "I will do what al-Mutawakkil did not do, what al-Muntasir did not do, what al-Mu'tasim did not do, what al-Wathiq did not do, and what al-Musta'een did not do; I will put poison in the food of Imam Ali al-Hadi (as)."

While Imam Ali al-Hadi (as) was dying, he wrote to his companions, "Do me one favor. The poison has affected my body…I beg of you, go to the grave in Karbala; go to the holy man who lies in the ground in Karbala." They would write back by saying to him, "O Imam, but aren't you his grandson? Do you not have the same affect with Allah?" He said, "Nobody has a relationship with Allah like my grandfather, Hussein."

That is why he would echo the words of Imam al-Sadiq (as) in the Ziyarah of Imam Hussein (as), "O Allah! Have mercy on those cheeks that rub themselves on the grave of Imam Hussein (as)."

Lecture 13

Imam Hassan b. Ali al-Askari (as)

Imam Hassan al-Askari (as) was born in the year 232 after Hijra and died in the year 260 after Hijra at the age of twenty-eight. He is a man from whose life many a lesson may be learnt and indeed many an example may be derived. He is a man whose life affects each and every one of our lives today, for he is known as the father of the final Imam of Aal Muhammad (pbuh), Imam Mahdi (ajfs).

Unfortunately, Imam Hassan al-Askari (as)'s life has not been examined in the way that it should be. There are many who know very little about the life of Imam Hassan al-Askari (as) and many who do not know about the political circumstances that surrounded the life of this great personality. It is unfortunate to see that there are not enough detailed commentaries on his life or analyzed biographies of what he faced. Indeed, he faced hardships more than any of the Imams of Aal Muhammad (pbuh) as the Abbasids knew that the time was near for the birth of the promised one from the line of Fatima (as). Therefore, there is a need for us to dissect his life, in addition to learning about his great companions, such as Fadl b. Shadhan and Abul Adyan.

His Parents and Siblings

Imam Hassan al-Askari (as) was born in the 232nd year after Hijra. His mother's name was Hudaifa, and in some narrations she was known as Saleel, and in other narrations she was known as Sawsan. But what is clear is that his mother's origin was from the southern part of Egypt. Therefore, again we find another Imam of the Ahlulbayt whose mother comes from an area in Africa. His mother was revered for being one of the most pious women who was alive at the time.

Imam Hassan al-Askari (as) was one of five children. He had an elder brother by the name of Muhammad, then himself, then a brother by the name of Hussein, and then Ja'far, and a sister by the name of Aliya.

Some of his brothers were very religious and some were not so religious. This highlights that the fact that, even in the lives of the Imams of Ahlulbayt, in one family you may have a brother who is very religious and then you may have a brother who is not necessarily religious at all. Imam Hassan al-Askari (as)'s elder brother Muhammad was one of the most pious sons of any Imams of Aal Muhammad (pbuh). Those of you who have had the honor of visiting Samarra...on the way back you might have stopped at Balad. There you may have gone to visit Sayyed Muhammad. He was the brother of Imam Hassan al-Askari (as) and is buried not too far away from Samarra, in the city of Balad. He was born three years before Imam Hassan al-Askari (as) and he died in the year 252 after Hijra at the age of twenty-three.

Imam Ali al-Hadi (as) used to love Muhammad very much because firstly, he was the eldest son and his older brother; this highlights the fact that our belief in the Imamate is not a belief in the primacy of the eldest son. Otherwise, Muhammad, son of Imam Ali al-Hadi (as), would have been the Imam. He was one of the most pious people of his time and the narrations say that nobody was as respected and as honorable or, indeed, as pious as Muhammad.

Thus, there are different reasons that are given for his death. One narration states that Imam Ali al-Hadi (as) had a piece of land in Balad. Muhammad went to collect the revenue of that land and he died there. Another narration says that he died a natural death in Balad. When Muhammad died, Imam Hassan al-Askari (as) is narrated to have ripped his shirt open when he heard the news. Now to show emotion like this is something unusual for an Imam of Ahlulbayt, so people came to Imam Hassan al-Askari (as) and said, "Imam, you are masum (infallible). How are you one who rips your shirt upon hearing the news of the death of your elder brother?"

He replied, "When Nabi Musa heard about the death of Nabi Harun he did the same thing." It is as if the chest gets enclosed, and there is a lack of breath. You want to rip open your shirt; it is sad news. It is highly recommended to visit Muhammad's grave, because amongst the gifts of Muhammad, son of Imam Ali al-Hadi (as), is that Allah answers the prayers performed under his dome, and especially the prayer of a family who cannot have children. If you go there you will see a cradle outside the haram; the reason there is a cradle there is that many people who are not able to have children went and did the ziyarah of Muhammad, the son of Imam Ali al-Hadi (as). After they came back, Allah granted them their request. Therefore, Muhammad, the son of Imam Ali al-Hadi (as) and the brother of Imam Hassan al-Askari (as), is remembered as a pious man.

Why is He Known as "al-Askari?"

"Al-Askari" refers to an army base. There are certain cities in Iraq that were originally army bases and not cities. So if the army was riding past an area, they would stop at the base for a while and move on. For example, Kufa was originally an army base situated on the outskirts of another city by the name of Aqulah. When Sa'ad b. Abi Waqas took his army there in the 17th year after Hijra, he said, "This area looks like an area where people can live." So Kufa was initially a base, but later became a garrison town after Sa'ad decided that people could live there. Likewise, Imam Hassan al-Askari (as) resided originally at an army base. Samarra was not a city; it was an army base. Why was it an army base?

During the time of al-Mu'tasim, Turkish soldiers became more powerful than the Abbasids. Some of these solders would ride their horses in the streets of Baghdad and harass people. For example, if they saw a woman walking on the street of Baghdad, they would snatch her bag or harass her. The people complained to al-Mu'tasim who was the caliph during the Imamate of Imam al-Jawad (as). They said to al-Mu'tasim, "These Turkish soldiers come and harass us while we live in Baghdad, and we are ready to fight you and your soldiers. We do not care that you are our caliph who lives in Baghdad!" He said, "What will you fight me with?" They said, "Dua al-Sahar." Notice they did not say with an army.

Al-Mu'tasim then decided that he needed to leave Baghdad and live somewhere else. On one of his journeys he went to an area called "Kartool," but he felt it wasn't a good place to live. Then he went to Samarra. One of the words "Samarra" comes from is "Surra man ra'a," which means "that which is pleasing to the eye." Those of you who have been to Samarra will know how beautiful it is. On the way there is the River Tigris and many forests and trees; it is a beautiful city. Al-Mu'tasim went there and decided that Samarra should not be an army base. He developed it into a city, but originally it was an "askar," or a base for an army.

After al-Mu'tasim, al-Mutawakkil took over. Here a famous incident took place after which the area was called the "Askariyayn." Imam Ali al-Hadi (as) and Imam Hassan al-Askari (as) are called "al-Askariyayn," meaning the two who were present in the "Mu'askar," or the area of the army. The incident is as follows: once al-Mutawakkil told all his soldiers, who numbered over a hundred thousand, to collect bags of wheat. He said, "I want all of you to come to the area where I am building my army base, and I want you to put all the bags together and make a hill for me on which I can ride to the top."

The narrations states that they all collected these wheat bags and then he and his representative, Fatha b. Khakan, stood at the top. When they looked down at Imam Ali al-Hadi (as), they said to him, "Look how grand our kingdom is? Where is your kingdom?" mam replied, "Look through my fingers and you'll see my kingdom."When al-Mutawakkil looked through his fingers, the narrations state that he immediately recognized what the Imam was implying - "You can build a place so high and you can have the highest peaks, but I have Allah's soldiers, who are even higher, to look after me."

His Childhood

From a very young age Imam Hassan al-Askari (as) was already showing qualities similar to his forefathers. One person narrates that, "I was walking one day when I saw these children all playing with toys, except one young child who had shed a tear. So I went up to him and said, 'Young man, I see you have shed a tear. Are you sad that you do not have any toys? Shall I go and bring you toys?' He looked at me and said, 'O man, this world was not meant for us to play with toys.' I looked at him, as I had never heard someone so young answer me like this, so I said to him, 'What do you mean?' He said, 'O man, have you not read the Quran?' I was staring at this child while he was talking to me about the Quran. I said to him, 'What do you mean? Which verse in the Quran?'

Look at Aal Muhammad; the Quran is part of their life. As their followers we must be the same. For three hundred and sixty five days of the year they had a relationship with the Quran. The child said, 'Have you not read surah 23, verse 115?' I was thinking to myself that I do not even know what it says, so I said, 'Tell me.' The child says, 'Do they think this world was created in vain and they will not return to Us one day?' I said, 'What do you mean by this?' He said, 'When I look at my mother moving the sticks to make fire, I wonder about this fire but I also wonder about the fire of the Day of Judgement. Am I going to be a part of the fuel of that fire?' I looked around and asked the people, 'Who is this child who is speaking to me like this?' They said to me, 'It is Hassan al-Askari.'"

His Imprisonment

From a young age Imam Hassan al-Askari (as) began to make his impression upon people and that is why the Abbasids knew that at any moment the Mahdi would be born. Was it al-Askari? Was it the one after him? The Abbasid caliph, al-Mu'tazz, had decided that it was better to kill this young man than to allow him to freely answer questions like Muhammad al-Jawad and Ali al-Hadi. His people told al-Mu'tazz, "But he is a young man." Al-Mu'tazz said, "I do not care. His father has now passed away and now it is time that we kill him. There is no need for these people in our territory." So he asked his companion ibn Saeed, "O Saeed, I want you to do something for me." "What is it?" "Take the young man towards the palace of ibn Ubair, and kill him on the way there; and when you have killed him, make an announcement on your return that it was an unfortunate accident, and that is why the young man is not present with us anymore."

Remember the Imam was around twenty-two when his father died. The Shi'a wrote letters to Imam Hassan al-Askari (as) saying, "O Imam, we were at a meeting between al-Mu'tazz, the caliph, and ibn Saeed, and he is planning to kill you on a journey." Imam said, "Do not worry. In a few days this person himself will be killed."

And just as Imam had said, within three days, the Turks had killed him. When the Turks killed ibn Saeed, the caliph decided that the best place for al-Askari was prison. That is why we find that Imam Hassan al-Askari (as), may Allah bless his soul, for six years, from the age of twenty-two until the age of twenty-eight, and this is where he died.

The Abbasids had two types of prisons: one was a public prison for thieves, rapists and people who have committed adultery. The other prison was a private prison where you were under house arrest in your own home. They have guards standing outside and you are not allowed to go out. There are narrations which state that, for two years in a row, for seven hundred and thirty days, Imam Hassan al-Askari (as) used to live on two loaves of bread and cold water.

It is surprising today to hear the complaints of the Shi'as of Aal Muhammad regarding what Allah has given them despite the innumerable blessings they have in their lives.

Narrations state that Imam Hassan al-Askari (as) entered the prison healthy, but by the end he was very frail. Sometimes they would go inside to check on him and they would see him on the ground and think he was dying. However, they would realize he was doing sujood to Allah (swt). Imam Hassan al-Askari (as) teaches us that sometimes you may be in your house and that may be a prison; and sometimes you may be in a prison but you make it a house. Make the best of whichever situation you may find yourself. "I'm in prison, but just because I am in prison does not mean I cannot serve Allah; I can serve Allah even by being in prison."

When you take a look at Islamic history, it is as if history repeated itself. Prophet Yusuf (as) also served Allah in prison. He worshipped Allah in prison and brought the inmates of the prison towards Allah. Some of the greatest personalities in history discovered Allah in prison or wrote their best books in prison. For example, Malcolm X came towards Allah in prison. A book by the name of al-Lum'ah ad-Dimashqiya is one of our greatest books on law, which has to be studied before you can even approach being a master of law. This book was written by Shaheed al-Awwal. According to certain sources he wrote this book in one week in prison.

If you read the book, you will wonder how a man could write it in seven days. It is a phenomenal text of law. ibn Khaldoon wrote al-Muqaddama in prison too.

In other words, some of the best works you can produce may be while you are in prison. Sometimes we are very negligent with our work with Muslims in prison. It's a shame. We have Muslims in prison but none of our scholars are going to the prisons. They are very active in the areas of nikkah and Salat ul-Mayyit, but their outreach work can also improve. We need more scholars who visit prisons to see the Muslims in prison and talk to them and guide them. Imam Hassan al-Askari (as) did not sit in prison and say, "Now that I am in prison I should just pray and fast the whole day." No. In fact he made the prison an avenue for spreading the word of Aal Muhammad. How did he do that?

First, his manners were such that they left an impression on anyone he came into contact with and that was the first way he made a difference. Saleh b. Wasit was a governor for the Abbasid caliph. He used to watch over Imam Hassan al-Askari (as) in prison. He narrates, "I sent two of the worst prison guards to Samarra into the prison of Imam Hassan al-Askari (as). I told them, 'Torture this man as much as you can.'"

The narrations mention that one day a group of people came to Saleh and said to him, "Saleh, you used to be very harsh, but you are not as harsh as you were before." He said, "What do you mean?" They said, "These guards that you are sending to Imam Hassan al-Askari (as) are not doing anything. We want them to whip him and kick him, but they are not doing anything." He said, "You go and ask the guards. Do not ask me." They went to the guards. These guards were the type you do not want to wake up to and face the first thing in the morning. They said to the guards, "Why have you not tortured Hassan al-Askari?"

The narrations state that they said, "How can we torture a man who in the daytime is fasting and in the night time is praying, and whenever we look at him we see his tongue moving in praise of Allah (swt)." These two guards came towards the Ahlulbayt because of Imam Hassan al-Askari (as). They went in to torture him but came out as lovers and followers of Aal Muhammad (pbuh).

There was another person who was appointed as a security guard for Imam Hassan al-Askari (as). He was told to keep a close eye on him. The guard came up to the Imam and said, "O Hassan b. Ali, here are some pomegranates. One of your Shi'a says that 'instead of having just two loaves and some water, here give him the pomegranates'; and I used to know this person from before, so take them."

So Imam Hassan al-Askari (as) took the five pomegranates and placed them by his side. This is tabligh: Imam Hassan al-Askari (as) did not eat them. He just kept them there. The guard kept on looking at the pomegranates. Imam looked at him and said, "Why don't you take a pomegranate, O guard?" The guard said, "No, no, keep it, keep it." Imam said, "O guard, I have seen you look at the pomegranate. Maybe the day is a hot today and because it is hot, maybe you are not getting fresh air. Take the pomegranate."

The guard took the pomegranate and then there were four pomegranates left. It was only a short time later when Imam Hassan al-Askari (as) looked at the guard and said, "O guard, I noticed that you are not eating the pomegranate. Why?" The guard said, "Do not worry, you do not need to ask." Imam said, "No, tell me." He said, "You know, I have young children at home and I want to save the pomegranates so that my children can eat them." Imam Hassan al-Askari (as) said, "Take the other four pomegranates." The guard said, "No." Imam said, "No, no, please. I cannot bear to think that your children will not have food."

After that incident, word spread among the other guards about what Hassan al-Askari was like, and the head of the guards found out. He was Turkish. Some narrations say his name was Ali b. Yarmash and some say it was Ali b. Utash. This head guard said to the other guard, "If you are not going to treat Hassan al-Askari in the way that he should be, by not whipping him while he is here, then I'm going to take him to my house, and I have received orders to even kill him."

Thus Imam Hassan al-Askari (as) was taken out of this prison and was transferred to the Turkish guard's house. As soon as the Turkish man walked into his house, his wife looked at him and asked, "Who is that you have brought with you?" He said, "Don't worry about it." "No, tell me." "Hassan b. Ali." "From whose lineage?" "From Muhammad's lineage." "Be careful; people like this are inheritors of knowledge. Do not hurt them." "Who are you to tell me not to hurt them? I have wild animals in my garden; I will leave the man with them. They have not eaten for a few days. Let them enjoy his flesh."

People ask, "Why did Allah make Imam al-Mahdi go into occultation (ajfs)?" Look at the way they were being treated. Do you think they would have left Imam al-Mahdi (ajfs) alone?

Thus the man put Imam Hassan al-Askari (as) in a cage with the wild animals. It takes a very hardened heart to actually do something like this. The guard then walked back to his house. His wife pleaded with him, but he did not listen. Then she said, "Now that they have killed him, at least have some respect and go back out and bury his body or what remains of it."

Ali b. Yarmash narrates, "I swear by God I walked back to the cage and I saw Hassan al-Askari prostrating with the animals all next to him. I could not believe that they were prostrating next to him as these animals had not eaten anything in days."

This same man, Ali b. Yarmash, who put Imam Hassan al-Askari (as) in the animal cage, went to visit Imam Hassan al-Askari (as) in prison when his son fell ill. He said, "Hassan b. Ali, I need a favor, and I know I have been harsh towards you, and I know I have been giving you the worst of guards, but I need one dua." Imam asked, "Why?" He said, "My son is ill and the doctors say he is going to die, and you are the only one who can pray for him; I beg you to please read a dua." Imam Hassan al-Askari (as) said, "No problem, recite the following dua with me." He began reciting the dua, and after it ended Imam said, "Go home now, your son will be okay." Ali b. Yarmash said, "I swear I went home and my son had recovered fully." This was the generosity of the Imams of Aal Muhammad (pbuh).

On one occasion they tried to mock Imam Hassan al-Askari (as). One day the caliph bought a horse which was too wild. The caliph said, "This wild horse has not been tamed and causes me trouble when I sit on it. Get Hassan al-Askari out of prison; let him sit on the horse so it can throw him off." Then he said, "But I know that if he is truly from the line of the Prophet that horse will never throw him off." When Imam Hassan al-Askari (as) sat on that horse, it became tame. Then the caliph told the man, "Come here, and take your horse back."

His Contributions to Humanity while in Prison

The first way Imam Hassan al-Askari (as) brought the people towards the Ahlulbayt while being in prison was through his manners; they would give him two loaves of bread and water, while he would show generosity back to them.

Imam Hassan al-Askari (as) also wrote two books while he was in prison. Of his great works is a fiqh collection called al-Muqni'a. This book is also present with us today. It is a book with all the jurisprudential questions that Imam Hassan al-Askari (as) answered in letters to his Shi'a. The scholars today answer questions by using the book of Imam Hassan al-Askari (as) and Imam Ali al-Hadi (as).

Furthermore, Imam Hassan al-Askari (as) would ask the people who came to see him in prison, "What's happening outside? Come and tell me. Do not keep me unaware so I can help and guide you in answering questions."

One day a person came to him and said, "O Imam, do you know Ishaq al-Kindi?" Yes." "Ishaq al-Kindi has written a book called The Contradictions in the Quran."

There are some verses in the Quran which sound contradictory; and unless you have strong knowledge of the Quran, which we need in this generation, then do not be surprised if you will be bamboozled by some of the questions about the contradictions in the Quran. For example, Ishaq al-Kindi said, "There is a contradiction in one verse of the Quran. In one verse God says marry one, two, three or four women; in another verse God says you can never treat them justly so stick to one. So how is it that in one verse God says marry four and in another God says you cannot treat them justly?" On the internet today this is a major question. Many object to the Quran saying it has contradictions.

The answer is that if you marry one, two, three or four, you can treat them justly financially; and you can also treat them justly with your time; but you can never treat them justly with love. So there is no contradiction. The first verse refers to justice in monetary and time issues, while the second is about justice in love.

Thus Ishaq wrote in his book that, "If the Quran was a book of God, then it wouldn't have contradictions." So the companions told the Imam about this book when he was in prison. Imam asked them, "Have any of you been able to refute it?" They said, "No." He said, "The refutation is easy. It does not need too many semantics." They said, "What's the refutation?" Imam said, "Go up to Ishaq and say to him, "O Ishaq, is there a possibility that the author of a book intends something different from its interpreter?" So when the companions asked Ishaq this question, he said, "Yes, there is."

The companions said to him, "So Ishaq, in regard to what you say about a contradiction, could Allah have meant something else? Or is your interpretation the only possible interpretation?" Ishaq said, "No. Allah could have meant something else." They said, "So, O Ishaq, why do you not then say, 'Maybe my conclusions are not correct and that Allah (swt) intended something else with this.'" Ishaq said to them, "Where did you get this answer from?" They said to him, "What do you mean?" He said, "No, tell me. Where did you get the answer from?" A companion said, "Oh, just from my own thoughts." He said, "None of you can think like this. Where did you get this from?" The companion said, "I got it from Imam Hassan al-Askari (as)." He said, "Only a man from the line of the Prophet can think like this. This is very true." Then he took the book and ripped it apart.

Imam Hassan al-Askari (as) tried his hardest to give out information to his followers and tell them about the beliefs of his religion. One of the most famous hadiths we have from Imam Hassan al-Askari (as) is when he explains the characteristics of his loyal Shi'a. He knew that in a short time his son Imam al-Mahdi (ajfs) would not be present as a locus for his followers. So he told his followers that, "There are five signs of a Shi'a" (so they could recognize each other in the ghayba).

1- "He prostrates on dust, and preferably the dust of Karbala." Some people ask why we Shi'as prostrate on the dust of Karbala and not on the carpet. We in the School of Ahlulbayt have clear evidence that the Prophet (pbuh) has a hadith where he says, "Innama jo'ilat li al-ardh masjidon wa tahura -The earth has been made a place which is pure and for prostration." Plus, there were no carpets in the time of the Prophet (pbuh). In both Shi'a and Sunni books of hadith, it is written that when the Prophet (pbuh) would sit up from sujood, and people would look up at his forehead, there would be marks of clay and mud. The Prophet (pbuh), therefore, did not pray on a prayer mat. He used to pray on earth because he said the earth has been made pure and has been made a place for prostration. The carpets and the prayer mats came into the Prophet (pbuh)'s mosque three hundred years after he died.

So people ask, "Does that mean that we must only prostrate on the dust of Karbala?" No. Any dust is fine, as long as it is natural and not something that can be eaten or be worn. Anything that is natural can be prostrated on.

2- "He prays fifty-one rakats of prayer a day." Sadly, at the moment, most of the Shi'as are struggling with the seventeen rakats. If we add Salat ul-Layl, it adds up to twenty-eight. So the rest of the rakats come from the sunnah prayers of Fajr, Dhuhr, Asr, Maghrib and Isha. If you add all of these together, it comes to fifty-one.

3- "He wears a ring on his right hand." If you look at many of the followers of the Ahlulbayt when you go on ziyarah, they will buy either a Durr al-Najaf, or Firuza (turquoise) or Aqiq Yamani (agate), or ruby or emerald. We have many hadiths from the Imams of Ahlulbayt about the importance of these stones. They protect you from envy of the people, they increase your sustenance and they prevent sudden attack from affecting your family.

4- "He says, 'Bismillah hir Rahman nir Rahim,' loudly before doing any act." Many people say "Bismillah" before praying, but then to forget to say it when they are eating, starting their work, or entering into their homes.

5- "He recites the Ziyarat Arba'een." Imam Hassan al-Askari (as) said one must never neglect the Ziyarat Arba'een of Imam Hussein. One of the ziyarahs has been narrated from Jabir b. Abdullah.

His Martyrdom

At the age of twenty-eight, Imam Hassan al-Askari (as) was poisoned. Al-Mu'tamid had said, "I put this man out of prison and the people love him; I put him back in prison and the people become followers of Ahlulbayt; it is better that I poison him."

The narrations state that Imam Hassan al-Askari (as) said to his companion, "O Abul Adyan! I am giving you some letters, go to Mada'in and deliver these letters. You will return in fifteen days; when you return to

Samarra, you will hear the people say, 'Al-Askari has died,' you will see the one who will succeed me from Aal Muhammad (pbuh), the al-Mahdi." Abul Adyan asked, "How will I know him?" Imam said, "You will know him because he will lead my prayers; he will ask you for the letters and he will know what is in the yellow bag." What were these letters he had to deliver? Imam Hassan al-Askari (as) used to stay up till midnight answering all the questions of his Shi'a.

Abul Adyan says, "I left; I went to Mada'in to meet Ahmad b. Hassan. I gave him the letters and I stayed with him for a few days. All I was thinking about was my Imam Hassan al-Askari (as). What would happen to him? Then I left Ahmad b. Hassan and returned to Samarra. When I entered Samarra, I saw people coming out crying and crying. I asked them what was wrong. They said to me, 'Hassan al-Askari has died.' I went to the house of Imam Hassan al-Askari (as) and saw his brother Ja'far standing there, about to lead Salat ul-Mayyit (the prayer for the one who is deceased). Ja'far was saying, 'I am now the Imam of the Shi'a,' and I thought, 'Ja'far? The one who is the liar? The one we have no respect for?' As Ja'far was about to begin the salat, a young five year old walked up to him and said, 'O Ja'far, move aside. I have a greater right to lead this salat than you do.' Ja'far was amazed at the young man and moved away."

After reading the salat, the young man went to Abul Adyan and said, "Where are the letters?" Abul Adyan knew that was a sign and gave him the letters. Then the narration states that a group of people had come from Qum. They had some khums in the bag. They said, "Who is the successor of Hassan al-Askari?" The people looked and said, "It is Ja'far." Ja'far also said, "It is me." The people of Qum said, "Then tell us, if you are his rightful successor, what is in the bag?" Ja'far said, "What? Do you think I have knowledge of the unseen?"

Then someone came and said, "There is one thousand and ten dinars in the bag." They said, "You are right. Who told you?" He said, "My Imam, al-Hujjah b. Hassan al-Mahdi (ajfs)." As soon as they heard that, they said, "Where is he?" Al-Mu'tamid also heard this and said, "Where is the young boy?" The Imam had disappeared.

Lecture 14

Imam Muhammad b. Hassan al-Mahdi (ajfs)

Imam Muhammad b. Hassan al-Mahdi (ajfs) was born on the 15th of Sha'ban in the 255th year after Hijra. He is revered by many as the Messiah of the religion of Islam. His life has to be examined in depth for he is the Awaited Savior of the religion - the one who will bring justice and remove all forms of oppression and indeed, all forms of cruelty and tyranny. The discussion concerning the Imam is a vital one which concerns each and every one of our lives. It is a discussion from which many a lesson may be learnt, and indeed, many examples may be derived, and many principles may be gained, whether they be theological, ethical, or jurisprudential.

The Mahdi - A Universal Concept

The discussion of the Mahdi has a historical basis and a contemporary significance, contemporary in a way that every religion in the world today believes in a Mahdi, or an Awaited Savior. If you were to study the scriptures of each and every religion in the world, you will find within their scriptures there is the discussion concerning an Awaited Savior, a Savior who will remove all forms of tyranny and oppression and instill justice and peaceful equality within the world in which we live. For example, if you were to study the Avesta, the Zoroastrian scripture, you'll find that it mentions the name of a man by the name of "Saoshyant." Saoshyant is the Awaited Savior - the one who will come and bring complete goodness in the universe.

If you were to study the Bhagavata Purana, one of the Hindu Scriptures, you will find that there is a person by the name of the "Kalki" who will come at a time when the politicians will be corrupt and full of deceit and will be abusing innocent people. They will come and remove all the corruption and all of the deceit from the world. In Buddhism, you will find that Gautama speaks of a final Buddha, a Buddha who will bring enlightenment to the earth at a time when it is full of darkness. Similarly, in the Jewish Scriptures, you will find that there is a discussion of a Messiah from the children of David who will come and remove all types of tyranny and injustice. In the Christian scriptures, too, there is a mention of the second coming of Jesus as the Messiah who will come with the word of God and will bring justice and equality to the world.

In other words, we find that the belief in the Mahdi is a belief not just for Muslims, but a belief of every religion in the world today. Likewise, when you look within the religion of Islam, you will find that the Sunni and Shi'a have more in common than they have differences on this issue. It is obligatory on every Muslim, both Sunni and Shi'a, to believe in the Mahdi, and the only difference between the different schools is whether he is alive or whether he is yet to be born. Other than that there are numerous traditions, both in Sunni and Shi'a literature, which refer to a man referred to as the Mahdi, from the sons of Fatima (as), whose name will be the same as the Prophet (pbuh), and who will establish justice. Therefore, on the first level, the need to dissect the biography of the Imam is due to its relevance to every world religion today.

And on the second level, the famous narration we have from the Holy Prophet Muhammad(pbuh) states, "The one who dies without knowing the Imam of his time dies the death of someone in ignorance."

So every Muslim has this belief that there is a need to know the Imam of Our Time, and that there is a need to understand his biography, and as a result of that, many questions arise concerning the Imam today. Some of them are as follows: "How many people did Imam Hassan al-Askari (as) talk to regarding Imam al-Mahdi (ajfs)?" "What is the origin of Imam al-Mahdi (ajfs)'s mother?" "Was Imam al-Mahdi (ajfs) with his parents for the first few years of his life or no?" "What was the need of a minor occultation and who were his representatives?" "What was the wisdom behind the major occultation?" "What are the signs of his reappearance?"

These are all the questions that are being asked today. There are certain elements within our own communities today who have begun to question the position of the Imam, but this allows for free thought and there is no harm in letting the people come and discuss things, with evidence and text, in order that we may be able to get acquainted with the biography of the Imam of Our Time.

Circumstances and Controversies Surrounding His Birth

When we discuss the life of Muhammad b. Hassan al-Mahdi (ajfs), we begin with his birth on the 15th of Sha'ban in the year 255 after Hijra. The question here arises, what was the environment surrounding his birth? As we know very well, his father, our eleventh Imam, was around twenty-two when he received his Imamate. There were two factions of people who were interested in identifying his successor.

The first of them were naturally going to be his own adherents, people from his own school, from the religion of Islam and from the School of Ahlulbayt. These people had traditions at the time which stated that there will be twelve Imams after the Prophet (pbuh) or that there will be twelve caliphs after the Prophet (pbuh). For example, from the time of our sixth Imam, people like Abu Saeed al-Asfari, Fadl b. Shadhan (a companion of the tenth Imam) wrote about this in their notebooks. During the era of our ninth Imam, Bukhari and Muslim mentioned this in their Sahihs; all of them either spoke of the names of the Imams of Aal Muhammad, noted that the number of caliphs after the Prophet would be twelve, or described the Mahdi from the line of the Prophet (pbuh).

For example Imam al-Bukhari, who was living at the time of Imam al-Jawad (as), Imam Ali al-Hadi (as) and Imam Hassan al-Askari (as), in his book, Sahih al-Bukhari, which is with us until today, has written about the fact that not only will there be twelve caliphs after the Prophet (pbuh), but that there will be a man by the name of Mahdi from the line of Fatima (as) who will come and bring justice and remove all forms of tyranny.

In other words, there were many texts that were available at the time which were already discussing the Mahdi. `Ali Mahzayar al-Ahwazi was a close associate of the ninth Imam, al-Jawad. He was appointed by the latter as his representative in al-Ahwaz and continued to remain in office throughout the reign of the tenth Imam, al-Hadi. He wrote two books, called Kitab al-Malahim and Kitab al-Qa'im, both dealing with the occultation of the Imam and his subsequent rising with the sword. Then between the years 260 and 329 his two sons Ibrahim and Muhammad became the authorised representatives of the Twelfth Imam in al-Ahwaz. It is on their authority that al-Kulayni and al-Saduq give important information concerning the communication methods employed in the underground activities of the Imamites.

In his work on the subject of al-Ghayba called al Mashyakha, al-Hassan b. Mahbub al-Sarrad records several anedoctes which are often attributed to the Imams. This work has been lost but several quotations from it are included in the available Imamite sources.

Al-Fadl b. Shadhan al-Nisaburi was a wellknown Imamite scholar and secured the trust and the praise of the eleventh Imam. He also compiled a book called al-Ghayba, but most of its material seems to have been quoted from the work of al-Hassan b. Mahbub. Since al-Fadl died two months before the death of the eleventh Imam , the importance of his work lies in the traditions he recorded indicating that the Twelfth Imam would be al-Qa'im. Many later writers like al-Tusi in his own work entitled al-Ghayba, relied on al-Fadl's work. Baha al-Din al-Nili also compiled a work entitled al-Ghayba by summarising al-Fadl's work. Despite the fact that the actual work of al-Fadl is lost, the works Kifayat al-Muhtadi fi Ma`rifat al-Mahdi by Mirlawhi and Kashf al-Astir by Mirza Husayn al-Nuri seems to be copies of his work. Therefore it is not unreasonable to make use of these later sources for our present purposes.

Another faction who was interested in the birth was the Abbasid caliphs. Naturally, today you will find some people who say, "What is your evidence that Imam al-Mahdi was born then? Imam al-Mahdi has not been born. Imam al-Mahdi will be born later."

Our reply is that, firstly, you already have texts which mention twelve Imams and his name is the last; and secondly, if there was no sign of the birth of Imam al-Mahdi (ajfs), then why would the Abbasid caliphs put Imam Ali al-Hadi (as) and Imam Hassan al-Askari (as) under house arrest? What did both of them have that was such a threat to the Abbasids? Huge armies? Did they have a hundred thousand people standing outside their homes? If you look at their lives, you will see that they had relatively few followers who had access to them. Therefore, today when someone says to you, "I do not believe Imam al-Mahdi was born. What is your evidence?" Alongside texts such as that of Fadl b. Shadhan or Abu Saeed al-Asfari, or for example, the texts which mention the Imams, say to them, "Then why were the Abbasid caliphs standing outside his house waiting for one of the women of the house to give birth?" If there was no fear of Imam Mahdi, then why would the caliph put Imam Ali al-Hadi (as) and Imam Hassan al-Askari (as) under house arrest?

Did Imam Hassan al-Askari (as) tell a lot of people about Imam al-Mahdi (ajfs)? If you research the sources, you will come to the conclusion that Imam Hassan al-Askari (as) did not tell many people. In fact, you may even realize that some of Imam Hassan al-Askari (as)'s closest confidants and advisors did not know about Imam al-Mahdi (ajfs)'s birth until the day of his birth. Only a very close group of people actually knew about Imam al-Mahdi (ajfs). Who were they? They were Abu Hashim al-Ja'fari, Ahmad b. Ishaq, Hakima (the aunt of Imam Hassan al-Askari (as) from his father's side, who is buried in Samarra) and Khadija (another aunt from Imam Hassan al-Askari (as)'s father's side); and also amongst the other close confidants were people such as Abul Adyan. Other than them it seems very unlikely that Imam Hassan al-Askari (as) told many people about the birth of Imam al-Mahdi (ajfs). Moreover, it is quite possible that Hakima may not have even known about the birth of the Imam until even the day of the birth. Why? Because Imam Hassan al-Askari (as) had to be very careful as to who exactly knew about his son.

The earliest Imamite scholar to give an account of the Twelfth Imam's mother is al-Mas'udi. He reports that she was a slave-girl called Narjis. Al-Shahid (d. 786/1384) states that her name was Maryam b. Zayd al-`Alawiyya, and other reports give her name as Rayhana, Saqil and Sawsan. ss It is possible that her name was in fact Narjis and the other names, except Saqil, were given to her by her owner Hakima bint Muhammad al-Jawad. People at that time used to call their slave-girls by different names as a form of flattery, and Narjis, Rayhana and Sawsan are all names of flowers.

The earliest report concerning the nationality of the Twelfth Imam's mother goes back to the year 286. This was written down for the first time by al-Saduq, on the authority of Muhammad b. Bahr al-Shaybani, who attributed his narration to Bishr b. Sulayman al-Nakhkhas. According to this report she was a Christian from Byzantium who had been captured by Islamic troops. Who was this lady?

Imam Ali al-Hadi (as) one day told his companion Bishr b. Sulayman, "O Bishr! You are from the people of Medina, the Ansar. I want you to go to the River Euphrates, on the banks of Baghdad. Here, take two hundred and twenty gold dinars with you." Bishr said, "Why, O Imam?" Imam said, "Go there, and you will see that a ship will arrive. There is a man who will take out a number of slaves. His name is Umar b. Yazid. He will come out with a number of slaves. You will see one particular slave, and people will be bidding on her. He will try and make her move her veil but she will say to him, 'Please do not touch my veil,' and when the people are bidding she will keep rejecting whoever bids; until eventually you will find someone who will say, 'I bid three hundred dinars and I will give you whatever you want.' She will turn around and say, 'Even if you gave me the kingdom of Sulayman, I will still not come towards what you want.' Then go forward and pay two hundred and twenty gold dinars and give this letter to her. When she reads the letter, you will see that she kisses it. Then she will come with you."

Bishr narrates, "I went, and the bidding began; I gave her the letter, she kissed it and she came with me, and then she began speaking in Arabic and told me her whole story. She said, 'I will tell you my story. My name is Malika. I am the daughter of the Caesar of Rome. My father wanted me to marry my cousin. He invited more than a thousand dignitaries, priests and all of the holy personalities. On the day we wanted to get married, there was lightening like a shaking in the building. The wedding was called off. Again there was a day when we wanted to get married, and again there was a shaking in the building and it was called off. My father was worried, why was this bad omen happening to us?

After all of this had happened, I saw Prophet Jesus in my dreams coming with all of his companions towards Prophet Muhammad and all of his sons. Prophet Muhammad said to Prophet Jesus, 'We want to ask for your daughter's hand in marriage for our son, Hassan al-Askari.' The Prophet Jesus said, 'It is our honor.' I woke up from this dream; fourteen nights later I saw another dream where I saw Fatima Zahra speak to Maryam. In this dream I asked, 'When will I see Hassan al-Askari?' and Fatima Zahra said to Maryam, 'When your daughter comes towards the religion of Islam, then there will be a union between the two of them.' I was waiting for this union to happen and then I was told by Imam Hassan al-Askari in a dream that 'there will be a war between the Muslims and the Romans; you will come on a riverbank and you will be sold for this amount. When the person offers this much and there is a Roman letter, accept it.' And that is how I came." Bishr said, "As I took her to Imam Ali al-Hadi (as), Imam Ali al-Hadi (as) said to her, 'You are honored by Allah on this earth.'" This is the narration about Nargis.

On the night of the 15th of Sha'ban, Hakima, the aunt of Imam Hassan al-Askari (as) herself, says, "I did not know which of the ladies was the one who was going to give birth." This was mainly because Nargis did not have the signs of pregnancy on her. Someone may say, "How can you not have the signs of pregnancy?"

To that we ask, "Did Musa's mother have the signs of pregnancy?" Why did she not have the signs of pregnancy? Because Pharaoh would have killed the baby. So Allah concealed her pregnancy. If Allah can conceal the pregnancy of the mother of Nabi Musa, why can't he conceal the pregnancy of the mother of Imam al-Zaman (ajfs)?

So Hakima said, "I did not know which of the ladies was going to give birth until my nephew came up to me and said, 'O aunt, tonight break your fast at my house. And I want you to stay in my house tonight, for Allah's proof on earth will be born.'

I went to the house at night and I looked at Nargis, and Nargis did not have the signs of pregnancy. Nargis came to clean my feet and I said, 'No, I have to clean your feet; you are going to be the mother of the Imam of this time.'

That night the baby was born and we heard a Quranic verse come out of the mouth of that baby." It was from Surah 28, verse 5, "And We intend to bestow favor upon those who were considered weak in the land, and to make them the Imams, and to make them the heirs…"

Therefore, not everybody around Imam Hassan al-Askari (as) or the Shi'a were told about the birth of the Imam because there were some you just could not trust. The first of them was Imam Hassan al-Askari (as)'s brother Ja'far. When Imam Hassan al-Askari (as) fell ill, Ja'far went behind his back and secretly told the Abbasid caliph, "Come home now. The Mahdi is going to surely lead his prayers."

Imam al-Mahdi (ajfs) was born in the year 255; Imam Hassan al-Askari (as) died in the year 260. When a baby is born in a house, let's say the soldiers have been outside that house monitoring it carefully, and the soldiers are surely going to recognize after six months, or a year, or eighteen months, or twenty-four months that there is a baby that they had never seen before, isn't it? So how could Imam live in Samarra that long without anyone knowing about him? And we believe that his Ghaybat al-Sughra (Minor Occultation) began at the age of five. So where was he?

If you say he was around Samarra for those five years, people will turn around and ask you, "Listen, are these soldiers blind? They cannot see a child walking around?"

Thus this proves that he wasn't in Samarra. His father sent him shortly after birth outside Samarra for forty days, and then after that his father sent him to stay with his grandmother, Hudaifa, in Medina. When Imam Hassan al-Askari (as) was going to pass away, that was when he was supposed to return to Samarra. So Imam al-Mahdi (ajfs)'s first few years were spent in Medina and not Samarra. That is why when some of Imam Hassan al-Askari (as)'s companions would come to him and ask, "Where is your son?" Imam Hassan al-Askari (as) would say, "If you go to Mecca for hajj, you will see him; and if you go to Medina, you will see him."

Finally, Imam Hassan al-Askari (as) told Abul Adyan, "In fifteen days I am going to die; here are the letters for my Shi'a in Baghdad. I have answered all of their jurisprudential issues. Go to them; you will see Ahmad b. Hassan there. When you go there, answer their questions. When you come back in fifteen days, you will hear that Hassan al-Askari has died; you will have the letters with you and you will see the one who asks you for them, and the one who prays over me, and the one who knows the answer to how much is in the yellow bag; he is my successor, O Abul Adyan."

Imam does not even tell Abul Adyan the exact identity of his son but he tells him to look out for the signs. Abul Adyan left, went to Baghdad and stayed there; then he came back and narrates, "When I came to Samarra, everybody had come out saying, 'Hassan al-Askari has died.' I went to Imam's house and I saw Ja'far saying that he was the new Imam. He almost began the prayers when someone came and removed him and said, 'I have a greater right on this prayer.'"

If Imam al-Zaman was living in Samarra all those years, would the people be confused as to who he was? On the contrary, they would be confused if someone out of the blue came after living in Medina and led the prayers. If Imam al-Zaman led those prayers, someone could turn around and say, "Are you telling me a five year old came to lead the prayer and nobody had ever seen him in Samarra before?" But he wasn't living in

Samarra, he was living in Medina and he came back to bury and to pray the salat of his father because an Imam always prays over an Imam.

So when the Imam came, Ja'far was bemused, "Who is this person?" If Imam was living in Samarra, would Ja'far be surprised? Now everyone was queuing up to pray and no one was concerned as to who was leading. They were trying to get there in time for the prayers. Just then the Imam came to Abu Adyan, and Abul Adyan narrates, "I was just standing there, and the five year old came to me and said, 'O Abul Adyan, give me the letters.'" Abul Adyan gave it to him because he remembered that Imam Hassan al-Askari (as) had told him there would be three signs; there would be someone who asks for the letters and leads the prayers, but before the third sign became apparent, Ja'far started getting suspicious and went and told the Abbasid caliph, "Quickly, the Mahdi is here. Come quickly."

The chief judge of Samarra came, and everybody else came. As they entered, a person from Qum entered too, saying, "Where is al-Askari? Ja'far said, "He has died." The people from Qum said, "Well, we have some khums to give him; how much khums is this if you are the real Imam?" Ja'far said, "What, do you think I know the unseen?" Then a person came and said to them, "One thousand and ten dinars." The people gave it to him. Abul Adyan said, "I looked at the man who took the money and said where are you going?" He said, "I am going back to my Imam al-Hujjah b. ul-Hassan al-Mahdi (pbuh)." Then, from that period onwards, Imam al-Mahdi (ajfs) went into the Ghaybat al-Sughra (lesser occultation).

In other words, the first five years of the life of Imam al-Mahdi (ajfs) are misunderstood in our communities and need more clarification. Many people wonder as to how all this happenened.

Ghaybat al-Sughra and His Representatives

Ghaybat al-Sughra was part of a system which began from the time of Imam as-Sadiq (as). Imam as-Sadiq (as) began an underground movement called "al-Wikala," or "the Deputies." Imam as-Sadiq (as) knew that soon it was going to be the beginning of the time when who would be in prison or house arrest or, indeed, under extreme government scrutiny. So Imam as-Sadiq (as) began the preparation for Ghaybat al-Sughra. He began the underground movement where, if you could not get access to an Imam because of the Imam being under house arrest, then the Imam appointed someone for you to go and see on his behalf.

Imam as-Sadiq (as) had, for example, Mualla b. Khunais; Imam al-Kadhim (as) had Uthman b. Isa ar-Rawasi; Imam ar-Ridha (as) had Safwan b. Yahya; Imam al-Jawad (as) had Abdur Rahman b. Hajjaj and Imam Ali al-Hadi (as) had Ayyub b. Nuh. Their role was to collect the zakat and khums of the Shi'a and answer the questions of the Shi'a on behalf of the Imam. Imam Hassan al-Askari (as) had families who were ready to do this for him. The Nawbakhti family, the Mahziyar family and the Hamadani family were all working under Imam Hassan al-Askari (as).

Imam al-Mahdi (ajfs) went into Ghaybat al-Sughra in order to prepare us for his absence, so that when he was absent, there were going to be people whom we could go to for solutions. Ghaybat al-Sughra lasted about sixty-nine to seventy years. Imam al-Mahdi (ajfs) had appointed four representatives during that time. The first of his representatives was Uthman b. Saeed. The narrations state that he used to work for Imam al-Jawad (as) from the age of eleven. Then he worked for Imam Ali al-Hadi (as) and then for Imam Hassan al-Askari (as); then Imam al-Mahdi (ajfs) made him his first representative. On many occasions the Shi'a would come to these four representatives and ask them questions. During Ghaybat al-Sughra these four na'ibs had direct access to Imam al-Mahdi (ajfs). After Uthman, his son became the representative of the Imam, and then Hussein b. Rooh.

The Shi'as would sometimes challenge these representatives to give them proof that they were truly in touch with the Imam. Once Ali al-Qummi came to Hussein b. Rooh and said, "O Hussein, my name is Ali al-Qummi." "Yes." "I am trying to have sons from my wife but I cannot have any. Can you ask the Imam to pray to Allah (swt) that Allah honors me with sons?" "Leave this to me. I will speak with the Imam, and as soon as I speak with him, I will come back with the confirmation."

When Hussein b. Rooh spoke to the Imam, the Imam told him, "Tell him the wife he has now will give him no children, but he is going to marry another wife from Dallam who is going to give him three sons, Muhammad, Hassan and Hussein. Muhammad and Hussein are going to be ulema of this ummah." And as the Imam had said, he had three sons. One of his sons, Muhammad b. Ali al-Qummi, is the man famously known as "Sheikh as-Saduq." Sheikh as-Saduq was born from the prayers of Imam al-Mahdi (ajfs). He is the author of many renowned texts in

Islam, one of them is *Man La Yahduruhu ul-Faqih*, which is one of our four main canonical books alongside al-Kafi by Sheikh al-Kulayni and the works of Shaykh al-Tusi. *Man La Yahduruhu ul-Faqih* is arguably the second most important book when it comes to the books of Imami law.

To the last of the deputies, Imam said, "In six days time, you will pass away and I am going to go into Ghaybat al-Kubra (Major Occultation); I will return when the hearts are hardened and the earth is full of wickedness. Tell my followers that if they sincerely want me to return I will return straight away."

Frequently Asked Questions about Ghaybat al-Kubra

Can we ever see the Imam in this period? The Imams of Ahlulbayt tell us in many narrations that the Imam visits a number of people a year and that there are three occasions in particular where the Imam is present. Of those occasions the first is the period of hajj; the second is the funeral of a man who has no debts; and the third is when someone is troubled and he calls out to the Imam.

Why did the occultation happen? There are three main reasons for this. The first and natural reason is for the protection of the Imam, as they wanted to kill him because of the prophecy of the Prophet (pbuh). The second reason was so that God would not allow the Imam to pledge allegiance to anyone in his lifetime; he would be his own leader. The third and most important reason is that it is a test for the followers of Imam al-Hujjah.

Many people say, "We are unfortunate that we cannot see our Imam; we wish we could see him." The narrations tell us that one day a person came to our sixth Imam and said, "Which is the greatest ever Muslim generation?" The Imam said, "The greatest ever Muslim generations are the followers and believers in Imam al-Mahdi (ajfs)." He was asked, "Why?" Imam said, "Because that generation believes in a man whom they cannot see, and if they work hard to prepare for his return, Allah will raise them as if they were martyrs alongside Prophet Muhammad (pbuh)."

How could a man so young have such great knowledge? We believe Jesus spoke from the cradle and when the Imam returns, Jesus will pray behind the Imam. So if Jesus can speak from the cradle with knowledge and he will pray behind the Imam when he returns, then what kind of knowledge must the Imam have?

If the Imam is alive today, he would be more than twelve hundred years old, how can this be? The Quran says Prophet Nuh (as) lived close to one thousand years. The Quran also says that when Nabi Yunus was in the belly of the whale, Allah said, "I wouldn't mind keeping you there till the day they are raised." How many years would that be?

Also, there is an existent entity by the name of Satan; he has been around for a very long time. Therefore, if someone believes in Satan being around for such a long time, then why don't you believe in a force of good being around for a long time?

How can you believe in an Imam you cannot see? He is not the first. Is Prophet Jesus alive? Yes.Can we see him? No.Similarly, Prophet Khidr and Prophet Idrees are alive.Can we see them? No. Do the Muslims believe in them? Yes. Even our Holy Prophet (pbuh), when he left in the night of Hijra to Medina...didn't Allah create a barrier for him where they could not see him leave the house? If Allah can do that for the grandfather of the Mahdi, why can't He do that for al-Mahdi himself?

Signs of Imam's Reappearance

There are many signs which we have to beware of which remind us about the Imam. Amongst those signs is the appearance of the Dajjal. Our sixth Imam (as) said, "The Day of Judgement will not come, nor the rising of the Imam, until thirty Dajjals appear." Dajjal is an ideology that represents opposition to the truth of the religion of Islam.

It is said that the Sufyani will appear and will control Syria and Palestine, Jordan and the Bilad ash-Sham, and will be from the lineage of Abu Sufyan. Are we aware who the Sufyani may be today? Or what is the Dajjal's system today?

Imam will rise with forty of his companions at hajj. The year before he rises he will be at hajj. The Imam will meet his companions at hajj and they won't leave hajj until the 15th of Dhul Hijja. From the 16th until the 22nd of Dhul Hijja, these companions will be with the Imam. Then the Imam will say to them, "Which one of you is willing to announce and stand up between the Rukn and the Maqam?" One of his companions, by the name of Nafs al-Zakiya (the Pure Soul), will stand up there. He will be killed, and it will then be only a matter of fifteen days, most probably on the tenth of Muharram, when the Imam will rise. When he rises, he will have an army of 313 generals who will be followed by over ten thousand soldiers who in turn will come to follow the Imam. It is said that the Imam will establish his central government in Kufa at Masjid us-Sahla.

Now the question arises, what are the signs which tell us that the time of Imam's reappearance is close?

Jabir b. Abdullah al-Ansari narrates, "One day I saw a dream and this dream really confused me. When I met Amir al-Mu'mineen, I told him about the dream. Imam Ali said, 'The signs in your dream are the signs of the return of the Imam.'" Jabir said, "The first thing that I saw in my dreams was that pieces of cloth were hanging from the sky and people were coming and taking pieces of the cloth but leaving other pieces. So I said, 'O Imam, what does this mean?' Imam Ali said, "Before the return of the Mahdi, Muslims will take some parts of the religion and neglect other parts of the religion."

We must ask ourselves today if we have taken some parts and neglected other parts of our religion. There are some parts which we may be very strict in, such as salat, fasting, but there may be other acts in which we show no strictness whatsoever; we have become "part-time" Muslims. When we feel like being religious in Ramadan and Muharram, all of us are religious, whereas when we do not feel like being religious, we do not mind breaking the rules in order to follow our own ways.

Then Jabir said, "O Imam, I saw sick animals and I saw healthy animals; I saw people milking the sick animals but not the healthy ones." Imam said, "That is the governments before the time of the Imam. They will take taxes from the poor and make sure that the rich do not have to pay any." Jabir said, "O Imam, I saw sick people and healthy people, but I saw the sick visiting the healthy and the healthy not visiting the sick." Imam looked at him and said, "In the period before the return of the Qa'im of Aal Muhammad, you will find that the sick are the poor, and they have to go and beg the rich for donations." Jabir said, "O Imam, I saw animals with two heads. What does that mean?" Imam said, "Before Imam al-Mahdi comes, you will find that the human will have two heads; they will earn money in halal and haram and they will not feel any remorse in doing this." We must ask ourselves if any of this applies to us today.

One of the acts which is recommended for us to recite in the Imam's occultation is Dua Nudba. Try and wake up on a Friday morning, after

Salat ul-Fajr, and read this dua. There are some memorable lines in this dua; amongst them is one where we say, "Ayn al-Hassan? Ayn al-Hussein? Ayna abna al-Hussein? Saleh ba'da saleh, wa Sadiq ba'da Sadiq… Where is Hassan? Where is Hussein? Where are the sons of Hussein?...." And it continues to lament saying, "Where are the suns? Where are the moons that used to light up this earth?..." and you continue in your talking towards the Imam, and say, "Where is that connector between the heavens and the earth? Where is that man who will come to avenge what had happened at Karbala?"

When the Imam returns he will bring justice as his mission is to remove tyranny from the world. The Imam will not just be for the Muslims. The Imam is for the Hindus, the Zoroastrians, the Buddhists, the Sikhs, the Christians and for the Jews; every single religion talks about the Imam in their scriptures. He will come back as a man who seeks to build a world free of tyrannical leaders and under the perfect rule of justice and equality.

Bibliography

Primary Sources

Ibn ʿAbd al-Barr, Yūsuf b. ʿAbdullāh, *al-Istīʿāb fī maʿrifat al-aṣḥāb*, ed. A. al-Bajjāwī, 4 vols. (Cairo, n.d.).

Ibn ʿAbd al-Ḥakam, ʿAbd al-Raḥmān b. ʿAbd Allāh, *Futuḥ Miṣr wa-Akhbāruha* (Baghdad, 1967).

Futūḥ Miṣr (al-Qāhirah: Maktabat al-Thaqāfah al-Dīnīyah, 1995).

Ibn Abī al-Ḥadīd, ʿIzz al-Dīn Abū Ḥamīd, *Sharḥ Nahjul Balāgha* (Cairo: Dār al-kutub al-ʿArabīyyah, 1944).

Ibn ʿAbd Rabbihī, Aḥmad b. Muḥammad, *al-ʿIqd al-farīd*, ed. Aḥmad Amīn, Aḥmad al-Zayn and Ibrāhīm al-Ibyārī (Cairo: Lajnat al-Ta'lif wa al-Tarjama wa al-Nashr, 1948).

ʿAlam al-Hudā, al-Sharīf Abū l-Qāsim ʿAlī b. al-Husain al-Murtaḍā aka Dhūl-Majdain, "*Majmu'a fi funūn min ʿilm al-kalām*" in *Nafā'is al-makhṭūṭāt,* ed. Muḥammad Ḥasan Āl-Yāsīn, 1st edition (Baghdād: al-Ma'arif, 1955).

"*al-Uṣūl al-itiqaḍīyya*" in *Nafā'is al-makhṭūṭāt,* ed. Muḥammad Ḥasan Āl-Yāsīn, 1st edition (Baghdād: al-Ma'ārif, 1955).

, *al-Shāfī fil Imāma* (Tehran, 1301/1884).

al-Amīnī, ʿAbd al-Ḥusayn, *al-Ghadeer* (Beirut: Dār al Kitāb al-ʿArabī, 1970).

al–Ghadīr fil Kitāb wal Sunnah wal Adab (Qum: Furū al-Dīn Publishers, 1995).

Asadābādī, ʿAbd al-Jabbār b. Aḥmad, *Fīraq wa-ṭabaqāt al-muʿtazilah* (Cairo: Dār al-Ṭibāʿah al-Jāmiʿīyah, 1972).

al-Mughnī (Cairo: al-Mu'assasa al-Miṣrīyya al-ʿāmma lil-ta'līf wal-anbā' wal-nashr, 1961-5).

Ibn ʿAsākir, ʿAlī b. al-Ḥasan, *Ta'rīkh Madīnat Dimashq*, ed. Muḥibb al-Dīn Abī Saʿīd ʿUmar b. Gharāma al-ʿAmrawī (Beirut: Dār al-Fikr, 1995-1998).

al-Ashʿārī, Abū al-Hasan ʿAlī b. Ismāʿīl, *Kitāb al-Ibānah ʿan uṣūl al-diyānah* (Hyderabad: 1321/1903); tr. by W.C. Klein as *The Elucidation of Islam's Foundation* (New Haven: 1940).

Abū al-Ḥasan Alī b. Ismāʿīl, *Kitāb al-Luma'*, text and translation in R. J. McCarthy, *The Theology of al-Ashʿarī* (Beirut: 1953).

Maqālāt al-Islāmiyyīn, ed. Hellmut Ritter (Istanbul, 1928).

al-ʿAsqalānī, Aḥmad b. ʿAlī Ibn Ḥajar, *al-Iṣābah fī tamyīz al-ṣaḥābah* (Cairo: Būlāq, 1328/1910).

Lisān al-mīzān (Beirut: Dār al-Fikr, 1987-1988).

Tahdhīb al-Tahdhīb fī rijāl al-ḥadīth (Beirut, 1968).

Ibn Aʿtham, *Kitāb al-Fūtūḥ*, 8 vols. (Ḥaydarabād: Dā'irat al-Maʿārif al-ʿUthmānīyyah, 1968-75).

Muḥammad b. ʻAlī, *Kitāb al-Futūḥ*, Istanbul Manuscript, Library of Ahmet III.

Ibn al-Athīr, Izz al-Dīn, *al-Bāhir fī Tārīkh ad-Dawllah al-Tatabanya,* ed. A. Tulaymat (Cairo: 1962).

al-Kāmil fi al-ta'rīkh, ed. C.J. Tornberg (Leiden: Brill, 1868-70).

al-Kāmil fī al-Tārīkh (Beirut, 1965).

al-Baghdādī, Abū Manṣūr ʿAbd al-Qāhir Tāhir, *Uṣūl al-dīn* (Istānbūl: Madrasat al-Ilāhīyāt bi-Dār al-Funūn al-Tūrkīyah, 1928), simplified translation in H.A.R. Gibb, "Constitutional Organisation" in *Law in the Middle East*, ed. Majid Khadduri and Herbert J. Liebesny (Washington D.C., 1955).

al-Balādhurī, *Ansāb al-Ashrāf* (published for the first time by the School of Oriental Studies, Hebrew University, Jerusalem, SDF Goitein Univ Press, 1936).

Ansāb al-Ashrāf, ed. Muḥammad Bāqir al-Maḥmūdī (Beirut, 1974).

Aḥmed b. Yaḥyā, *Ansāb al-Ashrāf*, ed. Iḥsān ʿAbbās (Wiesbaden: Franz Steiner, 1979).

Ansāb al-Ashrāf (Beirut: Dār al-Fikr, 1996).

Futūḥ al-Buldān, ed. M. de Goeje (Leiden: Brill, 1865).

Al-Bāqillānī, Abū Bakr Muḥammad b. al-Ṭayyib, *Manāqib al-aʿimmah al-arbaʿah,* ed. Samīra Farhat (Beirut: Dār al-Muntakhab al-ʿArabī, 2002).

al-Tamhīd fi al-Radd ʿalā al-mulḥidah al-muʿaṭṭalah wa al-rāfiḍah wa-l-Khawārij wa-l-Muʿtazilah (al-Qāhirah: Dār al-Fikr al-Islāmī, 1947).

al-Dīnawarī, Ābu Ḥanīfah Āḥmad b. Dawūd, *al-Akhbār al-ṭiwāl* (Leiden: 1888).

al-Farazdaq, Hammām b. Ghālib Abū Firās, *Dīwān*, ed. M.I.A. al-Ṣāwī (Cairo, 1936 and Beirut, 1960).

Ḥajjī Khalīf, Muṣṭafā b. ʿAbdullāh, *Kashf al-ẓunūn ʿan asāmī al-kutub wa-al-funūn,* ed. Gustav Flugel, 7 vols. (Leipzig and London: 1835-58).

al-Ḥamawī, Yāqūt b. ʻAbdallāh, *al-arīb ilā maʿrifat al-adīb al-Muʿjam al-ʿUdaba* (Dictionary of Learned Men), ed. D.S. Margoliouth, 7 vols., 2nd edition (London: 1923-31).

Ibn Ḥanbal, ʿAbd Allāh b. Aḥmad, *Musnad* (Cairo: Maymanya Publishers, 1313 AH).

Ibn Hishām, Muḥammad b. Aḥmad, *Ṣīrāt Sayyidna Muḥammad Rasūl Allāh*, ed. Ferdinand Wüstenfeld, 2 vols. (Göttingen, 1858-60; reprint, Frankfurt am Main, 1961).

al-Jāḥiẓ, Abū ʿUthmān ʿAmr b. Baḥr, *al-Bayān wa'l-tabyīn*, ed. A.S.M. Harun (Cairo, 1948-50).

Kitab al-hayawān, ed, A.S.M. Harun, 2nd edition (Cairo: Muṣṭafā al-Bābī al-Ḥalabī, 1965-1969).

Rasā'il al-Jāḥiẓ, ed. H. al-Sandubi (Cairo: Yuṭlab min al-Maktabah al-Tijārīyah al-Kubrā, 1933).

Rasa'il al-Jāḥiẓ, ed. A.S.M. Harun (Cairo, 1965).

Risālat al-ʿUthmānīyya, ed. A.S.M. Harun (Cairo: Dār al-Kitāb al-ʿArabī, 1955).

al-Jumaḥī, Muḥammad b. Sallām, *Ṭabaqāt fuḥūl al-shuʿarā'*, ed. A. M. Shakir (Cairo, 1952).

al-Juwaynī, ʿAbd al-Malik b. ʿAbd Allāh b. Yūsuf, *Ghiyāth al-Umām fi al-Tiyāth al-Ẓulam*, ed. A. Dīb (Qatar, 1400/1979).

Ibn Kathīr, Ismāʿīl b. ʿUmar, *al-Bidāyah wa al-Nihāyah* (Beirut: Maktabah al-Maʿārif, 1966).

al-Bidāya wa-l-nihāya, ed. ʿAlī ʿAbd al-Ṣāṭir (Beirut: Dār al-Kutub al-ʿIlmiyyah, 1985).

Ibn Khaldūn, *Muqaddimah* (Cairo, 1321), quoted by L. Gardet and M.M. Anawati in *Introduction à La Théologie Musulmane* (Paris: Librairie Philosophique J. Vrin, 1948).

Ibn Khallikān, Shams al-Dīn Abū al-ʿAbbās Aḥmad b. Muḥammad, *Wafayāt al-A'yān*, (Cairo, 1948).

al-Khaṭafā, Jarīr b. ʿAṭīyya b., *Diwān*, ed. M.I.A. al-Ṣāwī (Cairo 1353) and ed. N.M.A. Ṭāhā (Cairo 1969-70).

Ibn al-Khayyāṭ, ʿAbd al-Raḥīm b. Muḥammad, *Kitāb al-Intiṣar wa-al-radd ʿala Ibn al-Rawandī al-mulḥid,* ed. and tr. Albert Nader (Beirut: al-Matbaʿah al-Kathulikiyah, 1957).

al-Ṭabaqāt: riwāyat Abī ʿImrān Mūsā al-Tustarī, ed. Akram Ḍiyāʾ al-ʿUmarī (Baghdad: Maṭbaʿat al-ʿĀnī, 1967).

Tārīkh Khalīfah b. Khayyaṭ (Beirut: Dār al-Kutub al-ʿIlmīyyah, 1995).

al-Kindī, Abū ʿUmar Muḥammad b. Yūsuf, *Kitāb al-Wulāt wa Kitāb al-Quḍāt*, ed. R. Guest (Leiden, 1912).

al-Isfahānī, Abū al-Faraj ʿAlī b. al-Ḥusayn, *Kitāb al-Aghānī* (Cairo, 1285).

Kitāb al-Aghānī, ed. Naṣr al-Hurinī, 20 vols. (Bulāq, 1868).

Kitāb al-Aghānī (Leiden, 1905).

Kitāb al-Aghānī (Cairo, 1927-74).

Maqātil al-Ṭālibīyīn, ed. Aḥmed Saqr (Cairo, 1949; 2nd edtn, Tehran, 1970).

Maqatil al-Ṭālibiyyīn (Najaf: al-Maktabah al-Ḥaydarīyah, 1965).

al-Isfahāni, Ḥasan Muḥammad al-Raghib, *Kitāb al-mufradāt fī gharīb al-Qur'ān* (Beirut: Dār al-ma'rifah, n.d.).

al-Jaṣṣāṣ, Aḥmad b. 'Alī al-Rāzī, *Uṣūl al-fiqh al-musammā bi al-Fuṣūl fī al-uṣūl,* 4 vols., ed. U.J. Nashmī (Kuwait: Wizārat al-Awqāf, 1994).

Mālik b. Anas, *Muwaṭṭa' al-Imām Mālik b. Anas (*Jeddah: Dār al-Shurūq, 1985).

Ibn Manẓūr, Muḥammad b. Mukarram, *Lisān al-'Arab*, 20 vols. (Cairo: Būlaq, 1300-108 AH).

al-Maqrīzī, Ahmad b. 'Alī, *al-Khiṭaṭ,* ed. G. Wiet (Cairo, 1911-2).

al-Maṣrī, Imām Jamāl al-Dīn b. Manẓūr, *Lisān al-'Arab* (Beirut: Dār Ṣādir, 1955-56).

al-Mas' ūdī, 'Alī b. al-Ḥusayn, *Murūj al-Dhahāb wa Ma'ādin al-Jawhar*, ed. C. Pellat (Beirut: Université Libanaise, 1966-79).

Les Prairies d'or, ed and trans. Barbier de Maynard and Pavet de Courteille, 9 vols. (Paris, 1861-77).

'Alī b. al-Ḥusayn, *al-Tanbīḥ wa-l-ishrāf* (Leiden, 1894, rpt., Beirut: Maktabat al-Khayyāṭ, 1965).

al-Marzubānī, Abī 'Ubayd Allah Muḥammad b. 'Imrān b. Mūsā, *al-Muwashshah* (Cairo, 1924).

al-Māwardī, Abū al-Ḥasan 'Alī b. Muḥammad b. Ḥabīb, *al-Aḥkām al-Sulṭānīyyah* (Egypt, 1966).

al-Minqārī, Naṣr b. Muzaḥim, *Waq'at Ṣiffīn,* ed. A.S.M. Harūn (Cairo, 1365 AH).

Waq'at Ṣiffīn, ed. A.S.M. Harun (Cairo, 1382 AH).

al-Mufaḍḍal b. Salamah, *Fākhīr*, ed. C.A. Storey (Leyden: Brill, 1915).

al-Mufīd, Abū Abdullāh Muḥammad b. Muḥammad, *Awā'il al-maqālāt fi'l-madhāhib al-mukhtārāt*, ed. 'Abbāsqūlī S. Wajdī, with notes and introduction by Faẓl Allāh Zanjānī, 2nd edition (Tabriz: Charandabi, 1371).

al-Fuṣūl al-mukhtārah min al-'uyūn wa-al-maḥāsin (Tehran: Intishārāt-i Navīd, 1983).

al-Ifṣāh fi Imāmat Amīr al-Mu'minīn 'Alī ibn Abī Ṭalib, 2nd edition (Najaf: al-Haidariyya, 1950).

Kitāb al-Irshād, tr. I.K.A. Howard (London: The Muhammadi Trust, 1981).

Sharḥ 'aqā'id al-Ṣadūq (Beirut: Dār al-Kitāb al-Islāmī, 1983).

Taṣḥīh al-i'tiqād (Qum, 1951).

Ibn al-Murtaḍā, Aḥmad b. Yaḥyā, *Ṭabaqāt al-Mu'tazila/Die Klassen der Mu'taziliten von Ibn al-Murtaḍā*, ed. Sussana Diwald-Wilzer (Beirut: Imrimerie Catholique, 1961), as cited in L. Clarke, *Shī'ite Heritage*.

al-Najāshī, Abī al-'Abbās Aḥmad b. 'Alī, *Rijāl al-Najāshī* (Beirut: Dār al-Adwā', 1988).

al-Nīsābūrī, Muḥammad b. 'Abd Allāh al-Ḥakīm, *al-Mustadrak ala l-Ṣaḥīḥayn* (India: Dā'irat al-Ma'ārif al-Nād'imiyet al-Qā'ima fī l-Hind, 1913).

al-Nūmairī, Abū Zaid 'Umar Ibn Shabba b. 'Abida Zaid, *Tārīkh al-Madīna al-Munawarrah*, ed. Fahīm Muḥammad Shaltūt (Iran, 1989).

Nuwayrī, Aḥmad b. 'Abd al-Wahhāb, *Nihāyat al-'Arab fī funūn al-Adāb* (Cairo, 1342-48).

Al-Qāḍī al-Nu'mān, Abū Ḥanīfa al-Nu'mān b. Abī 'Abdillah Muḥammad b. Manṣūr al-Tamīmī, *Da'a'im al-Islam,* ed. A.A. Fyzee, 2 vols. (Cairo, 1951-60).

Qāsim b. Sallām, Abū 'Ubayd, *Kitāb al-amwāl* (al-Qāhirah: Dār al-Fikr, 1975).

al-Qurashī, Yaḥyā b. Adam, *Kitāb al-Kharāj*, ed. Th. W. Juynboll (Leiden: E.J. Brill, 1896).

Ibn Qutayba, 'Abdullāh b. Muslim, *al-Imāmāh wa'l-siyāsah* (Cairo, 1909).

Kitāb al-ma'arif, ed. Tharwat 'Ukāshah (Cairo: Maṭba'at Dār al-Kutub, 1960).

Ibn Sa'd, Muḥammad, *al-Ṭabaqāt al-kubrā* (Beirut, 1947-60).

al-Ṣafadī, Khalīl b. Aybak, *al-Wāfī bi-al-wafayāt* (Beirut: Dār Iḥyā' al-Turāth al-'Arabī, 2000).

al-San'ānī, 'Abd al-Razzāq b. Ḥammām, *Muṣannaf*, ed. Ḥabīb al-Raḥmān al-A'ẓamī, 11 vols. (Simlak, Dahbel/Beirut, 1391/1972).

Ibn Shahrāshūb, Rashīd al-Dīn Abī Ja'far Muḥammad b. 'Alī, *Kitāb Ma'ālim al-'ulamā'* (Ṭehrān: Maṭba'at Fardīn, 1934).

al-Shammākhī, Abū al-'Abās Aḥmad b. Sa'īd, *Kitāb al-Siyār* (Cairo, 1301).

al-Shīrāzī, Abū Isḥāq, *al-Ishārah ilā madhhab Ahl al-ḥaqq* (al-Qāhirah: Markaz al-Sīrah wa al-Sunnah, 1999).

al-Sijistānī, Abū Ya'qūb Isḥāq b. Aḥmad, *Kitāb al-Iftikhār,* ed. with notes and comments by Ismail K. Poonawala (Beirut: Dār al-Gharb al-Islāmī, 2000).

al-Ṭabarī, Abū Ja'far Muḥammad b. Jarīr b.Yazīd, *Ta'rīkh al-Rusul wal-mulūk,* ed. M.J. de Goeje, et al. (Leiden: Brill, 1881).

Tārīkh al-Rusūl wal-Mulūk (Cairo: al-Istiqāma Publishers, 1939).

Tārīkh al-rusul wa-al-mulūk, ed. Muḥammad Abū al-Faḍl Ibrāhīm, 11 vols. (Cairo: Dār al-Ma'ārif, 1960-1970).

Tārīkh al-Rusul wal-Mulūk, 13 vols. (Beirut: Dār al-Fikr, 1998).

al-Tabrīzī, Yaḥyā b. 'Alī Khaṭīb,*Sharḥ al-Ḥamāsah* (Cairo, 1916), vol. 1, 3.

al-Tamīmī, Sayf ibn 'Umar al-Asadī, *Kitāb al-Ridda wa'l-futūh and Kitāb al-jamal wa-masīr 'Ā'isha wa-'Alī: A Facsimile Edition of the Fragments Preserved in the University Library of Imām Muḥammad Ibn Sa'ud Islamic University in Riyadh* (Leiden: Smitskamp Oriental Antiquarium, 1995).

al-Tawḥīdī, Abū Ḥayyān ʿAlī b. Muḥammad, *al-Baṣāʾir wa-al-dhakhāʾir*, ed. Wadād al-Qāḍī (Beirut, 1988).

Kitāb al-imtāʿ wa-al-muʾānasah, ed. Aḥmed Amīn and Aḥmed al-Zayn (Cairo, 1953).

Risālat al-Saqīfah, published in I. al-Kīlānī, ed., *Thalāth rasāʾil lī-Abī Ḥayyān al-Tawḥīdī* (Damascus, 1951).

Ibn al-Ṭiqṭaqā, *al-Fakhrī fī al-adab al-sulṭānīyah wal duwal al-islāmīyya* (Cairo: al-Maktaba al-tijariya al-kubrā, 1927).

Ibn Ṭūlūn, Muḥammad b. ʿAlī, *Quḍāt Dimashq: al-thaghr al-bassām fī dhikr man wuliyya qaḍāʾ al-Shām*, ed. S. Munajjid (Damascus, 1956).

al-Ṭusī, *al-Fihrist*, ed. A. Sprenger/new ed. Maḥmud Ramyar (Mashhad, 1351).

Yaʿqūb, Abū Yūsuf, *Kitāb al-Kharāj* (1886).

al-Yaʿqūbī, Aḥmad b. Abī Yaʿqūb, *Kitāb al-Tārīkh* (Leiden: Brill, 1883).

"Kitab al-Buldan" in Ibn Rustah's *Aʿlāq al-nafīsah*, ed. M.J. de Goeje (Leiden: Brill, 1892).

al-Zubayrī, Abī ʿAbd Allāh al-Muṣʿab b. ʿAbd Allāh b. al-Muṣʿab, *Nasab Quraysh* (Cairo: Dār al-Maʿārif lil-Ṭibāʿah wa-al-Nashr, 1953).

Secondary Sources

Abbott, N., *Studies in Arabic Literary Papyri* (Chicago: University of Chicago Press, 1957).

al-ʿAdawī, Ibrāhīm Aḥmad, *al-Dawla al-Umawīyah* (Cairo: Maktabat al-Shabāb, 1987-88).

Afsaruddin, Asma, *Excellence and Precedence: Medieval Discourse on Legitimate Leadership* (Leiden: Brill, 2002).

The First Muslims: History and Memory (Oxford: Oneworld Publications, 2008).

"In Praise of the Caliphs: Recreating History from the *Manāqib* Literature", *IJMES*, 31 (1999).

Ahlwardt, W., *The Divans of the Six Ancient Arabic Poets*, 25, no. 23:11 (London, 1870).

ʿAlī, Jawād, "Mawarid *Tārīkh* al-Ṭabarī", *Majallat al-Majmaʿ al-ʿIlmī al-Iraqī*, 1 (1950).

al-ʿAlī, Ṣalih, "Muslim Estates in Ḥijāz in the First Century", *JESHO*, vol. 2 (1959).

ʿAlī, ʿAbdullāh Yūsuf, tr. *The Qurʾān* (New York: Tahrike Tarsile Qur'an, Inc., 2007).

Allard, M., *Le Probleme des attributs divins dans la doctrine d'al-Ashari et de ses premiers grands disciples* (Beirut, 1965).

Aqīl, Nabil, *Dirasat fi al-ʿaṣr al-umawī,* 4th edition (Damascus: University of Damascus Press, 1991-92).

ʿArafāt, W., "The Historical Background to the Elegies on ʻUthmān b. ʻAffān Attributed to Ḥassan b. Thabit", *BSOAS*, 33 (1970).

Arberry, A. J., *Arabic Poetry: A Primer for Students* (Cambridge, Cambridge University Press, 1965).

Arnold, T. W., *The Caliphate* (New York : Barnes and Noble, 1966 [1924]).

al-ʿAskarī, S. M. *The Role of ʿĀʾisha in the History of Islam: ʿĀʾisha in the Time of Muʿāwiya b. Abī Sufyān,* tr. Dr. ʿAlāʾ al-Dīn Pāzārgādī (Iran: Naba Organization, 2000).

Ashtiany, J. and J.D. Latham, *ʿAbbāsid Belles-Lettres* (Cambridge: Cambridge University Press, 1990).

ʿAṭwān, Ḥusayn, *Niẓām wilayāt al-ʿahd wa wirathāt al-khilāfah fī al-ʿasr al-Umawī* (Beirut: Dār al-Jīl, 1991).

ʿAẓamī, M. M., *On Schacht's Origins of Muhammadan Jurisprudence* (Oxford: Oxford Centre for Islamic Studies; 1996).

Studies in Early Ḥadith Literature (Indianapolis: American Trust Publications, 1992).

al-Azmeh, A., *Muslim Kingship* (New York: I.B. Tauris Publishers, 1997).

Bahar, Muḥammad Taqī, ed., *Tārīkh-i Sīstān* (Tehran, 1314).

Bakhit, M. Adnan, and Robert Schick, eds., *The History of the Bilād al-Shām During the Umayyad Period: Fourth International Conference of the History of Bilād al-Shām* (Amman: University of Jordan and Yarmouk University, 1989).

Bakhtin, M. M., *The Dialogic Imagination*, ed. Michael Holquist (Austin: Univeristy of Texas Press, 1981).

Barthes, Roland, *The Pleasure of the Text* (New York: Hill and Wang, 1975).

Bashear, Suliman, "The Title Fārūq and its Association with ʿUmar I", *Studia Islamica*, 72 (1990).

Bates, Michael, "The ʿArab-Byzantine Bronze Coinage of Syria: An Innovation by ʿAbd al-Mālik", *A Colloquium in Memory of George Carpenter Miles* (New York: American Numismatic Society, 1976).

Bayhom-Daou, T., "The Imām's Knowledge and the Qurʾān According to al-Faḍl b. Shādhān al-Nīsābūrī (d. 260 A.H./874 A.D.)", *BSOAS*, 64, 2 (2001).

Shaykh Mufīd: Makers of the Muslim World (Oxford: Oneworld, 2005).

Berg, H., *The Development of Exegesis in Early Islam* (Richmond: Curzon Press, 2000).

Birkeland, H., *Old Muslim Opposition Against Interpretation of the Qur'ān* (Oslo: Jacob Dybwad, 1955).

Brock, Sebastian P., "Syriac Sources for Seventh Century History", *BMGS*, 2 (1976).

"Syriac Views of Emergent Islam' in G.H.A. Juynboll (ed.), *Studies in the First Century of Islamic Society* (Carbondale and Edwardsville, 1982).

Brockelmann, C., "al-Ya'kubī", *Encyclopaedia of Islam*, 2nd edition (Leiden: Brill, 1954-66).

Brown, J., *Ḥādīth: Muhammad's Legacy in the Medieval and Modern World* (Oxford: Oneworld Publications, 2009).

Burton, J., *An Introduction to the Ḥadīth* (Edinburgh: Edinburgh University Press, 1994).

Busse, H., "Monotheismus und Islamische Christologie in der Bauinschrift des Felsendoms in Jerusalem", *Theologische Quartalschrift,* 161 (1981) as cited by Donner in *Narratives of Islamic Origins.*

Cahen, C., "History and Historians: From the Beginnings to the Time of al-Ṭabarī", *Religion, Learning and Science in the 'Abbāsid Period: The Cambridge History of Arabic Literature* (Cambridge: Cambridge University Press, 1990).

Calder, Norman, "The Qurrā and the Arab Lexicographical Tradition", *JSS*, 36, 2 (1991).

Cameron, A. J., *Abū Dharr al-Ghifārī: An Examination of His Image in the Hagiography of Islam*, Oriental Translation Fund, New Series, vol. 63 (London: Luzac and Co. Ltd. for the Royal Asiatic Society, 1973).

Cameron, Averil, "Images of Authority: Elites and Icons in Late Sixth-Century Byzantium", in M. Mullet and R. Scott (eds.), *Byzantium and the Classical Tradition* (Birmingham: University of Birmingham Press, 1981).

el-Cheikh, N., *Byzantium Viewed by the Arabs* (Cambridge, MA: Harvard Centre for Middle-Eastern Studies, 2004).

Cooperson, M., *Classical Arabic Biography* (Cambridge: Cambridge University Press, 2000).

Crone, Patricia, *God's Rule: Government in Islam* (New York: Columbia University Press, 2004).

Meccan Trade and the Rise of Islam (Piscataway, NJ: Gorgias Press, 2004).

Slaves on Horses: The Evolution of the Islamic Polity (Cambridge: Cambridge University Press, 1980).

"Were the Qays and Yemen of the Umayyad Period Political Parties?" *DI*, 71 (1994).

Crone, Patricia, and M. Cook, *Hagarism: The Making Of The Islamic World* (Cambridge: Cambridge University Press, 1977).

Crone, Patricia, and F.W. Zimmerman, *The Epistle of Sālim b. Dhakwān* (New York: Oxford University Press, 2001).

Coulson, N.J., *A History of Islamic Law, Islamic Surveys,* vol. 2 (Edinburgh: Edinburgh University Press, 1964; reprint, 1991).

Culler, Jonathan, *The Pursuit of Signs: Semiotics, Literature, Deconstruction* (London: Routledge & Kegan Paul, 1981).

Dabashi, Hamid, *Authority in Islam: From the Rise of Muhammad to the Establishment of the Umayyads,* 2nd edition (New Brunswick, NJ: Transaction Books, 1992).

Dakake, Maria, *The Charismatic Community: Shīʾite Identity in Early Islam* (Albany: SUNY Press, 2007).

al-Dīb, ʿAbd al-ʿAẓīm, *Imām al-Ḥāramayn* (Kuwait: Dār al-Qalam, 1981).

Dixon, A. A., *The Umayyad Caliphate 65-86/684-705: A Political Study* (London: Luzac, 1971).

Donner, Fred, *The Early Islamic Conquests* (Princeton: Princeton University Press, 1981).

"From Believers to Muslims: Confessional Self-Identity in the Early Islamic Community" in *The Byzantine and Early Islamic Near East, IV: Patterns of Communal Identity,* ed. Lawrence I. Conrad (Princeton: Darwin Press, 2003).

Narratives of Islamic Origins: The Beginning of Islamic Historical Writing (Princeton: The Darwin Press, Inc: 1998).

Dūrī, A. A., *The Rise of History Among the Arabs* (Princeton: Princeton University Press, 1983).

Elad, A., "The Beginnings of Historical Writing by the Arabs: The Earliest Syrian Writers on the Arab Conquests", *JSAI,* 28 (2003).

Ennami, A. K., "A Description of New ʿIbādī Manuscripts from North Africa", *Journal of Semitic Studies,* 15 (1970).

Farouq, Umar, *Khalīfah ibn Khayyaṭ Muʿarrikhān* (Baghdād: 1967).

Faris, N. A., "Development in Arab Historiography as Reflected in the Struggle Between ʿAlī and Muʿāwiyah" in *Historians of the Middle East,* ed. P. M. Holt and B. Lewis (Oxford: Oxford University Press, 1962).

Flood, Gavin, *Beyond Phenomenology: Rethinking the Study of Religion* (London: Cassell, 1999).

Fowden, G., *Quṣayr ʿAmra: Art and the Umayyad Elite in Late Antique Syria* (Berkeley: University of California Press, 1st Edition, 2004).

Fück, Johann, "Die Rolle des Traditionalismus im Islam", *Zeitschrift der Deutschen Morgenlandischen Gesellschaft,* 93 (1939) in Berg, H., *The Development of Exegesis in Early Islam,* (Richmond: Curzon Press, 2000).

Fyzee, A. A., "Qāḍī an-Nuʿmān: The Fāṭimid Jurist and Author", *JRAS* (1934).

Geyer, R., *The Divan of al-ʿĀʾisha* (London, E.J.W. Gibb Memorial series, N.S.6, 1928).

Gleave, R. "Between Ḥadīth and Fiqh: Early Imāmī Collections of Akhbār", *ILS*, 8, 3 (2001).

Goldziher, I., *Mohamedanische Studien* (first published 1890), vol. 2, tr. into English by C.R. Barber and S.M. Stern under the title *Muslim Studies*, vol. 2 (London: George Allen & Unwin, 1967-71).

The Principles of Law in Islam, vol. 8, 301, in *The Historian's History of the World,* ed. H.S. Williams (London, 1907).

Goriawala, M., *A Descriptive Catalogue of the Fyzee collection of Ismaili Manuscripts,* no. 24 and no. 49 entitled *Ithbāt al-Imāmah* (Bombay: University of Bombay, 1965).

Gorke, A., "The Historical Tradition about al-Hudaybīyya", in *The Biography of Muḥammad: The Issue of the Sources*, ed. Harald Motzki (Leiden: Brill, 2000).

Gruendler, B., "Verse and Taxes: The Function of Poetry in Selected Literary *Akhbār* of the Third/Ninth Century" in *On Fiction and Adab in Medieval Arabic Literature*, ed. Ph. F. Kennedy (Wiesbaden: Harrassowitz, 2005).

Gunther, S., "Assessing the Sources of Classical Arabic Compilations: The Issue of Categories and Methodologies", *BJMES*, 32, 1 (2005).

Halm, Heinz, *Shī'ism* (Edinburgh, 1992).

Hamda, Muḥammad Māhir, *Dirāsa wathā'iqīyya li-l-Tārīkh al-Islamī wa-maṣadirihī; min 'ahd banī umayyah ḥata al-fatḥ al-'Uthmānī li-Sūriyah wa-Miṣr 40-922 AH /661-1516 CE* (Beirut: Mu'assassat al Risāla, 1988).

Hasson, Isaac, 'La conversion de Mu'āwiya ibn Abī Sufyān', *JSAI*, 22 (1998).

Hawting, Gerald R., *The First Dynasty of Islam* (London: Routledge, 2000).

"The Origins of the Muslim Sanctuary at Mecca", in G.H.A. Juynboll (ed.), *Studies on the First Century of Islamic Society* (Carbondale and Edwardsville, 1982).

"The Significance of the Slogan *La Ḥukma illa Lillah* and the References to the *Ḥudūd* in the Traditions about the *Fitna* and the Murder of 'Uthmān", *BSOAS,* 41 (1978).

el-Ḥibrī, T., *JSTOR*, vol. 118, n.1.

Reinterpreting Islamic Historiography: Harūn al-Rashīd and the Narrative of the 'Abbāsid Caliphate (Cambridge: Cambridge University Press, 1999).

Hinds, Martin, "The Banners and the Battle Cries of the Arabs at the Battle of Ṣiffīn (657 AD)", *al-Abḥāth*, 24 (1971).

"Mu'āwiya I", *The Encyclopaedia of Islam*, New Edition (Leiden: Brill, 1993).

"The Murder of the Caliph 'Uthmān", *IJMES*, 3 (1972).

"Sayf b. 'Umar's Sources on Arabia", *Studies in the History of Arabia*, 1: ii (1979).

"The Siffin Arbitration Agreement", *JSS,* 17 (1972).

Hitti, Philip K., *History of the Arabs* (Basingstoke: Palgrave Macmillan, 2002).

Hodgson, Marshall, "How Did the Early Shi'a become Sectarian", *JAOS*, 75 (1955).

Horst, Heribert, *Die Gewahrsmanner im korankommentar at-Ṭabarī: Ein Beitrag zur kenntnis der exegetischen Uberlieferung im Islam* (Rheinische Friedrich-Willhelms-Universitat zu Bonn, Ph.D dissertation, 1951) in Berg, H., *The Development of Exegesis in Early Islam* (Richmond: Curzon Press, 2000).

Hoyland, R., "Sebeos, the Jews and the Rise of Islam", *SMJR,* 2 (1996).

Seeing Islam as Others Saw It (Princeton: Darwin Press, 1997), quoting George of Resh'aina, "An Early Syriac Life of Maximus XXIII".

Humphreys, R. S., *Islamic History: A Framework for Inquiry* (Princeton: Princeton University Press, 1991).

Mu'āwiya ibn Abī Sufyān: From Arabia to Empire (Oxford: Oneworld Publications, 2006).

Ibrāhīm, Maḥmood, *Merchant Capital and Islam* (Austin: The University of Texas Press, 1990).

The Social and Economic Background of the Umayyad Caliphate (University of California, Los Angeles, Ph.d. dissertation, 1981).

Ivanow, V., "Early Shī'ite Movements", *JBBRAS* (1941).

Izutsu, T., *Ethico-Religious Concepts in the Qur'ān* (Montreal: McGill University Press, 1966).

God and Man in the Koran: Semantics of the Qur'ānic Weltanschauung (Tokyo: The Keio Institute of Cultural and Linguistic Studies, 1964).

al-Jabburī, K. S., *Nuṣūs min Tārīkh Abī Mikhnaf Lūṭ b. Yaḥyā b. Sa'īd al-Jāmidī al-Azdī l-Kūfī l-Mutawaffa* [157 H] (Beirut: Dār al-Rasūl al-Akram, 1999).

Jones, J.M.B., "The Chronology of the *Maghāzī*: A Textual Survey", *BSOAS*, XIX (1957).

Juynboll, G.H.A., *Muslim Tradition: Studies in Chronology, Provenance and the Authorship of Early Ḥadīth* (Cambridge: Cambridge University Press, 1983).

Studies on the First Century of Islamic Society (Carbondale, IL: Southern Illinois University Press, 1982).

Kaegi, Walter, "Initial Byzantine Reactions to the Arab Conquests", *CH,* 38 (1969).

Kassis, H. E., *A Concordance of the Qur'ān* (Berkeley: The University of California Press, 1983).

Kennedy, Hugh, *The Prophet and the Age of the Caliphate: The Islamic Near East from the Sixth to the Eleventh Century* (London: Longman, 1986).

Al-Ṭabarī: Studies in Late Antiquity and Early Islam (London: Darwin Press, 2008).

Keshk, Khaled, *The Depiction of Mu'āwiya in the Early Islamic Sources* (Chicago: University of Chicago, 2002).

The Historian's Mu'āwiyah: The Depiction of Mu'āwiyah in the Early Islamic Sources (Saarbrucken: VDM Verlag Dr Muller, 2008).

"The Historiography of an Execution: The Killing of Ḥujr ibn 'Adi", *Journal of Islamic Studies* 19, 1 (January 2008).

Khālidī, T., *Arab Historical Thought in the Classical Period* (New York: Cambridge University Press, 1994).

Images of Muhammad (New York: Doubleday, 2009).

Kohlberg, Etan, "Evolution of the Shī'a", *JQ,* 27 (1983).

"From Imāmīyya to Ithnā-Asharīyya", *BSOAS*, 39 (1976).

"Imām and Community in the Pre-Ghayba Period", in *Authority and Political Culture in Shī'ism*, ed. Sa'īd Amīr Arjomand (Albany: State University of New York Press, 1988).

"The Term *Muhaddath in Twelver* Shī'ism", *Studio Orientalia D.H. Baneth Dedicata* (Jerusalem: Magnes Press, 1979).

Kristeva, Julia, *Desire in Language: A Semiotic Approach to Literature and Art* (New York: Columbia University Press, 1980).

Lalani, Arzina, *Early Shī'ī Thought: The Teachings of Imām Muḥammad al-Bāqir* (London: I.B. Tauris and the Institute of 'Ismā'ilī Studies, 2004).

Lambton, A., *State and Government in Medieval Islam* (Oxford: Oxford University Press, 1981).

Lammens, Henri, *Etudies sur le regne du Calife Omiyade Mo'awiya I* (Leipzig, 1908).

"Mu'āwiya", *The Encyclopaedia of Islam,* 2nd edition (Leiden: Brill, 1954-66).

Lapidus, Ira M., *A History of Islamic Societies* (Cambridge: Cambridge University Press, 1988).

"Knowledge, Virtue, and Action: The Classical Muslim Conception of *Adab* and the Nature of Religious Fulfillment in Islam" in *Moral Conduct and Authority: The Place of Adab in South Asian Islam,* ed. Barbara D. Metcalf (Berkeley: Univeristy of California Press, 1984).

'The Separation of State and Religion in the Development of Early Islamic Society", *IJMES* 6 (1975).

Lassner, J., *Islamic Revolution and Historical Memory* (New Haven: American Oriental Society, 1986).

Lecker, Michael, "The Estates of 'Amr b. al-Āṣ in Palestine: Notes on a New Negev Arabic Inscription", *BSOAS*, 52 (1989).

Leder, Stefan, "The Literary Use of the *Khabar*: A Basic Form of Historical Writing" in *The Byzantine and Early Islamic Near East I: Problems in the Literary Source Material*, ed. Averil Cameron and Lawrence I. Conrad (Princeton: The Darwin Press, 1992).

Lewinstein, K.,Journal of the American Oriental Society, 121, 2 (2001).

Lindsay, J., *Ibn Asākīr and Early Islamic History* (Princeton: Darwin Press, 2001).

Macdonald, D. B., *Development of Muslim Theology: Jurisprudence and Constitutional Theory* (New York: Charles Scribner's Sons, 1903).

MacIntyre, Alasdair, *A History of Ethics* (London: Routledge & Kegan Paul, 1967).

McCarthy, R. J., "Al-Bāqillānī", *Encyclopaedia of Islam*, 2nd edition (Leiden: Brill, 1954-66).

The Theology of al-Ash'ārī (Beirut: 1953).

McCutcheon, Russell T., "General Introduction" in *The Insider/Outsider Problem in the Study of Religion*, ed. Russell T. McCutcheon (London: Cassell, 1999).

McDermott, Martin J., *The Theology of Shaykh al-Mufīd* (Beirut, 1978).

Madelung, Wilferd, *The Succession to Muḥammad* (Cambridge: Cambridge University Press, 1996).

Madelung, Wilferd, "Early Sunnī Doctrine Concerning Faith as Reflected in the Kitāb al-Imān of Abū 'Ubayd al-Qāsim b. Sallām" (d. 224/839), *SI*, 32 (1970).

"The Hāshimīyāt of al-Kumayt and Hāshimī Shī'ism", *SI*, 70 (1989).

Margoliouth, D. S., *Lectures on Arab Historians* (Calcutta: University of Calcutta, 1930).

Marsham, Andrew, *Rituals of Islamic Monarchy, Accession and Succession in the First Muslim Empire* (Edinburgh: Edinburgh University Press, 2009).

Martensson, U., "Discourse and Historical Analysis: The Case of al-Ṭabarī's History of the Messengers and the Kings", 16 (2005).

Mattson, I., *JR 78.2* (1998).

Miles, G. C., 'Early Islamic Inscriptions Near Ṭā'if in the Ḥijāz', *JNES,* 7 (1948).

Millward, W. G., "Al-Ya'qūbī's Sources and the Question of Shī'ī Partiality", *Abr Nahrain*, 12 (1971-1972).

Modarressi, Hossein, *Crisis and Consolidation in the Formative Period of Shī'ite Islam: Abū Ja'far ibn Qiba al-Rāzī and His Contribution to Imāmite Shī'ite Thought* (Princeton: Darwin Press, 1993).

Tradition and Survival: A Bibliographical Survey of Early Shī'ite Literature (Oxford: Oneworld Publications, 2003).

Montgomery, J., "al-Jāḥiẓ" in *Dictionary of Literary Biography*, vol. 311: *Arabic Literary Heritage 500-925, ed.* S.M. Toorawa and M. Cooperson (Detroit: Layman, Brucoli & Clark, 2005).

"Jāḥiẓ's *Kitāb al-Bayan wa-l-Tabayin"*, in Julia Bray (ed.), *Writing and Representation: (London: Muslim Horizons,* 2006).

"Of Models and Amanuenses: The Remarks on the Qaṣīda in Ibn Qutaybah's *Kitāb al-Shi'r wa-l-Shu'arā*", in R. Hoyland and P. Kennedy (ed.), *Islamic Reflections, Arabic Musings: Studies in Honour of Alan Jones (*Oxford: Gibb Memorial Trust, 2004).

Morony, M., trans., *History of Ṭabarī: Between Civil Wars: The Caliphate of Mu'āwiyah*, vol. 18 (Albany: State University of New York Press, 1987).

Iraq after the Muslim Conquest (Princeton: N.J.; Princeton University Press, 1984).

NES, 59, 2 (2000).

Motzki, H., *The Biography of Muhammad: The Issue of the Sources* (Leiden: Brill, 2000).

Ḥadīth: Origins and Development (Aldershot: Ashgate, 2004).

'The *Muṣannaf* of 'Abd al-Razzāq b. Ḥammām al-San'ānī as a Source of Authentic *Aḥādīth* of the First Century AH', *JNES*, 50 (1991).

Mubarak, Z., *al-Nathr al-Fannī* (Cairo, 1934).

Muir, W. *The Caliphate: Its Rise, Decline and Fall* (London: Religious Tract Society, 1891).

al-Najjar, M., *al-Dawla al-Umawīyya fi al-sharq* (Cairo, 1962).

Nallino, C. A., "Appunti sulla natura del 'Califatto' in genere e sul presunto 'Califatto ottomano'", in *Raccolta di scritti editi e inediti* (Rome, 1941) as cited in Watt, W. Montgomery,"God's Caliph: Qur'ānic Interpretations and Umayyad Claims", *Iran and Islam*, ed. C. E. Bosworth (Edinburgh: Edinburgh University Press, 1971).

Noth, A., and L. Conrad, *The Early Arabic Historical Tradition: A Source-Critical Study* (Princeton: Darwin Press, 1994).

Ostrogorsky, George, *History of the Byzantine State* (Oxford: Blackwell, 1968).

Palmer, A., S. Brock, and R. Hoyland, *The Seventh Century in the West-Syrian Chronicles* (Liverpool: Liverpool University Press, 1993).

Pellat, C., *The Life and Works of Jāḥiẓ: Translation of Selected Texts* (Berkeley: University of California Press, 1969).

Petersen, E., "'Alī and Mu'āwiya: The Rise of the Ummayad Caliphate 656-661", *Acta Orientalia*, 23 (1955).

'Alī and Mu'āwiya (Copenhagen: Munksgaard, 1964).

Poonawala, Ismail K., *Al-Qaḍī al-Numān and his Urjuza on the Imāmate* (University of California, Los Angeles, Ph.d. dissertation, 1970).

al-Qāḍī, Wadād, *Bishr ibn Kubar al-Balawī*; *Namūdhaj min al-nathr al-fannī al-mubakkir fī al-Yaman* (Beirut: Dār al-Gharb al-Islamī, 1985).

"al-Raka'iẓ al-fikrīyyah fī naẓrat Abū Ḥayyān al-Tawḥīdī ilā l-mujtama", *al-Abḥāth*, 23 (1970).

"The Religious Foundation of Late Umayyad Ideology and Practice", *Saber Religioso y Poder Politico en el Islam: Actas del Simposio Internacional,* Granada, 15-18 octubre 1991 (Madrid, 1994).

"The Term 'Khalīfa' in Early Exegetical Literature", *DWI,* 28 (1988).

Quṭb, Sayyid, *Social Justice in Islam,* tr. John Hardie (New York: Octagon Books, 1970).

Quṭbuddin, T., "*Khuṭba*: The Evolution of Early Arabic Oration", in *Classical Arabic Humanities in their Own Terms: Festschrift for Wolfhart Heinrichs on his 65th Birthday*, ed. Beatrice Gruendler (Leiden: Brill Academic Publishers, 2008).

Reinink, G.J., "The Beginnings of Syriac Apologetic Literature in Response to Islam", *Oriens Christianus,* 77 (1993).

Richards, D. S., "Ibn al-Athīr and the Later Parts of the *Kāmil*: A Study for Aims and Methods" in *Medieval Historical Writing in the Christian and Islamic Worlds*, ed. D.O. Morgan (London: SOAS, University of London, 1982).

Rippin, A., "Literary Analysis of the Qur'ān, *Tafsīr* and *Sīrah*: The Methodologies of John Wansborough" in *Approaches to Islam in Religious Studies*, ed. Richard C. Martin (Tucson: University of Arizona Press, 1985).

Robinson, C., *'Abd al-Mālik: Makers of the Muslim World* (Oxford: Oneworld Publications, 2007).

Islamic Historiography (Cambridge: Cambridge University Press, 2003).

Robson, J., "The *Isnād* in Muslim Tradition", *Transactions of the Glasgow University Oriental Society,* 15 (1953-4).

Rosenthal, F. A., *Knowledge Trimuphant : The Concept of Knowledge in Medieval Islam* (Leiden: Brill, 1970).

History of Muslim Historiography (Leiden: Brill, 1968).

The History of Ṭabarī (Albany: State University of New York Press, 1989).

Rubin, Uri, "The Eye of the Beholder: The Life of Muhammad As Viewed By the Early Muslims, A Textual Analysis", *Studies in Late Antiquity and Early Islam*, 8 (Princeton: The Darwin Press, 1995).

al-Sāmarrā'ī, Ibrahīm, *Fī al-Muṣṭalaḥ al-Islāmī* (Beirut: Dār al-Hadāthah, 1990).

Schoeler, G., *The Oral and the Written in Early Islam,* tr. Uwe Vagelpohl (London: Routledge, 2006).

Serjeant, R. B., "The Caliph 'Umar's Letters to Abū Musā and Mu'āwiya", *SS*, 24 (1984).

Sezgīn, F., *Geschichte des Arabesque Schriftums, Band I: Qur'ān Wissenschaften, ḥadith, Ge-*

schichte, Fīqh, Dogmatik, Mystik bis ca. 430 H, tr. H. Berg (Leiden: E.J. Brill, 1967).

Sezgin, U., *Abū Mikhnaf: Ein Beitrag zur Historiographie des umaiyadischen Ziet* (Leiden: Brill, 1971) as cited in C. Robinson.

Shaban, M. A., *The Abbasid Revolution* (London: Cambridge University Press, 1970).

Islamic History: A New Interpretation A.D. 600-750 (Cambridge: Cambridge University Press, 1971).

Shahid, Irfan, *Byzantium and the Arabs in the Fifth Century* (Washington D.C., Dumbarton Oaks Research Library Collection, 1989).

Byzantium and the Arabs in the Sixth Century (Washington D.C. Dumbarton Oaks Research Library Collection, 1995).

Byzantium and the Arabs in Late Antiquity (Bruxelles: Byzantion, 2005).

Sharon, Moshe, "Notes on the Question of Legitimacy of Government in Islam", *IAO*, 10 (1980).

"The Umayyads as Ahl al-Bayt", *JSAI*, 14 (1992).

Shepard, W., "The Development of the Thought of Sayyid Quṭb as Reflected in Earlier and Later Editions of 'Social Justice in Islam'", *DWI*, 32 (1992).

"Sayyed Quṭb's Doctrine of Jaḥilīyya", *IJMES*, 35 (2003).

Schacht, J., *Origins of Muhammadan Jurisprudence* (Oxford: Oxford University Press, 1950).

Shackle, Christopher, and Stefan Speri, "Qạsīda Poetry in Islamic Asia and Africa"2 vols., in *Studies in Arabic Literature*, vol. 20 (Leiden: Brill, 1997).

Silverstein, A., *Postal-Systems in the Pre-Modern Islamic World: Cambridge Studies in Islamic Civilization* (New York: Cambridge University Press, 2007).

Speight, M., "A Look at Variant Readings in the *Ḥādīth*", *DI*, 77 (2000).

Stetkevych, Jaroslav, *Arabic Poetry and Orientalism* (Oxford: St John's College Research Centre, 2004).

Stetkevych, S.,*Early Islamic Poetry and Poetics: The Formation of the Classical Islamic World* (Farnham, Surrey: Ashgate Variorum, 2009).

The Mute Immortals Speak: Pre-Islamic Poetry and the Poetics of Ritual (Ithaca, NY: Cornell University Press, 1993).

Stewart, Devin, "*Saj'* in the Qur'an: Prosody and Structure", *JAL*, 21 (1990).

Stroumsa, S., "The Blinding Emerald: Ibn al-Rawandī's *Kitab al-Zumurrud*", *JAOS*, 114 (1994).

"Ibn al-Rawandī's *Su' adab al-mujadala*: The Role of Bad Manners in Medieval Disputations" in H. Lazarus-Yaffe, et al. (eds.), *The Majlis: Interreligious Encounters in Medieval Islam, Stud-*

ies in Arabic Language and Literature (Wiesbaden: Harassowitz, 1999).

Taqqush, M. S., *Tārīkh al-dawla al-Umawīyya* (Beirut: Dār al-Nafā'is, 1996).

Thompson, Willie, *Postmodernism and History* (New York: Palgrave Macmillan, 2004).

Tyan, E., *Histoire de l'organisation judiciare en pays d'Islam* (Paris, 1938-1943; 2nd edition, Leiden, 1960) in Watt, W. Montgomery,"God's Caliph: Qur'ānic Interpretations and Umayyad Claims", *Iran and Islam*, ed. C.E. Bosworth (Edinburgh: Edinburgh University Press, 1971).

'Uways, Abd al-Ḥalīm, *Banū Umayyah bayn al-suqūt wa al-intiḥār; dirāsah ḥawl suqūṭ Banū Umayyah fī al-mashriq* (Cairo: Dār al-Sahwa, 1987).

al-Wakīl, Muḥammad al-Sayyid, *al-Umawīyun bayna al-sharq wal-gharb: dirāsah waṣfīyah wa-taḥlīlīyah lil-dawlah al-Umawīyah* (Damascus: Dār al-Qalam, 1995).

Walmand, M. R., *Toward a Theory of Historical Narrative* (Columbus: Ohio State University Press, 1980).

Watt, W. Montgomery, *The Formative Period of Islamic Thought* (Edinburgh: Edinburgh University Press, 1973).

"God's Caliph: Qur'ānic Interpretations and Umayyad Claims", *Iran and Islam*, ed. C.E. Bosworth (Edinburgh: Edinburgh University Press, 1971).

Muḥammad at Mecca (Oxford: Clarendon Press, 1953).

"Shī'ism under the Umayyads", *JRAS* (1960).

Wansborough, J., *Qur'ānic Studies: Sources and Methods of Scriptural Interpretation* (Oxford: Oxford University Press, 1977).

Weber, Max, *Max Weber on Charisma and Institution Building: Selected Papers*, ed. S.N. Eisenstadt (Chicago: University of Chicago Press, 1968).

Wellhausen, J., *The Arab Kingdom and its Fall*, tr. Margaret Weir (Beirut: Khayats, 1963).

The Religio-Political Factions of Early Islam, ed. R.C. Ostle, trans. R.C. Ostle and S.M. Waltzer (Amsterdam: North Holland Publishing, 1975).

White, Hayden, *Metahistory: The Historical Imagination in Nineteenth-Century Europe* (Baltimore: Johns Hopkins University Press, 1973).

Wolfson, H., *The Philosophy of the Kalam* (Cambridge, MA: Harvard University Press, 1976).

Printed in the USA
CPSIA information can be obtained
at www.ICGtesting.com
LVHW012128120224
771669LV00050BA/1255

9 781908 110053